D1241464

TOWARD
NEW
TOWNS
FOR
AMERICA

TOWARD
NEW
TOWNS
FOR
AMERICA

BY
CLARENCE S.
STEIN

**With an
introduction
by
LEWIS
MUMFORD**

THE M.I.T. PRESS

**Massachusetts Institute of Technology
Cambridge, Massachusetts, and London, England**

First M.I.T. Press Paperback Edition, March, 1966

Copyright 1957 by Clarence S. Stein

Printed in the United States of America

Library of Congress Catalog Card Number: 57-6538

CONTENTS

FOREWORD   7

FOREWORD TO THE REVISED EDITION   9

INTRODUCTION BY LEWIS MUMFORD   11

TOWARD NEW TOWNS FOR AMERICA   19

1 SUNNYSIDE GARDENS, *New York City*   21

2 RADBURN, *New Jersey*   37

3 CHATHAM VILLAGE, *Pittsburgh*   75

4 PHIPPS GARDEN APARTMENTS (I), *New York City*   87

5 HILLSIDE HOMES, *New York City*   93

6 PHIPPS GARDEN APARTMENTS (II), *New York City*   109

7 VALLEY STREAM PROJECT   114

8 GREENBELT, *Maryland*   119

    GREENHILLS, *Ohio*   178

    GREENBROOK, *New Jersey*   183

    GREENDALE, *Wisconsin*   185

9 BALDWIN HILLS VILLAGE, *Los Angeles*   188

INDICATIONS OF THE FORM OF THE FUTURE   217

APPENDIX   228

BIBLIOGRAPHY   249

REFERENCES   255

PHOTOGRAPHIC CREDITS   257

INDEX AND LIST OF ILLUSTRATIONS   259

TO ALINE

FOREWORD

The purpose of re-exploring this series of experiences in community building was to find guidance for all of us in making the next step toward building New Towns. I had in mind that both in America and in Europe the time is ripe for complete change in the form of urban environment. I believe that the best and easiest way to start that change is to build New Towns on new sites, as Sir Ebenezer Howard suggested. The opportunity to do this may come sooner than we had reason to expect. The creation of towns for industry and for living, of moderate size, widely separated from each other, may be imminent as a defense measure. This could be the beginning of a new era of nation-wide decentralization. For fortunately here the best policy for peace and for defense are the same: orderly, related dispersal of workers and working places in limited-sized communities, surrounded by open country.

On the other hand, as a result of the Redevelopment powers under the Housing Act of 1949 the way is now open for large-scale rebuilding of decaying sections of old cities. It is equally important that both the building of New Towns and the redevelopment of old ones shall be part and parcel of the future.

In the case of the redevelopment projects it seems clear to me that they will fail in their purpose and be merely patches on the past and passing framework of the old cities unless they are all conceived, planned, and carried out as large-scale units of new cities — new cities even though they are on the old sites. In finding the form of these future cities the preliminary experiments of which this book tells will, I hope, be of help to both planners and administrators.

Although this book deals with American experience it has strong ties with Great Britain. Much of the philosophy and experience in housing and city building from which Henry Wright and I and the rest of us started had its roots in English experience and thinking. To a great extent we carried on the work begun by Ebenezer Howard and Raymond Unwin. By a happy chance, much of this book was written during 1949 in Wyldes, the former home of Sir Raymond Unwin. The articles were prepared for a British publication, *The Town Planning Review*, edited by Gordon Stephenson of the Department of Civic Design at the University of Liverpool. It was he who suggested that I tell the story of some of my experiences in connection with the creation of new communities in America.

FOREWORD

I was at the time preparing a book on the three Greenbelt Towns. I put this aside to start on a series of articles because I had come to the conclusion that the Greenbelt Towns were only three links in the chain of experiences that led from Sunnyside and Radburn through Baldwin Hills Village toward the future New Towns of America. This fortunately resulted in its splendid presentation by the Liverpool University Press and to my association with Gordon Stephenson. To his thoughtful understanding and editorial guidance this book owes much of its form and beauty. So here I offer my affectionate thanks to Gordon Stephenson—and may I add to his American wife, who edited this in the American language in such a way that my British and European friends could understand it.

Of the many other friends and associates to whom I owe gratitude for their help in research or in reading the manuscript I can mention only a few. For research I thank Louise Blackham, Elizabeth Coit, Kate Edelman, and Helena Newman.

For suggestions and correction of manuscript I have had the assistance of those who promoted, planned or managed the various developments, including: Alexander M. Bing, Ralph Eberlin, and Herbert Emmerich on *Sunnyside* and *Radburn;* Ernest Schofield on *Phipps Garden Apartments;* Nathan Straus and Frank Jordan on *Hillside Homes;* Charles T. McDonald, James Gobbel, Samuel Ashelman, Jr., Win McCamy, and Mary Jane Kinzer on *Greenbelt;* Walter Kroening and Elbert Peets on *Greendale;* Lawrence Tucker and Roland A. Wank on *Greenhills;* and Lewis Wilson, Ray Knisely, Robert E. Alexander, and Edwin Merrill on *Baldwin Hills Village.*

For the living pictures of Radburn and Greenbelt, most of which were taken in the summer of 1949, we owe deep appreciation to Gretchen van Tassel. For assistance in the bibliography my thanks are due to Katherine McNamara, Librarian, Departments of Landscape Architecture and Regional Planning, Harvard University.

Finally, for inspiration and general assistance, my heartfelt gratitude to Benton MacKaye, Hugh Pomroy, Albert Mayer, and Lewis Mumford.

New York
November 1950

FOREWORD TO THE REVISED EDITION

Six years have passed since this book was published: six years of unprecedented production of mass housing, redevelopment, even New Towns. The ideas and forms that it describes have become widely accepted—even if not so widely practiced.

This book was called *TOWARD New Towns for America* because, although it described communities that were thoroughly contemporary, none of them was comprehensive enough in scale or functions to fully deserve the title of New Town.

Since then, that has changed. At least one such municipality has been planned and is being built in America, though not in the United States. Kitimat in British Columbia is the direct descendant of the communities that are the subject of this book. It has the same basic physical elements. The procedure by which the plan was developed grew out of the experience that is described here.

The influence of the Radburn Idea has travelled far. I am finding that even if the seeds of ideas are slow in propagating close by, they often are carried to distant points, there to bloom more fully. This is true of Vallingby, a veritable New Town for 60,000 people, built as an addition to Stockholm, which was started about when this book was written and is now practically complete—and fully inhabited.

The Radburn Idea is a basic element of the plan of Vallingby, conceived by the brilliant community architect Sven Markelius. It is carried out with much originality, imagination, and variety, to fit the special requirements of the site and of the people of Stockholm. The plan further develops the related Radburn elements of superblocks with central open greens forming a continuous chain of parks toward which buildings face, and specialized types of paths and roads completely separated from one another.

The same principles, modified to meet quite different local customs, in large part set the pattern for Chandigarh, the new capital of East Punjab, India, both as first laid out by Mayer and Whittlesey and as now being built according to the plans of Le Corbusier.

Thus three of the outstanding New Towns or cities of this decade demonstrate on a city-wide scale the principles and practices which were the basis of the pioneer communities with which this book deals. In Sweden, India, and British Columbia the New Towns toward which we in the United States have been moving these last thirty years have actually come into existence.

New York
November 1956

FOREWORD TO 1966 EDITION

This third edition of *Toward New Towns for America* follows the text of the 1956 edition without revision.

I have, however, added a short supplementary bibliography containing a few outstanding and particularly pertinent references with some description of their contents.

New York
November 1965

INTRODUCTION

BY

LEWIS

MUMFORD

Except for colonial times, hardly a beginning has been made, up to now, on the history of American city development and urban design. Not the least merit of Clarence Stein's account of the housing and planning experiments that began with Sunny-side Gardens in the nineteen-twenties is the fact that it is a valuable document toward this unwritten history. But it is happily far more than that: it is an account of certain new ideas in planning the urban environment; and it is a critical appraisal —often a strict self-appraisal—of the results. No book in this field could be more pertinent to our present task, or more salutary; for both the housing and the city planning movement have reached a point where, to justify their existence, they must depart from their familiar stereotypes and strike off boldly along the lines indicated by the planning work of Clarence Stein and Henry Wright, correcting the weaknesses time has disclosed and carrying further their many valuable contributions.

Seen in perspective, the positive phase of city planning began in America with the work of Frederick Law Olmsted, first in Olmsted and Vaux's plan for Central Park; while the positive phase of housing began, after the Civil War, with the building of the series of White model tenements in Brooklyn, dwellings whose good qualities never received adequate analysis or awakened emulation. Though Olmsted's was a reflective mind, his own work failed in some degree to produce the impression it might and should have had on a later generation. Perhaps one of the reasons for this was the fact that he did not write such a detailed account of his own achievement as Mr. Stein wisely has here attempted, with the providential and patient encouragement of Mr. Gordon Stephenson. Even the two-volume biography of Olmsted, published

in our generation, centers almost exclusively on one aspect of his work, park planning, and does not do justice to his many pioneering contributions, not merely to urban design but to regional culture.

Since the work of such strong individuals has been so easily forgotten—despite Olmsted's immense influence on his contemporaries—it is not perhaps singular that the excellent early planning of mill villages, like Lawrence and Lowell in Massachusetts and Manchester in New Hampshire, was passed over without even comment, till Mr. John Coolidge published his recent *Mill and Mansion*. Even more significant American initiatives in urban layout and site planning were forgotten: I refer not merely to the planning in long parallel rows in Jefferson's University of Virginia (triumphantly invented a century later by German planners) but to the creation of the super-block, with entrant cul-de-sacs. This admirable device for lowering road costs, increasing the amount of green space, and creating tranquil domestic quarters free from through traffic long antedated the motor car; in fact, it was widely employed in Cambridge and Longwood (both near Boston, Mass.) before the middle of the nineteenth century. Curiously it never attracted any later attention, not even from nearby planners like Olmsted and John Nolen, though the latter had his office in Cambridge and must have repeatedly visited these very super-blocks on friendly, if not on professional, errands.

The transition to modern planning and housing in America did not take place on any scale until the First World War. So far from building on American traditions, the planners turned mainly to England for their models: reverting to an old colonial habit. In 1915 Charles Harris Whitaker, the redoubtable editor of the Journal of the American

INTRODUCTION

Institute of Architects, then to enter on its most brilliant decade, began to publish reports of the new war housing communities built in England under Raymond Unwin. Mr. Frederick L. Ackerman made a special visit to England to gather materials for one of these articles; and the discussions that followed laid the foundations for the new housing policy courageously instituted by the Federal Government under Woodrow Wilson. The current shortage of housing in industrial towns, even before the United States entered the war in 1917, made it imperative for the government to plan and construct housing estates for munitions workers and shipbuilding workers: indeed, Washington created two independent authorities to plan and build adequate quarters in these respective fields.

Working in a realm where they had little preparation and less formal training, the accomplishment of American architects and planners was remarkably high; and the new housing communities, like the Black Rock development at Bridgeport and the Yorkship Village near Camden, gave an immense stimulus to socially minded architects throughout the country. Two such architects, F. L. Ackerman and Henry Wright, had worked on the United States Shipping Board's War Housing, under Mr. Robert D. Kohn, he who was to become first head of Public Works Administration housing under President Roosevelt in 1933; and sometime after the war Mr. Kohn, already associated professionally with Mr. Stein, brought Wright and Stein together. That meeting began their close association, a partnership in every sense but the legal one, which lasted for a decade. The results of that synergy are visible in this book.

In the post-war period, Mr. Whitaker performed one further service to the planning movement, when he moved his offices from Washington to New York: he brought together in friendly intercourse the group that was to become, in 1923, the Regional Planning Association of America; and he opened the pages of his Journal to reports and discussions on community planning, in a special department edited by Mr. Stein. To understand the scope of Stein's and Wright's contributions to planning, one must do more than appraise their individual work: one must also examine the close

group in which they played such a dynamic part. But first a word about their own personalities.

As is usually the case in a good partnership, Clarence Stein and Henry Wright each possessed special abilities that complemented those of the other. Henry Wright was both an able technician and a dreamer: a man with a quick mind, fertile in suggestions, never rigidly committed even to his own best ideas, but ready to go off on a new trail at the first gleam of an opening. Trained as a landscape architect, he had settled down in St. Louis and raised a family of four, a large family for his generation. Wright's experiences with the difficulties and opportunities of a middle class household made him a most sympathetic interpreter of the needs of his new clients in low income housing: here he counter-balanced Stein, who had long been a bachelor, accustomed to the apartment house life of Paris or New York. Wright even lived with his family in Sunnyside, during its early days, and learned at first hand its advantages and drawbacks. He recognized the necessity of both lowering the cost of housing and doing a better job of it; and his analysis led him to emphasize the way in which control over the over-all pattern could contribute to both ends.

Henry Wright was a great lover of chess; and he used to say that his skill in chess made a better planner of him, ready with alternative solutions, able to think many moves ahead, trained to coordinate many variables; certainly planning itself had for him all the excitement of that noble game; and as with chess, he never thought he could exhaust all its possibilities. Both as a human being and as a thinker, he retained a youthful eagerness that matched his capacity for growth. This readiness to learn helped to make him an excellent teacher; and his openness to new ideas in architecture put him into sympathetic relations with the younger architects and planners, whom he gathered round him in a small summer school on his New Jersey farm. Some of the best of the younger generation, people like Robert Mitchell and Chloethiel Woodard Smith, were Wright's students. Wright had the independence and freedom of the unfettered intellectual, who has never been bribed into submission by the fleshpots; but his very independence and his occasional hot temper needed a moderating influence; and this, among many other things, his associate, Stein, provided.

Clarence Stein is a rare combination of artist and organizer; a man of fine taste, delicate discrimination, and a background of adequate means that gave him wide opportunities, not only for the exercise of these qualities but for travel as well. He had been chief designer for Bertram Gosvenor Goodhue and had been in charge of the planning of a model mining town at Tyrone, New Mexico. But during the years of his greatest activity, the organizer in Stein was perhaps uppermost: it was he who not merely kept the office running, but organized the Regional Planning Commission, and deployed the little squad of thinkers and technicians who surrounded him with such skill that their opponents treated them as respectfully as if they were a regiment. If Wright was the zealous bird-dog who was always picking up a new scent, Stein was the hunter who never forgot that he had to bring home the game. Stein combined an extremely conciliatory manner with a will of steel; and he had a happy faculty of being all things to all men: he was capable of smoking a long black cigar with Governor Smith or admiring a Renoir that Alexander Bing had recently purchased; of chewing over contractors' estimates with his engineer and man-of-all-work, Frank Vitolo, or of reacting intelligently to the latest idea MacKaye or Wright had evolved overnight.

Stein was an excellent appraiser of both men and ideas; and best of all, for the purpose in hand, he never permitted himself to lose sight of the broader social goals through overemphasis on any single set of details. Stein's persistence often kept Wright on the main track when the latter's curiosity or his love of intellectual adventure might have led him off along ultimately less rewarding paths; this very persistence was partly responsible for the final appearance of that early landmark in regional planning thought, the Plan for the State of New York: a task from which at one moment Wright was inclined to withdraw—only to come forward finally with the most brilliant historical summation, and a radically new concept of decentralization.

So close was the relation of the two men during the decade of their active association that it is hardly possible to assign credit to one or the other for any particular part of the work; and it was of the essence of their relation to disregard such matters; for a good partnership, like marriage, disdains any close accountancy of personal disbursements and receipts. By training, however, Wright was the planner, with a specially fine eye for site planning and grouping; while Stein was predominantly the architect. When their association terminated, however, Stein devoted himself increasingly to planning. If the architecture always remained more traditional than the planning in the work they did together, this was at least partly because salesmen, contractors, and financiers, making principles out of prejudices, all fancied themselves as having more competence in the architectural department. So preposterous was the prevailing conservatism here in the twenties that it was only after a serious struggle that the planners of Sunnyside were permitted to paint the interior doors, instead of giving them the conventional hideous mahogany stain, or to use common brick throughout, instead of using special face-brick on the street side.

But, to sum up, what Wright and Stein had in common was even more important than what they held separately: they were united in personal modesty and generous public aims, in an absence of competitive self-display, in a keen sense of the essential values in art and life, in a desire to make the good things of our civilization available to all its members: above all, they shared a warm, abiding humanity. But for Wright's early death in 1936, it is conceivable that the two men might have come together again professionally; indeed each, independently, had a part in the development of Greenbelt.

In the case of Clarence Stein one further element must be added: his keen sense of public issues. Until his influence began to be felt, the housing movement in New York had confined itself, under Mr. Lawrence Veiller's leadership, almost exclusively to restrictive legislation. Even the model tenements built in New York by philanthropic groups were only a few shades better than those allowed by law; while the notion of having the State supply the capital and even take the initiative in publicly condemning land for housing purposes and subsidizing, further, the lowest income groups would

INTRODUCTION

have been regarded by the original housing reformers with more horror than the slums themselves. More than any other single person, Clarence Stein changed all this. As the dynamic chairman of the Commission for Housing and Regional Planning, he not merely established the widespread need for new housing for the lower income groups, ill-served by private enterprise: he also showed the need of large scale enterprise, both private and public, to do the job effectively; and pointed out that money at low interest rates would be far more effective in reducing costs than any conceivable economy in construction. Stein also pointed to the need, now only beginning to be recognized, to build on open land, in order to eliminate wasteful street patterns, provide open spaces, reduce density, and drain off sufficient population from the central areas to lower the grossly inflated land value based on anti-social standards. Early and late, Stein advocated a public policy working for decentralization, industrial dispersal, new towns, and regional reconstruction.

Without Clarence Stein's initiative, New York State's constructive leadership in publicly aided State housing in the late nineteen-twenties would not have come about; and without this leadership, the Roosevelt administration would not, in all probability, have been able to evolve the comprehensive national housing policy that it actually embarked on with such readiness. Finally, had it not been for the ideas that the Regional Planning Association of America, under Stein's presidency, had put into circulation during the twenties, the Greenbelt Towns undertaken by the Resettlement Administration in 1934 would have been inconceivable, and the germs of an American New Towns policy—still unfortunately aborted—would not have been implanted in Washington.

The important thing to realize, then, is that the work Clarence Stein took part in as architect and planner, though largely of a private nature, up to Greenbelt, went on against this background of wider public education and effort; and it had as its ultimate aim the use of the power and wealth of the State to co-ordinate all the forces that create communities and to make them serve public, rather than private and selfish ends, even though the enterprise itself was privately financed. Stein treated

these experiments in housing as Ebenezer Howard treated the Garden City: as a proving ground for methods that would later be used, if successful, on a far wider scale. First private initiative to test the validity of the new planning; then public enterprise, to extend it and co-ordinate it, when private enterprise lagged or retreated or proved impotent. Stein's purposes found a sympathetic echo in Alexander M. Bing, a public spirited citizen, who fortunately was also a shrewd and experienced real estate operator, accustomed to handling large enterprises. At the height of his business success, Mr. Bing put his abilities at the service of housing improvement, with the ultimate purpose of building a garden city; and without such valiant practical co-operation Stein would probably never have gone so far in community design. As it was, Stein became something more than an architect and planner: he was the foremost exponent in his generation of urban statesmanship.

Having sketched in this political background, I must complete it by outlining the intellectual foundations of Stein's and Wright's work: the vivid interchange of ideas that took place within the Regional Planning Association, where the civic ideas of Geddes and Howard, the economic analyses of Thorstein Veblen, the sociology of Charles Horton Cooley, and the educational philosophy of John Dewey, to say nothing of the new ideas in conservation, ecology, and geotechnics, all had a part in transforming the cut-and-dried procedures of the earlier planners. The Regional Planning Association of America—not to be confused with the Regional Plan Association of New York, a later organization created to carry on the work of the Russell Sage Foundation plan—is perhaps worth more than a mere mention here, for its composition and nature should be well understood by those who erroneously believe that important movements can be carried out only by mass organizations, supported by a heavy budget. The charter members of this group, which first met in 1923, were the following: F.L. Ackerman, Frederick Bigger, A.M. Bing, John Bright, Stuart Chase, R. D. Kohn, Benton MacKaye, Lewis Mumford, C. S. Stein, C. H. Whitaker, and Henry Wright. In time, a handful of others joined the association, including Edith Elmer Wood, Tracy Augur, and Catherine Bauer; but at no time were there as many as twenty members.

This group made up in intensity what it lacked in extension. A core of members met at least two or three times a week, sometimes more, for lunch or dinner; and from time to time somewhat more formal meetings were held over a weekend, at the Hudson Guild Farm in Netcong, New Jersey, for strenuous systematic discussions. (The members came with their wives and incidentally were among the first urban groups to revive the square dances and the Appalachian folk-ballads, under the guidance of MacKaye: the great geotect who conceived the Appalachian Trail, as a means of both using and conserving that primeval area.) Patrick Geddes was present at the first weekend meeting in May 1923; and at one of the last weekends, before Radburn was launched, Clarence Perry took an active part. But essentially this little group was a society of friends: people so close in aim, so freely co-operative in act, that the principle of unanimity, of laboring with each other till they had clearly focussed their agreements, spontaneously operated. On such a basis neither factionalism nor desire for priority or publicity marred the work in hand. This group's active years spanned the decade between 1923 and 1933; and its last public effort was to conduct a week's meeting on Regionalism for the Institute of Public Affairs at the University of Virginia. On that occasion, the principal address was delivered by Franklin D. Roosevelt, then Governor of the State of New York, soon to bring before the American people the ripest fruit of two generations of regional thinking, from Marsh and Olmsted onward—the Tennessee Valley Authority act.

After 1933, the members of the Regional Planning Association scattered, many of them to work actively on the projects for which the group had, with no thought of such early realization, laid the theoretic foundations and outlined the practical tasks. Both the public and the private work carried on by the members of this association was affected by the constant cross-fertilization of ideas that took place between its members; for their prime object was to re-educate themselves, rather than to diffuse the existing stereotypes. They could shift from one task to another without narrowing their objectives or losing sight of their goals: the building of balanced communities, cut to the human scale, in balanced regions, which would be part of an ever widening national, continental, and global whole, also in balance. They could dream, with Walt Whitman, of 'the place where the great city stands,' the city of the most faithful friends, because they had wrought that ideal into their own lives. Ultimately, it was out of this group as a whole, rather than simply out of those directly responsible, that some of its best products came forth: the Regional Planning Number of the Survey Graphic (May 1925), the Final Report of the New York State Commission for Housing and Regional Planning, (1926), and the Radburn plan itself.

Playing over Stein and Wright, then, as thinkers and planners, was the constant stimulus of this wider group, sympathetic yet critical, idealistic but shrewd, not committed to immediate success but working patiently and effectively toward ultimately practical goals. Because of the general misdirection of effort in housing and planning during the nineteen-twenties, with its sprawling cities, its extravagant subdivisions, its areas of standardized blight, hastily sold off (under the aegis of the Own Your Own Home movement) to people already sufficiently insecure without this extra burden—because of this Stein and Wright were the only living links, along with Ackerman, between the admirable community planning of the war communities in 1918 and the efforts in housing and urban re-development undertaken, all too ignorantly of past efforts, in the early days of the Roosevelt administration.

Without this link, that work could hardly have gotten off to such an early start. Yet here, perhaps, is the place to make an observation entirely outside Mr. Stein's province as historian: namely, that the inadequate employment of Henry Wright and the all but total neglect of Mr. Stein in the housing and planning work of the thirties was, to speak in the mildest terms possible, one of the great oversights of the Roosevelt administration. And the country has paid for that neglect in dull stereotyped plans, in poverty of amenities and social facilities, in the notable lack of the human touch, which characterizes so much of the public housing and planning in the United States during the last 15 years. That work has been unexpectedly large in quantity, compared with the modest hopes entertained in the

INTRODUCTION

twenties; but it has been unnecessarily low in quality, compared with Sunnyside, Radburn, Greenbelt.

If the significance of the work of Stein and Wright had been fully understood, the reckless overcrowding of the land that has now become standard practice in urban re-development—piously concealed under the 'low-coverage' which its density makes almost meaningless—could never have taken place. Projects like the Metropolitan Life Insurance Company's Parkchester and Stuyvesant Town, and the New York City Housing Authority's many slum clearances of equal density, should have been unthinkable, in view of these better precedents, had not wilful indifference to the side-reaction from this overdensity, upon both the occupants and the city, become almost a qualification to posing as an allegedly practical expert on these matters. The invisible costs of such projects— the increased burden on non-existent parks, playgrounds, schools, the excessive costs of traffic congestion and avenue widening in cities developed now for five or six times their original density— heavily outweighs all the visible economies. Stein and Wright had demonstrated on the basis of a careful cost analysis, which included long term as well as immediate costs, that the prejudice in favor of high buildings and high densities simply could not stand up under rigorous appraisal. In short, they had verified for themselves Sir Raymond Unwin's dictum: Nothing gained by overcrowding. In community development it is not the first costs but the final costs that count.

If in housing Stein and Wright's work carried on the wartime traditions in group housing and row (terrace) housing that were otherwise being abandoned or forgotten, on the side of community planning they were conscious disciples of Barry Parker and Raymond Unwin, and unconscious disciples of their own great precursor, Olmsted. Olmsted's complete separation of pedestrian walks from vehicular and horseback traffic, by means of overpasses and underpasses, in Central Park, was certainly the major forerunner of the Radburn plan. Unfortunately, Olmsted himself never apparently grasped the general significance of this separation for modern planning, particularly on land whose contours offer different levels. But one can hardly doubt that Stein's daily walks through Central Park during this formative period encouraged him to hold to it tenaciously, once Radburn was built: more so than Henry Wright, who, when he came to plan Greenbrook in 1935—it was never built—went back to a more traditional layout. In Hampstead Garden Suburb, on the other hand, Parker and Unwin had explored the possibilities of the superblock even in the early units, and had used it in the same fashion as the earlier subdividers around Boston. But these English planners never erected the super-block into a universal principle of laying out a modern residential quarter: hence they never carried it through as systematically as the planners of Radburn did. Similarly, Parker and Unwin had, in Hampstead, created on a limited scale the continuous inner park; but they did not follow this to its logical conclusion by interweaving this continuous green throughout the whole development. But it was the systematic application of these two planning elements that created a radically new urban layout, the Radburn plan, in which the avenue itself was pushed to its logical conclusion to function solely as a means of circulation, not as a promenade for shops and offices. This is not indeed the only possible solution for the problem of traffic in a motorized age; but it is one that had many excellent features never before utilized.

Like Olmsted, Stein and Wright dared put beauty as one of the imperative needs of a planned environment: the beauty of ordered buildings, measured to the human scale, of trees and flowering plants, and of open greens surrounded by buildings of low density, so that children may scamper over them, to add to both their use and their aesthetic loveliness: a freedom not possible, incidentally, on land occupied at a density over a hundred persons to the acre, where the green exists only to be looked at, not used. These planners insisted on including open spaces and generous plantings as part of the essential first costs of housing. In the effort to achieve utmost economy, at a time when building costs were still prohibitively high, they doubtless sometimes allowed the inner quarters of the house to become a little cramped. Their excessive economy here was re-enforced, probably, by their memory of the fate of Forest Hills, the garden suburb built on Long Island before the First

World War by the Russell Sage Foundation: meant to serve as a working-class community, but destined by the very generosity of its housing to become an entirely middle class, indeed upper middle class, community. When they came to Radburn their parsimony—say rather their prudence—somewhat relaxed, though never so much as a long term view would have justified; but even in the earliest work they provided generous open spaces and play areas, in a fashion hitherto unknown in New York since the middle of the nineteenth century. The results of their open designs speak for themselves; and they will continue to speak for many years; for their communities—and later ones patterned after them, like Baldwin Hills Village in Los Angeles and Fresh Meadows in New York—will sturdily resist that endemic disease of urbanism, blight: a disease that fatally overtakes places people quickly cease to love, once the first glow of possession is over, because they were never in fact lovable.

Comeliness and neighborliness are the qualities that Clarence Stein and Henry Wright wrought into their designs. Before Clarence Perry wrote his able treatise on the Neighborhood Unit, Stein and Wright had, in Sunnyside, carried out many of his theoretic suggestions in concrete detail. Their growing attention to the promotion of social life, through the timely provision of schools, shopping centers, community meeting rooms, informal outdoor meeting places, and even, in Radburn, swimming pools, distinguishes the work here presented from the more rigorous but somewhat less genial schemes that were current in Europe, particularly in Germany, during the same period, a moment when the tenants' 'minimum of existence' seemed to represent the modern architects' maximum of desire. These American planners had indeed something to learn, in clean modern form, from the best of their colleagues in Zurich, Berlin, and Frankfurt-am-Main; and Wright spent the better part of a year in Germany and Switzerland, zealously familiarizing himself with the fresh work there, which reached such a high level in Zehlendorf, Roemerstadt, and Neubuehl. But in turn these Americans had something to teach their European colleagues; and in current healthy reaction against a one-sidedly mechanistic mode of planning, in which the main human objec-

tives are forgotten, Stein and Wright still have something to teach to the younger generation. Stein's direct influence on Greenbelt, Md., and Baldwin Hills Village, and his indirect influence on Fresh Meadows, have contributed in no small measure to their excellence.

No one knows better than Clarence Stein that the work he has here described is but a beginning. What he and Wright demonstrated are not forms to be copied, but a spirit to be assimilated and carried further, a method of integration to be perfected, a body of tradition to be modified and transmitted—and in time transmuted into new forms that will reflect the needs and desires and hopes of another age. But the educated man is he who can best make use of the wisdom of the past, economizing his own time by not blindly and ignorantly repeating experiments that have failed, or by following blind trails that lead to bankrupt enterprises. Those who would go beyond the work Mr. Stein has spread before the reader in the following pages must at least catch up with it; and some of those who fancy themselves most in advance of it are actually lagging far behind: witness such a Fourierist antique as the new skyscraper village in Marseilles.

Sunnyside Gardens and Radburn and the Greenbelt towns were but finger exercises, preparing for symphonies that are yet to come: preliminary studies for the new towns that a bolder and more humane generation, less victimized by the false gods of finance, will eventually build. These planners dreamed generously; and their dreams will survive the weaknesses and imperfections of their execution. They achieved an outstanding degree of success, even when the economic tide was running against them, and when the more favorable political currents, represented in America by the New Deal and the more constructive elements in the labor movement, were not yet in motion. Their relative success and increasing influence is a pledge of what may be attained in the future under happier conditions.

Let the planners of the coming generation ponder this testament.

LEWIS MUMFORD
AMENIA, NEW YORK
1951

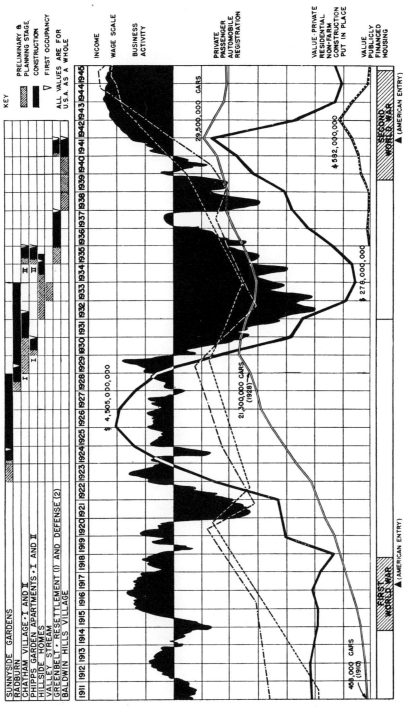

Fig. 1—Chart showing the years in which the various projects described were planned and constructed, and the time relation to the general economic climate. Sources included: U. S. Dept. of Labor: Poliak Foundation for Economic Research; Twentieth Century Foundation.

TOWARD
NEW
TOWNS
FOR
AMERICA

After the First World War there was a strong surge of enthusiasm for a better world. A group of us, including Lewis Mumford, Stuart Chase, Benton MacKaye, Charles Whitaker and Henry Wright, formed the Regional Planning Association of America, to discuss regional development, geotechnics and New Communities. New York's great democratic governor, Al Smith, planned to replace the slums in which he had grown up. As a result, there was created the Commission of Housing and Regional Planning. He made me Chairman. Up to that time in America our attack on housing had been regulatory—legal don'ts. I went abroad in search of more constructive action. In England 'New Towns' and 'New Towns after the War' were attempting to chart a new way; the second Garden City, Welwyn, was being built. I returned to America a disciple of Ebenezer Howard and Raymond Unwin.

Soon after, I walked uptown with Alexander M. Bing, the successful developer of massive apartments and skyscrapers. His war work had been connected with labor problems. He was trying to decide whether he would be more useful in the field of labor or housing. I suggested the building of a Garden City.

That is how it started. We intended to create a Garden City in America. But time and place and the so-called economic cycle mold the ultimate reality of our dreams. So we first built Sunnyside, a community within the rigid framework of New York's gridiron. Then Radburn, realistically planned for the Motor Age, but not a Garden City as Howard saw it.

Before either of these we planned a Garden Community for a population of 25,000 on a square mile, at the undeveloped edge of New York City.[1] Here, in association with Henry Wright, the brilliant city planner and analyst, we developed the theoretical basis of land and community planning that was afterwards applied at Radburn, Chatham Village, the Greenbelt towns, and Baldwin Hills.

But the Garden Community was never realized: the purchase of the property could not be financed quickly enough to prevent the land being subdivided and thrown into the speculative market.

Fig. 2—Preliminary study of a proposed garden community in the New York region, 1923. In the normal subdivision plan, lower right, a street area of 190 acres, or 32.8 per cent of the whole, was required. In the proposed plan, upper right, 135 acres of streets, or 23.5 per cent, make ample provision for all needs, and park areas and space for other community needs are gained. The diagram below shows the use areas for apartments, row houses, communal space, parks, allotment gardens, light industry and store groups in the various centers.

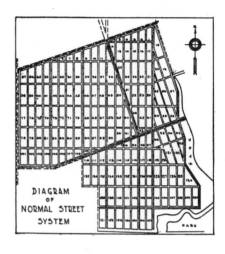

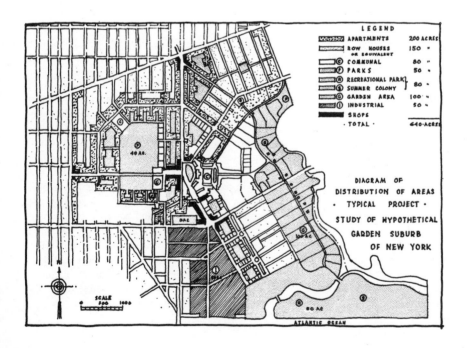

1

SUNNYSIDE
GARDENS

Clarence S. Stein and Henry Wright,
Town Planners
Clarence S. Stein, Chief Architect
Frederick L. Ackerman,
Architect of Blocks of Houses

The first development of the City Housing Corporation, the limited dividend company which Mr. Bing organized in 1924 for the ultimate purpose of building an American Garden City, was less spectacular than our proposed Garden Community. During the early years the Corporation required practice in large-scale planning, building, and community organization. Cautious, safe investment seemed a wise first step. Therefore we started in the Borough of Queens, on a large undeveloped site close to Manhattan's business center.

Construction of moderate-cost housing was once more slowly getting under way. It had been arrested during and after the First World War. This was in spite of the tremendous need, the crowding of our slums, and the doubling up of families. Building costs had almost doubled between 1914 and 1924.

Speculators feared the competition of lower future building costs. Ultimately, as the result of the tax exemption[2] offered by the city in 1920, a housing boom started in the practically undeveloped area across the East River. Land values were low, but street or utility improvements and recreational space were practically non-existent. Endless rows of cramped shoddy wooden houses and garages covered the land and destroyed natural green spaces (Fig. 7). The Metropolitan Life Insurance Company, as a result of tax-exemption, built, in Queens Borough, large-scale apartment groups to rent at $9 a room.

Near the largest of these the City Housing Corporation, in early 1924, purchased an undeveloped area which had been held by the Long Island Railroad for use as a railroad yard. With additional purchases, there were about 77 acres, 55.82 of which were used to create the Sunnyside Community of 1,202 family units. These were built during 1924-1928 as a continuous large-scale operation.

THE SITE was convenient for workers in the office centers of Manhattan. The rapid transit station at the corner of the property was 15 minutes travel time from the 42nd Street center. Land was cheap, averaging 50¢ per square foot, not including streets. It offered little difficulty, through rock or soil, for large-scale methods of excavating. Main utilities came to the edge of the property. We found it more economical to install sewers, and to build streets under City specification, than to have this done by the municipality. Our work was programmed so that each unit of building was completed without leaving vacant lots, and utilities were installed only as needed. This saved greatly on carrying charges as compared with the typical spotty methods of development.

1924-1928 were good years financially and for employment. Sunnyside houses were sold and apartments rented as soon as they were completed.

The City Housing Corporation had profited when in the autumn of 1928 it had finished its building of Sunnyside. This was not only because of good management, low-cost land close to rapid transit, economical planning, and orderly large-scale building in the brief period of 1924-1928. It was also a result of fortuitous circumstances. Among these were (1) the colossal post-war de-

SAINT PETER'S COLLEGE LIBRARY
JERSEY CITY, NEW JERSEY 07306

SUNNYSIDE GARDENS

mand for homes, which filled houses as soon as they were finished; (2) and as a result of (1) the rapid rise of land costs. The 671 thousand square feet of land purchased by the corporation, but not used, increased in value from 50¢ a square foot (plus 15¢ carrying and improvement cost) to $1.62 a square foot.[3]

Objectives

PURPOSE.—The ultimate aim of the City Housing Corporation was to build a garden city. Knowledge and experience gained at Sunnyside was intended to serve that objective. The immediate purposes, as stated by Mr. Bing in 1926, were 'to produce good homes at as low a price as possible: to make the company's investment safe; . . . to use the work of building and selling houses as a laboratory in which to work out better house and block plans and better methods of construction and financing.'

These objectives guided us in planning Sunnyside.

1. It was a laboratory, an experiment, a voyage of discovery, and an adventure.

2. Economy in planning and building was essential. Most earlier well-intentioned American attempts at community housing for low-income workers had been tempted, by planners' delight in spacious elaboration, into becoming middle-class suburbs. Wright and I were determined to simplify and even squeeze our house plans so as to make them available at as low a price as possible. Economical spaciousness we hoped for as a result of judicious group planning.

LAND COST.—One of the principal reasons given for unhealthy, inhuman congestion is generally the high cost of urban land.

What we demonstrated for America, by our site and group planning at Sunnyside, and even more at Radburn, was the possibility of preserving open spaces for natural green, for recreation, for light, for healthful living, and for more spacious and beautiful living without additional cost, in fact at less than the normal price.

The basic theories by which we worked were not new. In England, Raymond Unwin, at the beginning of the century, in his revolutionary pamphlet 'Nothing Gained by Overcrowding,' had adequately proved that large open spaces could be preserved in block centers at practically no additional cost per lot, and with far less investment of capital or labor. Henry Wright brilliantly applied these principles to American conditions.

The division of land costs at both Sunnyside and Radburn illustrate the discrepancy between raw and improved land. The land at Sunnyside had been out of farm use for thirty to thirty-five years. During that period of 'ripening' the cost of the land rose from 3.3 cents per square foot in 1892 to the 48.5 cents that the City Housing Corporation paid the railroad for property it had held out of use for 18 years. There was no profit in this difference of 45 cents.

The increased value was mainly in carrying charges, taxes and interest. Up to the time of the City Housing Corporation's purchase in 1924, the railroad in 18 years had built up 38.3 cents production cost, of which less than one cent was for public improvements. The City Housing Corporation, through speedy use, minimized the carrying charges on the land. Of the production costs of $33\frac{1}{3}$ cents between purchase and use for construction, 24 cents per square foot went for public improvements and interest on these, as compared with $8\frac{2}{3}$ cents for taxes and interest on investment.[4]

Planning Sunnyside

THE GENERAL PLAN (Fig. 3).—There never was time to study the plan of Sunnyside as a whole. As soon as the tract of land owned by the Pennsylvania Railroad was purchased in February, 1924, planning for the first unit was started. Building actually commenced on April 1st, two months later.

Our previous studies, in 1923, of a garden community had proved the unnecessary costliness of developments based on the typical gridiron layout.[5] But the Sunnyside area was already laid out in city blocks 190 to 200 feet wide and about 600 to 900 feet long (Fig. 3). In spite of the evidence of economy and better living conditions shown in the various studies made by Wright, for the elimination of certain thoroughfares that became dead-ends by the railroad, the Borough Engineer's Office would have nothing of it. The streets were on the map

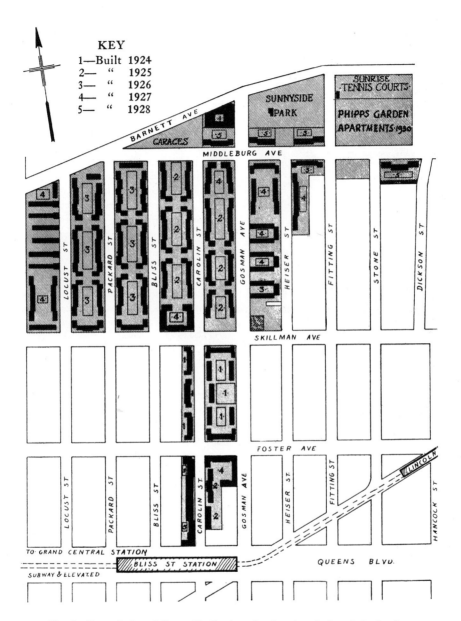

Fig. 3—General plan of Sunnyside Gardens showing the relation of the development to the city block system of layout, the position of the rapid transit station, and the site of Phipps Garden Apartments. The years in which the various stages of construction were completed are indicated. These streets have had their names changed. Locust, Packard, Bliss, and Carolin are now 44th, 45th, 46th, and 47th Streets, respectively. Middleburg Ave. is now 39th Ave., Foster Ave. is now 43rd Ave.

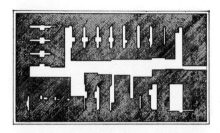

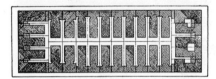

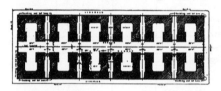

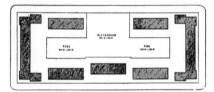

Fig. 4—Comparison of four ways of developing blocks in New York City. In the first three examples the subdivision into lots is the controlling factor in design. In the third, by the Metropolitan Life Insurance Company, the inner green space is greatly increased, but the persistence of lot subdivision causes bad side-lighting. In the fourth example, lot subdivision no longer controls design.

and there they must remain. A variation would be a dangerous precedent! Ultimately, only a few short ends of streets near the railroads were closed. These were advantageously used for garage groups, the Park, and in the end for the Phipps Garden Apartments. Elsewhere we were forced to fit our buildings to the blocks rather than the blocks to the living conditions, as we afterwards did at Radburn.

GROUP PLANS.—The first unit, built in 1924, was designed as a separate community (Fig. 5). By surrounding the perimeter of the block with narrow buildings, leaving no projecting wings, a great part of the block could be held for common use, even after allowing for private gardens connected with the single and two-family houses (Fig. 6). Playground and common garden space was dedicated as a private park for the use of surrounding residents, under the control of block trustees (Fig. 8). Experience showed that the single tennis court was an impractically small unit for operation. The playground activities were found annoying and noisy by those who dwelt around them (Fig. 5).

During the second and third years the use of the common block centers was continued, but in a somewhat different form. The long 900-foot blocks were divided into smaller quadrangles, almost completely enclosed and in scale with humans and their two-story houses. These interior garden courts were the equivalent of a park, some three-quarters of a mile in length and totalling six acres in area. Their appearance contrasted sharply with the typical speculators' developments nearby on similar blocks, crowded with garages and access roads, a mass of gray cement and roofs, barren of trees and grass. The characteristic Sunnyside block interior was some 120 feet wide between the rear of buildings. Each house had its private garden space, about 30 feet deep. The central areas, some 60 feet wide, though legally the property of the various owners, were used in common by all those in the surrounding houses under a 40-year easement agreement (Fig. 12). These common greens were intended for restful gatherings or for quiet play. They were not to be used as playground for any but the very young (Fig. 13). Adequate space was left between the rear of the end buildings to open up a vista through the length of the block. Between the three-family buildings, paths cross from street to street

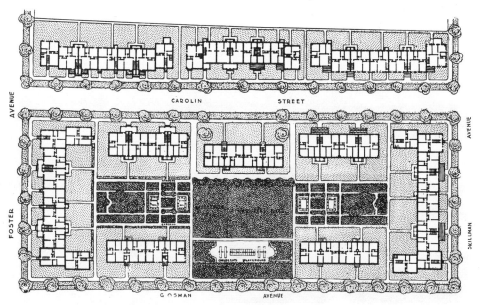

Fig. 5—*The first unit of Sunnyside, built in 1924.*

Fig. 6—*The interior of a block in the first development, showing the landscaping soon after completion in 1924. Apartment buildings and two-story single and two-family houses are on the perimeter. The central space is for common use and there are private gardens. From foreground to background may be seen decorative gardens, infants' play space with pergola, young children's recreation space, and then tennis courts. In the distance is the rapid transit line to midtown New York. Photo taken in 1924.*

SUNNYSIDE GARDENS

Fig. 7—The character of miles of boom development in Long Island City at the time when the Sunnyside Gardens project was conceived.

Fig. 8—Children's playground in court of the first unit, built in 1924. Photo taken in August 1949.

and give access to the center of the blocks. These cross-walks were staggered so as to create interesting vistas with terminal facades (Fig.9).

The carrying of coal, ice and food to the rear of row houses meant in the early work two areaways allowing passageway through the cellar. Later, on the basis of our observation in the English Garden Cities, Henry Wright and I decided to try passageways through the ground floor of some houses. These were not successful; they complicated the plans, and were difficult to maintain and police.

GARAGE COMPOUNDS.—The preservation of the Sunnyside block interiors required some other location of garages. They were grouped at the other side of Middleburg Avenue near the railroad. This was a daring thing to do, especially as the nearest house in the first unit was fully a thousand feet away, and there was nothing but barren waste between. However, this did not prevent the quick sale of houses. The parklike courts more than compensated for the lengthy walk to the garages.

The garages, which were grouped behind a brick wall, were factory-made metal units. They served well the first decade or so; they are now rather obsolete. Our large automobiles are cramped both in the garages and in the roads. The metal exteriors are rusted and worn. We have found masonry garages, in the later developments, more lasting. A little additional cost in construction, and above all in spaciousness, to prepare for possible change is generally a good investment.

At a later date, a large two-story concrete garage was erected nearby by the corporation. It was heated, and service was expensive. Therefore it was necessary to charge more rent, much more than most Sunnyside residents could afford. The large garage never paid. It has been my experience that in communities of this kind the simple type of low structure is the most successful and most satisfactory. Expensive, large structures require too much in overhead costs.

COURTS AND GARDENS.—In the last years at Sunnyside, at the edges of the property, we built courts opening off the streets. Our purpose was to front as few houses as possible toward the outside builders' monotonous rows. The continuous rows of buildings on three sides of a common green have

a pleasant sense of enclosure. Architecturally I find them more satisfactory than the broken line of free-standing houses on typical Radburn culs-de-sac (Fig. 11).

These courts worked very well at Sunnyside in spite of being fitted into the gridiron street pattern. There is a great deal of privacy on the garden sides, augmented by the height above Gosman Avenue of the three eastern groups (Fig. 14). The varied landscape design is rich with twenty years' growth, and has a restful beauty. The livingrooms and most of the bedrooms face toward gardens instead of streets. Services come directly to the kitchen or cellar entrance by private paved service lanes which connect two public streets.

Lewis Mumford, who lived in Sunnyside for 11 years, most of this time on one of these courts, has this to say:[6] 'It has been framed to the human scale and its gardens and courts kept that friendly air as, year by year, the newcomers improved in the art of gardening and the plane trees and poplars continued to grow . . .

'So, though our means were modest, we contrived to live in an environment where space, sunlight, order, color—these essential ingredients for either life or art—were constantly present, silently molding all of us.'

PLANNING ECONOMIES.—These courts opening off the street suggested methods of replacing some through streets with parks, as was afterwards done at Radburn. Let us compare their cost with a group of the same number of similar houses around the typical earlier inner courts. About the same amount of main street front is required on two streets for the two arrangements of two three-family houses, two two-family houses and 12 single-family dwellings. However if we had been permitted to close every second street without installation of main line utilities and street paving, wiring, etc., we would have had a goodly saving. This would have more than paid for adequate turn-arounds at private lane ends, or even for narrow U-shaped roads around each second dead-end group. It would also have covered the costs of replacing half the streets with well-planted parks, sixty feet wide.

GROUPING.—We mixed the different house types in the same rows throughout the development:

SUNNYSIDE GARDENS

single-family-home-owners next to landlord and tenant in flats. In spite of the speculative operators' fear of such indiscriminate grouping, and the zoners' preoccupation in keeping dwellings of similar types together, we found this did not cause sales resistance. I have heard of no social difficulty resulting from it. The tenants on the second floor were members of the Sunnyside Association as well as the house owners, and so were those of the apartment houses, both in the co-operatives and those operated by the Corporation as landlord.

In the block which was developed during the first year we grouped three-floor apartment buildings with the two-story rows of mixed single and two-family houses. The varied heights give far more interest than could any amount of pattern, horizontal or vertical massing of windows, or lines of brick ornament. Such a combination would not have been permitted if Sunnyside had been classified within the zoning laws as *residential*. Luckily, as a proposed site of a railroad yard, Sunnyside was mainly classified as *industrial*. Therefore we were free to design for community and aesthetic objectives.

We continued to experiment in this manner by locating an apartment building around a court which opened on the central green of the block. This gave the apartment tenants a view for 800 feet over trees and lawns and gardens and pergolas.

UNIT PLANS.—We aimed to simplify construction, heating and plumbing; to make every internal inch serve, to eliminate waste movement, to minimize frontage and thus utility costs. We studied every detail so as to save money and thus serve as low an income group as possible. We counted on the spaciousness of our gardens to compensate for any undue tightness inside houses.

The types of houses at Sunnyside were limited in number (Fig. 10). We did our best to standardize so as to keep down costs and resulting selling price. All residences were two stories high above a basement. They had maximum cross-ventilation as none was more than two rooms deep. The depth of 28-ft. 4-in. which was used through all five years, and for all single and two-family houses as well as for the earlier apartments, was based on stock framing lengths.

After a careful cost analysis was made by Henry Wright in 1925, we made some minor changes. The operation of all mechanics was carefully followed and timed, so as to find ways of improving plans and construction without increasing costs. What we learnt was very useful in developing broader types of economical houses at Chatham Village.

The *two-family* house had identical plans on both floors. The typical apartment, 25-ft. wide, had two bedrooms besides kitchen and livingroom. The end houses, 28-ft. wide, had in addition a diningroom that could be used as an additional bedroom. These were very economical houses. The first year we used identical plans for our first apartment building which was three stories high, for the purpose of comparing construction costs.

The *three-family* house was planned primarily as the end enclosure of our garden courts. It also filled the needs of larger families in the first floor apartments, and the two upper apartments, each with a single bedroom, livingroom and kitchen, served well for the newly-wed families.

These houses had windows on all four sides and were almost free-standing, having very little attachment to the row. They had more than the usual garden space. In fact, the family on the ground floor, in a number of cases I have noted of late, not only grows flowers, but even vegetables.

Both two- and three-family houses were purchased by single owners at Sunnyside, on the basis of the upper-floor tenants helping to pay operation charges and maintenance. As a result, all disputes between owner and tenant eventually came to the management office of the City Housing Corporation. When hard times came and rents could not be paid or tenants moved out, the owners of these multiple-family houses were in much worse straits than the individual house owners.

The predominant type of *apartment dwelling*, the four-room unit (which was similar to that of the two-family house), had one outstanding defect. One bedroom opened into the livingroom and not into the passageway leading to the bathroom. Another less important objection was that access to all rooms except kitchen was through the end of the livingroom. In spite of this the houses and apartments were popular. Therefore I continued to use these two types, because of their great economy and

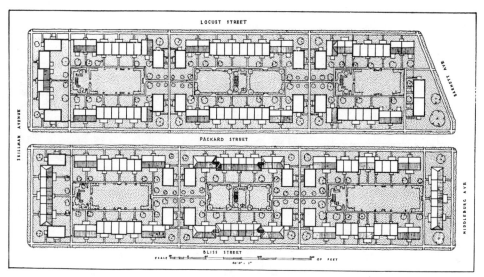

Fig. 9—Plan of two blocks with inner courts, built in 1926.

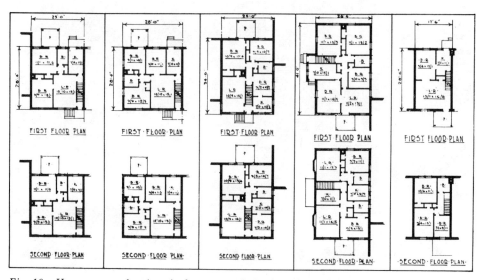

Fig. 10—House types, showing single, two- and three-family houses.

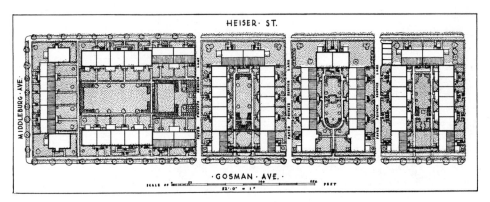

Fig. 11—Plan of part of a block with an inner court and three courts opening off the street, built in 1927.

Fig. 12—An inner court built in 1926. Photo taken in August, 1949.

minimum corridors for walk-up apartments, for years, gradually increasing the depth from 28 feet to 34. We must have built thousands of them at Sunnyside and Phipps. Then I finally developed a plan with all bedrooms leading to the corridor for Hillside, and used it again for the second unit of Phipps Homes (Fig. 97).

The Corporation looked upon Sunnyside as a social and economic, as well as an architectural, experiment. Therefore they tried co-operative ownership of the first apartment buildings. Only a few experiments in co-operative ownership of low-priced apartments had been tried in New York. These were mostly by groups of the same ancestry, from countries such as Finland where there had been practical experience in co-operation. The Sunnyside purchasers were of varied racial, religious and social background, and perhaps because of this the co-operatives were not successful. In later co-operative schemes success has been achieved. Perhaps we were too early with the Sunnyside experiment.

BASEMENT.—There is much to be said for and against cellars in single or two-family dwellings. Most governmental houses have been built without them, but they never have enough storage space. I am for cellars, ground conditions and water level permitting. A house should be lifted up a few steps as protection against rain and snow. In the north, footings have to go down below the frost level. Slightly more depth will suffice for a cellar. If ground is not rocky, a bulldozer will clear the whole space under the house as easily as cutting for footings and foundations only. It gives the cheapest possible space for heating and storage. If the ground slopes a little, as at Chatham Village, a large window can be put in at one end for a work-room or children's play space.

Brick Exteriors

USE OF BRICK, we found, had certain difficulties, such as leaking. This was not due to the use of comparatively cheap local (Hudson River) bricks, instead of the more extravagant face bricks. The leaks, experts told us, were through the joints—too much lime in our mortar. Keppler, the great master-builder of Amsterdam, said when I discussed our difficulties with him: 'In Holland we have built our walls almost exclusively of bricks for a thousand years. We should be experts, but they still leak.'

There is an architectural harmony at Sunnyside because of the common use of brick, as well as the repetition of simple details and the continuous roof lines. After twenty years or so, I am still strongly impressed by the advantage of brick over wood as an exterior material, whether it is used for bearing walls, as in Sunnyside's first year, or merely as a facing, as it was later used there and at Radburn. I am thinking of its effective appearance in a setting of natural green. That is the dominant feature at Sunnyside. The street trees that were so thin and scraggly when Marjorie Cautley, the Landscape Architect, planted them two decades ago now almost arch over the streets. The varied Hudson River brick, our common brick in New York City, forms a beautiful and contrasting background for the trees. And then there are the inner courts! In midsummer they seem almost too rich and luxuriant. But the dwellers in the surrounding houses are probably thankful for the protection from the sometimes torrid summer sun and in part from rain, as well as for the everchanging play of light and shadows on the opposite buildings. The courts seem well enough cared for after all these difficult years of depression and war. The planting of the little private gardens in many cases shows care and affection for natural beauty. There are even some home-owners who are growing vegetables, mainly in the larger lots around the three-family houses.

The brick exteriors remain more harmonious than wood because they are not painted. Therefore, there is no danger of assertive souls expressing their individuality, to the dismay of their neighbors, by coloring their dwelling with an inharmonious pigment. The natural quality of the brick eliminates the need of one expensive item of upkeep.

Life in Sunnyside

Although the orderly community character of Sunnyside drew to it teachers, artists, and writers, the intellectuals never were a dominant portion of the Sunnyside population. A census of house-owners in 1928 showed that non-professional workers—116 mechanics, 79 office-workers, 55

Fig. 13—An inner court built in 1926. Photo taken in August 1949.

Fig. 14—A court opening off the street, built in 1927.
Photo taken in 1949.

SUNNYSIDE GARDENS

small tradesmen, 5 chauffeurs, 49 salesmen, etc.—were about four times as numerous as actors, artists, musicians, teachers, architects, engineers, doctors, and other professionals.

The Sunnyside population was a cross-section of those of moderate means (in 1926 the median income was $3,000). They were not the very poor who were afterwards to be housed by the Housing Authority with the aid of a governmental subsidy.

It was the pupose of the City Housing Corporation to create a setting in which a democratic community might grow. The Corporation supplied the place and equipment for community gathering and activity. In the beginning it also employed playground directors and encouraged the organization of a community association. Tenants and house owners had equal voice in community undertakings. The Corporation enthusiastically cooperated in the rapid development of social activity.

In the beginning there was no time to prepare a general community or physical plan. The two grew together. The neighborhood unit idea was still to be developed in America. Sunnyside was a pioneer in the community field as well as in housing.

As construction was gradually completed, court or block groupings served as centers for social activity and block organizations sponsored the program. Ultimately a recreation park served as a social center for the whole community.

In 1926 the City Housing Corporation set aside a park of three and a half acres and fully equipped it for the recreational use of children of all ages, as well as adults. A house already on the site was adapted to serve as a Community Building. The park was deeded to the Community Trust to be held in trust for the use of the 1202 families of Sunnyside.

With the establishment of this physical center for activity came the organization of a single Sunnyside Community Association. This was more effective than the several separate 'block' organizations. However, for the protection of property interests of the house owners and the maintenance of the block centers, the property owners' associations which had been organized for each block were continued.

Later, at Radburn, because of the Sunnyside experience, a single association was formed in the beginning with much broader functions than the Sunnyside Community Association.

The economic depression affected the people of Sunnyside as it did the great many who lived in the thousands of houses which sprang up in the Borough of Queens during the building boom period of the twenties. There was unemployment, savings were spent, and people were unable to pay the interest and amortization on their mortgages. In the end, many lost the homes they had thought were theirs.

There was one important difference between the people of Sunnyside and the others. Sunnyside was a community of people accustomed to meeting and doing things together—a real neighborhood community. The others were lone individuals with no organized social or other relations with the people who lived next door. At Sunnyside a home-owners' group was quickly formed; it comprised a majority of the community. The home-owners, as a community group, were soon ready to ask, and if necessary to fight, for a postponement of or a decrease in mortgage payments. In the end, they went on strike and, as a group, refused to make payments. Their attack was aimed at the City Housing Corporation. In this they were wrong, no matter how just might be their resentment.

The City Housing Corporation, in regard to the collection of charges on mortgages, was only the agent of the lending institutions that held the principal mortgages. The financial organizations had no personal contact with the home-owners of Sunnyside, or with any others who were being dispossessed. They insisted that the legal terms of the mortgages be fully carried out; basic economic conditions or sentiment were not within their province. The City Housing Corporation, though powerless, took the full brunt of the attack from the organized people of Sunnyside. The irony of the situation was that it had stimulated and helped community organization, and those living in Sunnyside had thus become accustomed to forming their own organizations.

The disunion growing out of the conflicts in the community, at that time, ended the most constructive development of community life, and Sunnyside has never regained its sense of unity as a neighborhood. However, the green commons, and their continued care by the block groups, have served as a basis of local unity; and, most important perhaps, the beauty of the garden-community, within the framework of the busy city, has been preserved. This pointed the way toward the 'Radburn Idea.'

Conclusions

I. GREEN COMMONS in block centers can be developed, even within the limitations of the characteristic American gridiron street pattern. They make a peaceful and beautiful setting for the surrounding homes.

Private deed restrictions can preserve such common green areas which are likely to disappear if protected solely by zoning.

II. THE GROUPING OF BUILDINGS of different heights and bulk, if well organized, increases the architectural interest and distributes the advantages of open spaces.

A combination in rows or groups of single-family, two-family and apartment houses, inhabited partially by tenants and partially by home-owners, need not cause social difficulties or sales resistance.

III. THE SIMPLE RECTANGULAR FORM of apartment unit gives maximum livability at minimum cost.

IV. SUCCESSFUL INVESTMENT HOUSING DEVELOPMENT for those of limited incomes requires:

1. *Low cost land,* adequate in size and easy of development.
2. *Transportation* to take people easily to working places in relatively short time.
3. *Continuous large scale building* of complete sections with installations of utilities and streets paralleling construction of buildings, the building to be followed immediately by marketing and use.
4. *Rapid development* so as to minimize carrying charges.
5. *Simple standardized units.*
6. *Grouping* for unity and variety of appearance as well as to add to the feeling of spaciousness given by the open areas.
7. *Limited interest rate* on capital invested.

All these elements existed in the development of Sunnyside. As a result it was a financial success until it was blighted by the depression. The disastrous results, both to the inhabitants and the City Housing Corporation, that followed were accentuated by the system of mortgage financing that functions to the advantage of owner or tenant only in the limited periods between economic deflation.

These periods, as shown (in Fig. 1), have been shorter, in the past, than the time required to pay off most residential mortgages. As the 'home-owner' has only a minority holding on his house, when inevitable depression comes, he discovers that 'home-ownership' for those with low incomes is a myth.

V. RESEARCH AND ANALYSIS should form an essential part of all community development. Every job should be a laboratory. Customary plans, forms or construction methods should be constantly questioned and analyzed. Fresh exploration and investigation is required to keep both architecture and community organization alive and contemporary.

Fig. 15—Houses and landscape are united in a spacious composition.

2 RADBURN

**Clarence S. Stein and Henry Wright,
Town Planners
Clarence S. Stein, Chief Architect
Frederick L. Ackerman, Architect of Blocks
of Houses and Radburn Building
Andrew J. Thomas,
Architect of Apartment Buildings
James Renwick Thomson,
Associate Architect for House Groups**

Economic Background

Early in 1928, after four years of success at Sunnyside, the City Housing Corporation was prepared to carry out its original objective, the building of a complete Garden City.

It had an experienced organization of technicians practised in economical planning, large-scale building, real-estate management, and community organization. It had confidence based on increasing success. By the end of the year Sunnyside would be completed; 1200 units would be sold or rented; 8 million dollars would be invested in Sunnyside, and after paying operating and carrying expenses and full annual 6 per cent stock dividend, a good surplus would remain to invest in the new venture. Mr. Bing was convinced of the security of the investment. He said[7] 'The larger the company becomes, the safer its operations will be, the greater the economy . . . of the company's work.' Land prices had risen so that ultimately the 20¾ acres at Sunnyside not used in the development were sold at a profit of over $646,000 — almost three times its cost. In short the Corporation was riding high on the waves of prosperity and booming real estate.[8]

The economic atmosphere in which Radburn was born was very different. The first home-owners moved into Radburn in May, 1929; that autumn the Wall Street market collapsed. Building went on around New York for a while, and for some years the City Housing Corporation continued to buy land and build at Radburn, though at a diminishing rate (twelve houses were built in 1933). Mean-

while the home owners of Radburn lost their jobs and incomes, and many of them their homes. The depression gave them the time and leisure to use the community opportunities provided by the physical and social plan. But it left a deep scar on their lives and little hope for the successful completion of Radburn. The City Housing Corporation was ruined. It lost most of the land outside the two developed superblocks. But in these there was enough to demonstrate a new form of town and community building: the Radburn Idea.

Conception of the Radburn Idea

Sunnyside was a dress rehearsal, but on a stage so limited that the authors' style was cramped. During the final year's performance, a search was started for an adequate theater in which to produce an American Garden City.

In our minds' eye we still had the theme that Ebenezer Howard had created so vividly in his book 'Garden Cities of Tomorrow.' We believed thoroughly in green belts, and towns of a limited size planned for work as well as living. We did not fully recognize that our main interest after our Sunnyside experience had been transferred to a more pressing need, that of a town in which people could live peacefully with the automobile—or rather in spite of it. The limitations which we found in the gridiron street pattern at Sunnyside, as a setting for safe motor-age living, made clear to all the staff what we planners had long seen and had planned to eliminate. So it was not surprising that at a staff discussion of the next project, the

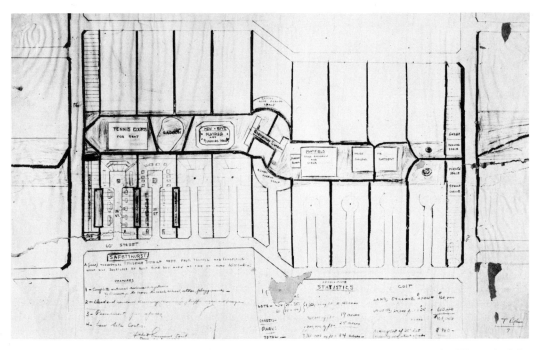

Fig. 16—*Sketch plan made by Herbert Emmerich on December 3, 1927. The principles developed by the architects of Sunnyside are here set down by an administrator, who had joined in many discussions and was thoroughly conversant with the experience of Sunnyside. He called his superblock "Safetyhurst: a (highly) theoretical residence district free from traffic and congestion—which will doubtless be built someday when we tire of auto risks!"*

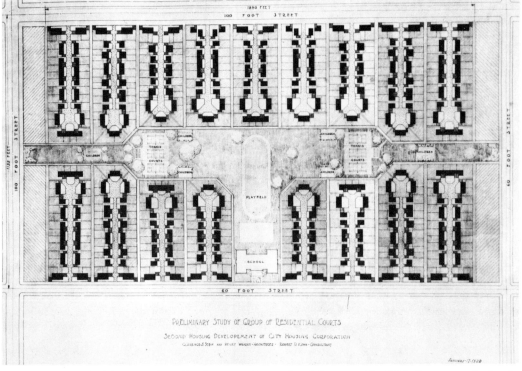

Fig. 17—*Theoretical study of a superblock, dated January 17, 1928. It was made by the architects at the time when the idea was being discussed by all concerned, including Mr. Emmerich. It was soon to be the basis of the Radburn Plan.*

young general manager, who was later to become head of the Federal Public Housing Authority, Herbert Emmerich, appeared with a crude, but complete, diagram of a superblock, which formed a neighborhood (Fig. 16).

The preliminary theoretical diagram of a rectangular superblock that the architects drew on January 17, 1928, included all the elements of the Radburn Idea (Fig. 17). The superblocks built at Radburn, although less geometric as a result of the topography—and therefore more interesting—were basically the same.

The Site

After examining some 50 possible sites, a large tract of undeveloped fertile farm land in the Borough of Fairlawn, New Jersey, only sixteen miles from New York, was chosen.

The speculative builders, who were already ruthlessly destroying the appearance of the land toward the proposed George Washington Bridge, had found this property too expensive. The good farmers, descendants of the Dutch, who had worked the land since Colonial days, were content and not anxious to sell. Careful maneuvering by real estate agents was required to prevent land prices from soaring beyond the possibilities of moderate cost housing.

The site was attractive, with rolling ground, but only a slight pitch at most places. Groups of houses could be arranged around courts without too much grading. There were some moderate hills that offered attractive locations for buildings of importance, such as the high school. Very little of the land was marshy. Most of it was good for economical large-scale building, with little rock that would require heavy blasting.

The property lent itself very well to the development of a new street system. Fairlawn Avenue, which appears on George Washington's military map, was the only existing road of importance. The large open areas to north and south we later connected by an overpass where the avenue dipped below the land at either side. The Borough of Fairlawn, then mainly a rural community, had not yet been sold an official road plan or a zoning ordinance. For this we offered thanks; we were free to design a functional town plan.

About two square miles of irregularly-shaped land on which to build Radburn was ultimately secured by the City Housing Corporation. There was an area sufficient for three neighborhoods, with a total population of about 25,000.

Not a Garden City

There was not, however, adequate area to surround the proposed town with a broad protecting greenbelt. This essential element of the garden city was sacrificed because of the greater emphasis on our other objectives. All that remained of green belt in the general plan was the proposed narrow parkway as northern boundary, and the recreation field along Saddle River to the east. That these would have been insufficient to give the essential protection was proved by what happened. The unrelated, badly conceived products of the speculative builder now hem it on every side. Fortunately, Radburn can still look into the center of its superblocks for peaceful green (Fig. 49).

Industrial opportunities seemed good, according to the rules that were generally followed. The town was served by the Erie Railroad; it was near Paterson, which had been one of the great silk industry centers; an express highway was planned to the great bridge which was being constructed to link New York with New Jersey.

We made our decisions quickly in those days. Our preliminary plans showed spacious sites for industry adjacent to the proposed express highway and the railroad. But the railroad was a secondary branch that went nowhere of importance. The Hudson River bridge to New York and the proposed through highway were both in the future; industry lives in the present, we found. Perhaps it was the bad times that kept factories away; but I think that section of New Jersey was on the downward trend, industrially. Certainly Paterson was losing its principal industry—the manufacture of silk (the fact that it has had an industrial revival since was of no help then). Most of the workers in the Paterson plants were too poorly paid to afford Radburn houses. This was only partially due to the quality of planning and building and the high standard of community facilities and organization at Radburn. At that time the provision of decent homes for low paid workers was an

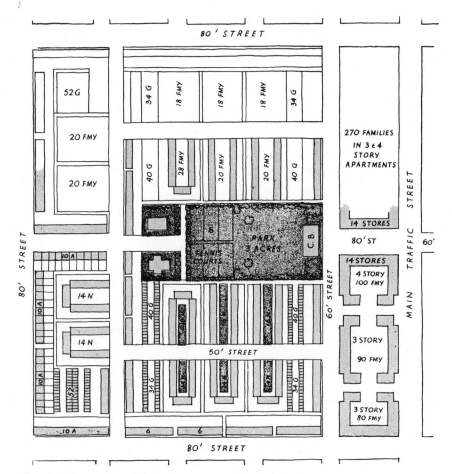

Fig. 18—Diagram reproducing a sketch in the "Study of Application of Sunnyside Planning Principles to a Larger City Area," a report prepared by Henry Wright in December 1924. The idea of the Radburn superblock with an inner park is emerging.

economic impossibility. It would still be so now, if there were no governmental subsidies, low rate loans or insured mortgages. Government aid in housing was non-existent at that time Radburn was built.

Thus two of the basic Garden City ideas, green belt and industry, were eliminated, and Radburn had to accept the role of a suburb. Though some engineers and executives of New Jersey public utility companies and other corporations purchased houses, most of the inhabitants were, and still are, 'white-collar' commuters from New York City.

At that period, access to Manhattan was difficult. The Erie Railroad service was poor and expensive; and the journey had to be completed by ferry and streetcar. By the time the George Washington Bridge and the connecting superhighway were completed, the depression had blighted all hope of success of Radburn, which required quick growth to balance carrying charges of land, plant and management organization.

CO-ORDINATION OF ECONOMIC WITH PHYSICAL AND SOCIAL PLANNING.—The failure of Radburn to become a Garden City, and its limitations as a suburb of New York, emphasize the dominant importance of the convenient and economic relation of working and living places in the choice of site of any new town. Generalizations are not sufficient. Good timing is essential to succesful New Town planning. Future transportation, or tomorrow's highways, do not market houses to workers now. It was not only at Radburn, but in the choice of sites for the three Greenbelt towns, that the economic and industrial studies were not sufficiently specific and realistic.

The Radburn Idea

Radburn's ultimate role was quite different from our original aim. It was not to be a Garden City. It did not become a complete, balanced New Town. Instead of proving the investment value of large-scale housing it became, as a result of the depression, a financial failure. Yet Radburn demonstrated for America a new form of city and community that fits the needs of present day urban living in America, and it is influencing city building throughout the world.

We did our best to follow Aristotle's recommen-

dation that 'a city should be built to give its inhabitants security and happiness.'

THE NEED FOR RADBURN.—American cities were certainly not places of security in the twenties. The automobile was a disrupting menace to city life in the U.S.A.—long before it was in Europe. In 1928 there were 21,308,159 automobiles registered (as compared with 5 in 1895). The flood of motors had already made the gridiron street pattern, which had formed the framework for urban real estate for over a century, as obsolete as a fortified town wall. Pedestrians risked a dangerous motor street crossing 20 times a mile. The roadbed was the children's main play space. Every year there were more Americans killed or injured in automobile accidents than the total of American war casualties in any year. The checkerboard pattern made all streets equally inviting to through traffic. Quiet and peaceful repose disappeared along with safety. Porches faced bedlams of motor throughways with blocked traffic, honking horns, noxious gases. Parked cars, hard grey roads and garages replaced gardens.

It was in answer to such conditions that the Radburn plan was evolved. For America it was a revolution in planning; a revolution, I regret to say, which is far from completed.

Elements of the Radburn Plan

'The Radburn Idea,' to answer the enigma 'How to live with the auto', or, if you will, 'How to live in spite of it,' met these difficulties with a radical revision of relation of houses, roads, paths, gardens, parks, blocks, and local neighborhoods (Figs. 19, 20 and 21). For this purpose it used the following elements:

1. THE SUPERBLOCK in place of the characteristic narrow, rectangular block.

2. SPECIALIZED ROADS PLANNED AND BUILT FOR ONE USE INSTEAD OF FOR ALL USES: service lanes for direct access to buildings; secondary collector roads around superblocks; main through roads, linking the traffic of various sections, neighborhoods and districts; express highways or parkways, for connection with outside communities. (Thus differentiating between movement, collection, service, parking, and visiting.)

3. COMPLETE SEPARATION OF PEDESTRIAN AND

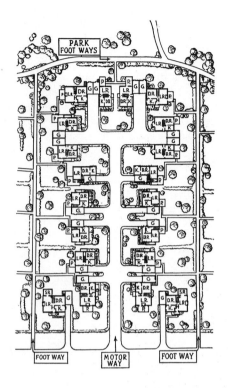

Fig. 19—Plan of a typical "lane" at Radburn. The park in the center of the superblock is shown at the top; the motor ways to the houses are at right angles to the park.

Fig. 20—Typical transverse section of a "lane" in the first unit of Radburn.

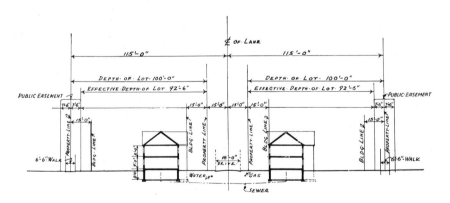

Fig. 21—Plan of the residential districts, dated November 1929.

AUTOMOBILE, or as complete separation as possible. Walks and paths routed at different places from roads and at different levels when they cross. For this purpose overpasses and underpasses were used.

4. HOUSES TURNED AROUND. Living and sleeping rooms facing toward gardens and parks; service rooms toward access roads.

5. PARK AS BACKBONE of the neighborhood. Large open areas in the center of superblocks, joined together as a continuous park.

Geddes Smith described Radburn compactly in 1929 as:[9]

'A town built to *live* in—today and tomorrow. A town "for the motor age." A town turned outside-in—without any backdoors. A town where roads and parks fit together like the fingers of your right and left hands. A town in which children need never dodge motor-trucks on their way to school. A *new* town—newer than the garden cities, and the first major innovation in town-planning since they were built.'

Precedents

None of the elements of the plan was completely new. The distinctive innovations of Radburn were the integrating superblocks, specialized and separated means of circulation, the park backbone, and the house with two fronts. Radburn interwove these to form a new unity, as a practical and attractive setting for the realities of today's living.

There were precedents for all the elements.

SUPERBLOCKS with great green interiors had been built in America. Before 1660, the Dutch in *Nieue Amsterdam* (New York) built their homes around the periphery of large blocks, with farms behind and sometimes with a great garden core (Fig. 22). However, throughout the nineteenth century and the early twentieth, most city growth was based on the repetitious geometric gridiron; a plan for facile plotting, surveying, legal recording—but not a plan for living. So Henry Wright and I went to Britain, on a special investigation to study superblocks with culs-de-sac, before we started planning Radburn. We concluded that, because of the greater use of the automobile in America, we were justified in increasing the size of superblocks over those at Welwyn, Letchworth and Hampstead Garden Suburb. The Radburn blocks were 30 to 50 acres in size. Their outlines were determined by their internal needs and by topography. Because of our heavier automobile traffic we faced fewer houses on main highways than most of the British examples. The English experiences helped us greatly, but if the superblock had not existed logic would have forced us to invent it. A rational escape from the limitations of the checker-board plan in which all streets are through-streets, with the possibility of a collision between auto and pedestrian every 250 feet, compelled it.

CULS-DE-SAC.—The dead-end lane had served in England for peacefulness and for economy of roads and utilities. Culs-de-sac had been used occasionally in our colonial villages. But the typical early American arrangement of houses was along the main, and sometimes only, road. This was more neighborly, and it was easier to shovel snow away in winter. The costliness of through street pavement and main line utilities was not yet a factor of economic importance. Later the extravagance was not understood. Real-estate and municipal engineering customs perpetuated obsolete forms.

I have already spoken of our experience with courts opening off streets at Sunnyside.

SEPARATION OF DIFFERENT MEANS OF COMMUNICATION had an excellent nearby precedent, Central Park in New York. Here, almost half a century before the invention of the automobile, Frederick Law Olmsted and Calvert Vaux planned and executed what they described in 1851 as:[10]

'. . . A system of independent ways; 1st, for carriages; 2nd, for horsemen . . .; 3rd, for footmen; and 4th, for common street traffic requiring to cross the Park. By this means it was made possible . . . to go on foot to any district of the Park . . . without crossing a line of wheels on the same level . . .' (Fig. 25).

The automobile has multiplied the need of separating antagonistic uses of streets. The need is

Fig. 22—*Nieue Amsterdam in 1660. Redraft of the Castello Plan, by John Wolcott Adams and I. N. Phelps Stokes, 1916.*

Fig. 23—Air view of Radburn. Photo taken in 1929.

recorded in the statistics of automobile accidents—
33,410 deaths in 1946, to say nothing of the million
or more cripples.[11] At Radburn we proposed to
unscramble the varied services of urban streets.
Each means of circulation would take care of its
special job and no other: through traffic only on
the main highways; with street intersections decreased about two-fold; most parking as well as
garages, delivery, and other services, on the lanes;
walks completely separated from autos by making
them part of a park instead of a street, and by
under- or over-passing the roads; finally, children's
play spaces in the nearby park instead of in busy
roads.

SPECIALIZED HIGHWAYS were in their infancy in
the U.S.A. at the time that Radburn was conceived.
There was not much more than the differentiation
of parkways and pseudo-expressways from the ordinary city or town street. To plan or build roads
for a particular use and no other use required a
predetermined decision to make specialized use
permanent or rather long-lived. That was contrary
to the fundamentals of American real estate gambling, to serve which the pattern of ordinary highways had become the basis of city planning. I say
this in spite of the fact that the 1920's were the
heyday of zoning. None of the realtors, and few
city planners who accepted zoning as their practical
religion, seemed to have faith enough in the perm-
anency of purely residential use to plan streets to
serve solely that use. No, not even when the economy of so doing was clearly proved by Henry
Wright and Raymond Unwin. Zone for dwellings?
Yes, but don't give up the hope that your lot may
be occupied some day by a store, gas station, or
other more profitable use.

The Radburn Plan proposed to protect the residents, 1st, by planning and building for proposed
use, and no other use; 2nd, by private restrictions
rather than by wishful zoning.

THE HOUSE TURNED ROUND.—The creation of
the Radburn Idea and of the Radburn Plan was a
group activity. It was not merely the conception of
its architect-planners. It took form out of actual
experience at Sunnyside. It was influenced by the
character and diversified abilities and experience
of the technicians and the staff of the City Housing
Corporation. But there can be no question that

Fig. 24—The underpass is a safe way between home, recreation ground, school, and swimming pool.

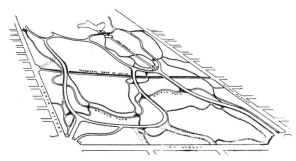

Fig. 25—Perspective sketch showing the separation of routes for vehicles, equestrians, pedestrians and outside traffic at the south end of Central Park, New York City. Greater comfort and safety is attained on all routes by the elimination of grade crossings, as planned by Frederick Law Olmsted a century ago.

the seed from which the Radburn idea grew was conceived by that imaginative genius Henry Wright. Luckily we have in his own words 'The Autobiography of Another Idea'[12]—that is, the Radburn idea.

'In 1902, as an impressionable youth just out of architectural school . . . at Waterford . . . Ireland, . . . I passed through an archway in a blank house wall on the street to a beautiful villa fronting upon spacious interior gardens. That archway was a passage to new ideas. . . . I learned then that the comforts and privacy of family life are . . . to be found . . . in a house that judiciously relates living space to open space, the open space. . . being capable of enjoyment by many as well as by few.'

From that time on Henry started 'to face kitchens and service rooms toward the street, and living-rooms inward toward the garden.' At Sunnyside we both wanted to turn all the houses that way, as we ultimately did at Radburn, but conservative opposition only permitted placing some of the porches on the lovely garden side.

ECONOMY OF THE RADBURN PLAN.—The parks that formed the interior core of the Radburn superblocks were secured without additional cost. Or rather the savings in expenditure for roads and public utilities at Radburn, as contrasted with the normal subdivision, paid for the parks. The Radburn type of plan requires less area of street to secure the same amount of frontage. In addition, for direct access to most houses, it uses narrower roads of less expensive construction, as well as smaller sized utility lines.

The superblock of 35 to 50 acres is surrounded by wide streets, but it replaces the greater number of wide broad streets of the normal checkerboard plan with service roads only 18 to 20 feet wide. The use of these is limited to 15 or 20 families living on each cul-de-sac, and they carry no through traffic going elsewhere. Therefore they can be of lighter construction, and sewers and water lines are of lesser size and cost than the main lines on the through highways. In fact the area in streets and the length of utilities is 25 per cent less than in the typical American street plan.

The saving in cost of these not only paid for the 12 to 14 per cent of the total area that went into internal parks, but also covered the cost of grading and landscaping the play spaces and green links connecting the central block commons. The greater part of this expenditure was for improvement. The land itself—in spite of its value for spinach-growing —cost only six cents a square foot. What makes subdivided land costly, even with the financing, carrying charges, taxes, and profits, is not the land itself. It is the roads and walks, sewers, water lines, electric, gas and other utilities that surround it. This land in lots along streets or lanes costs 6 cents gross or 10 cents per square foot, but an additional 25 cents must be added to pay its share of the improvement that lead to it. A park or playground in a regular town surrounded directly by improved streets would cost as much as it would with houses as a frontage. But not at Radburn—there land is just land (except for surrounding walks). There are no streets. So before landscaping the land, the cost of the parks was less than a fifth of what it would have been had dangerous highways encircled it.

The Plan of Radburn

The time between the purchase of land in Fairlawn and the starting of construction was too short to develop a plan of Radburn as a whole. This was vaguely in the back of our minds, to be given more definite form later. Our immediate problem was to relate the superblocks to the form of the land. We began with an area near the railroad station (Figs. 23, 26 and 49). As we did not want direct access to culs-de-sac from Fairlawn Avenue, which promised to become a main thoroughfare, we left a strip, an ordinary block wide (200 feet), between it and our first superblock. If we had had time to study our whole plan carefully before deciding on the first superblocks, we probably would have eliminated all of the old forms of block and separated the superblock from Fairlawn Avenue merely by a parallel service road. For these blocks have not lent themselves as well to practical development for modern living or shopping.

NEIGHBORHOODS.—At Radburn, I believe, the modern neighborhood conception was applied for the first time and, in part, realized in the form that is now generally accepted.

The neighborhoods were laid out with a radius of half a mile, centering on elementary schools and

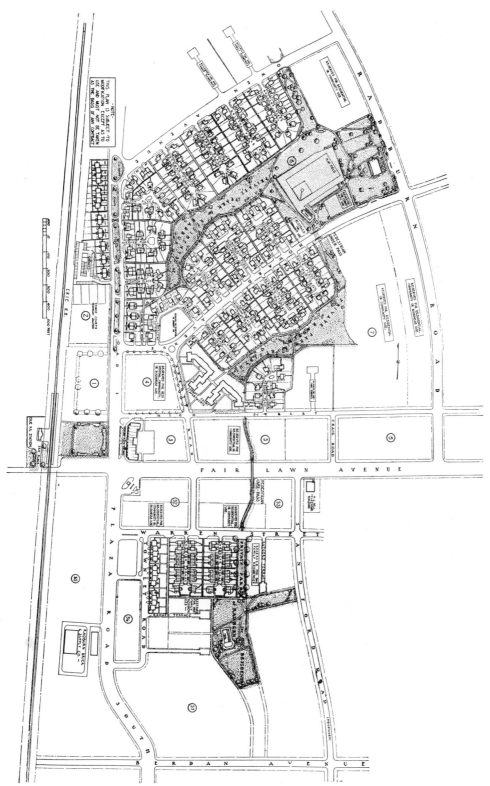

Fig. 26—Plan of the development completed by 1930.

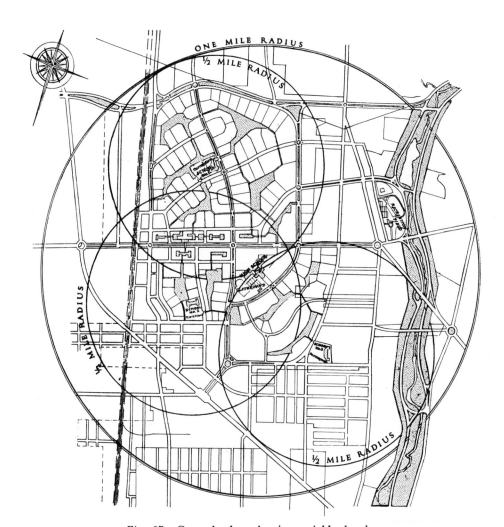

Fig. 27—General plan showing neighborhoods.

playgrounds. Each was to have its own shopping center. The size of the neighborhood was determined by the number of children cared for by a single school. So as to allow for flexibility in development, we tentatively overlapped our half-mile circles (Fig. 27). This left lee-way for somewhat greater concentration of population in apartments or row houses, where it would be found most advisable to place these as building progressed. All parts of each neighborhood were to be connected by over- and under-passes.

The neighborhoods were planned for 7,500 to 10,000—this to depend on the most desirable number of pupils in a school—a matter that was then, and I believe still is, open to a wide diversity of opinions. Although a start was made in the building of two of the neighborhoods, ultimately neither was completed.

TOWN PLAN: THE TOWN AS A WHOLE.—As a main educational and cultural center we chose a point nearly equidistant from the three proposed elementary schools, within a mile radius of all future houses. This was close to the intersection of the main north-south and east-west avenues. We planned to set the high school and town community building on a beautiful hill. Below was a low nearly marshy area. This, although not desirable for residential purposes, was excellent for the central recreational field, to serve both high school and town athletic needs.

The main commercial center might, we felt, serve as a regional market. So we located it close to the proposed state throughway at the main entrance to Radburn, rather than in the physical center. We assumed that most of the regional market's clients would come by automobile. Therefore we planned superblocks, with an interior area of some 400,000 square feet, to permit the parking of some 1,250 cars. This parking area was to be used in the evenings by the nearby Regional Theater.

For industry the section to the south of the State Highway was planned. This would have had direct access not only from the main entrance highways, but also from a spur from the railroad (Fig. 28).

How the Radburn Plan Worked

Those who live in Radburn and have lived there for any great length of time find that it has served its objective of making home and community life more reposeful, pleasant and safe—and particularly safe for children. The physical plan of central parks, superblocks without through traffic, safe walks, houses facing on gardens and parks along with the convenience of service have, they find, given them a quality of living that, as medium-income folks, they could not find elsewhere. My associates and I have observed the actions and reactions of the people. We have talked it over with a good many of them, and we have studied the investigations of others. We find that the general feeling, after twenty years of trial, is enthusiastic approval. This does not man that there are not adverse criticisms of details. But these are secondary in the minds of the people.

SAFETY FOR CHILDREN.—Radburn is above all a town for children. The safety features, the free safe life in the open, is what drew young parents to it in the beginning. The first forty families who moved into the town were young folks in their thirties with children of early or pre-school age. Although Radburn was affected by the national shifting of population during 1939-1945, stability has returned to the town. Old residents are re-appearing. Former Radburn children have married and have come back to bring up their own youngsters. Seventy-five per cent of the present Radburn men are veterans of the recent war. They are starting their married life in Radburn apparently because they want their families, and particularly their children, to have the same background for free living which they knew as youngsters.

In regard to safety, let us look at the figures. In Radburn's 20 years there have been only two road deaths. Both were on main highways, not in lanes. There has been only one serious accident on any lane, which resulted in a little girl's arm being broken.

That the small proportion of auto fatalities is due to the physical plan is indicated by the record of other towns that have followed in general the Radburn scheme. In 1949, when Greenbelt, Maryland, Greendale, Wisconsin, and Greenhills, Ohio, were all over ten years old, only one pedestrian had been killed by a car. The fatal accident was in Greenbelt. There had not even been a severe injury at Greendale, and only one at Greenhills—a boy who did not look round after getting off a bus—(and he is all right now). That is quite a good record for four towns of 2,500 to 7,500 population, compared with other towns of similar size. In 1945, there were 1,240 deaths in towns of 2,500 to 10,000 in the United States (a rate of one death per 100,000 population), and the ratio of injuries to fatalities is about 30-35 to 1.

This does not mean that pedestrians are kept 100 per cent apart from autos at Radburn. No, they are human—old habits stick—the sense of exploration and curiosity leads youngsters into forbidden places.

PLAY PLACES—The playgrounds, the central greens, and the swimming pools in summer, are the favorite recreation places for Radburn children. But the paved lanes are also used for playing. I have studied the reasons for this so that in the future we might keep children and autos apart to an even greater degree. We never will do so completely, nor do I think we should attempt to. The spirit of adventure should not be extinguished.

Young children play in the lanes because their mothers, who spend much of their time in the kitchen, want to keep them in sight. We put the kitchen on the service side of the house, because that was where things would be happening—delivery of goods and fuel, the coming of postman, husband, even visitors. But I think that in the future we should use (as we did in Burnham Place) a type of house with a combination kitchen-diningroom running through from garden to lane side. Then the mother can easily go from one side to the other, and keep a watchful eye on the kids on the quiet side as well as on the life of the cul-de-sac (Fig. 34).

There is another reason why children play in the lanes. They are paved, and so wheeled toys run better than in the grass, and with less objections from parents. They can use the walks, it is true, but these are crowded enough already. Even roller skates and bicycles are often found to be an inconvenience on the paths.

A solution might be wider paved areas for wheeled toys on the walk side of house groups—a couple of them, perhaps, one near the park and the other midway between main highway and park. For bicycles we should have special paths, as in

Central Park. This might lead to a greater use of bicycles and thus cause a decrease in the use of autos for trips to market and recreation places.

THE UNDERPASS.—The underpass permits safe passage from home to school, playground and swimming pool. The younger children religiously obey parents' injunctions to use it. When asked where they live they invariably say 'through the underpass and so many houses farther.' Cyclists find it convenient. Older children use it to a much lesser degree. A young Radburn boy, old enough to test his own judgment, scrambles up the hill beside the pass and braves the perils of traffic rather than walk a step out of his way. To be effective, such a pass must follow the shortest distance between two points, and the bank beside it must be steep and thickly planted.

The underpass is closer to the swimming pool than to the school, and therefore is used by most of those in bathing suits.

THE OVERPASS.—The overpass crossing the busiest highway, Fairlawn Avenue, and connecting the north and south sections of Radburn, was reached by a gradual slope on the north and easy steps on the other side. Both ways were much easier than climbing down steep slopes to the road. It was therefore much used.

SAFETY goes beyond the physical plan of pathways far from traffic, of underpasses and overpasses at crossings, and of playgrounds, even beyond the provision of recreation supervisors.

Paradoxically, the very position of some of these precautions for safety can encourage enough relaxing on the part of busy mothers in the supervision of their children to create some safety problems. The fact that there is a playground and supervised play, provided and paid for out of the community pocketbook, gives some parents a vague confidence that all is well with the children all the time—and family responsibility is lessened.

This kind of all-out care cannot be given in any community. Recreation staffs can take responsibility only for those children who come under their supervision voluntarily. Usually the children in Radburn and similar towns find so much of interest in school, home and playground that there is little need for concern. It is possible, however, for youngsters to fall between the relaxed parental attention

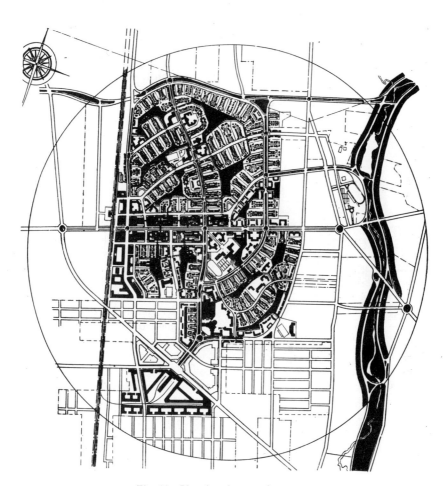

Fig. 28—Plan for the complete town.

Fig. 29—Typical plan of one of the early Radburn Houses. It has three separate entrances. Later houses had two.

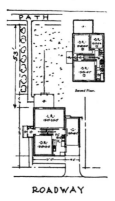

Fig. 30—An experimental plan of four attached two-family houses used in one place only. The eight families have separate stairs to their own basements and their own gardens.

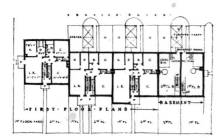

and the limited community control, leaving them more free for unconventional activity than the child in a traditional environment. Some parents feel that this is good, making for independence and self-reliance, and for some children this is probably true. Others think that it is an unsafe situation conducive to destructiveness and a lack of consideration for others. These thoughts are based on disturbing experience through the years, of broken street lamps and school windows, and of automobiles mischievously rolled down hill.

Unit Plans

SINGLE FAMILY HOUSE.—The development of the first house with two fronts, one for convenient service, the other for peaceful living, took much time and study. Customary planning habits had to be suppressed and replaced. The house interior had to be reorganized, so that it would fit naturally into the whole Radburn pattern. Changes in the relation between house, garden, path and highway were not to seem extraordinary if the logic of our answer to auto-age requirements was to be accepted by the prospective owner and his future visitors. Plan requirements were: living room, porch and as many bedrooms as possible facing the garden; kitchen and garage and cellar storage easily accessible from service lane; the main entrance door leading directly by corridor or stairs to all rooms. These were satisfied in the early plan, with the exception of that affecting the kitchen (Fig. 29). Experience and use showed that the principal entrance should be most conveniently accessible to both public path and service road, as visitors might park their car in the latter or walk from a main road across the inner park. The three exterior doors in the early plans were afterwards cut to two for economy and simplicity.

The disorderly loose appearance of the free-standing houses in relation to each other, and the insufficient space left on either side of the small buildings, lead us to join houses by coupling garages—the most interesting grouping of two houses was that in which garages and houses were joined by porches, through which summer breezes could play.

Cheaper houses were later designed by attaching two or three houses to each other as in Burnham Place (Fig. 34). These compact units have a com-

Fig. 31—An inner park, beautiful as the estate of an 18th century country gentleman.

Fig. 32—Small children play in safety on the footpath adjacent to the brick and clapboard houses.

Fig. 33—The turning circle at the end of the service lane in Burnham Place, showing the additional space gained by a grouping of houses.

Fig. 34—Plan of Burnham Place. This, with its grouped houses and turning circle, is the most spacious cul-de-sac at Radburn. The turning circle allows vehicles to turn and get away more easily, and it provides an island for planting.

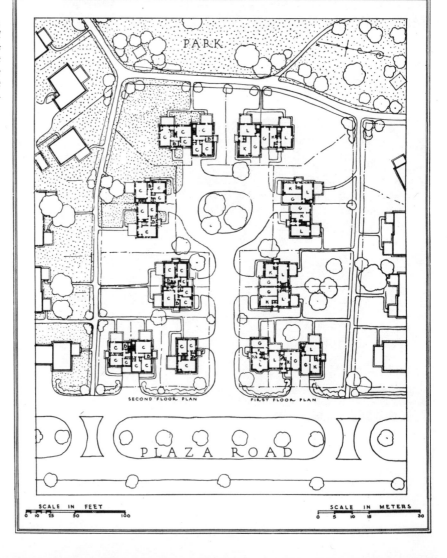

bined kitchen and dining space running through the house. This gives the mother in the kitchen an opportunity to watch the children playing in the garden, an advantage I have already indicated.

Longer rows of single family houses were ultimately built on Randolph and Reading Terrace in what was to have been the second neighborhood. The topography and soil were such that we could cut the service roads a story below the main entrance on the garden side. Thus the garage, service entrance and laundry are in the basement. The two fronts of the houses are connected externally by stairs at the ends of each group of four (Fig. 48).

THE ECONOMY OF SPACIOUS PLANS.—Habits of economy of space in house planning, developed at Sunnyside, were carried over to the early days of Radburn. The bathrooms and kitchens in particular were tightly planned, though they held the required fixtures in an orderly manner and there was room for essential and convenient movement. Experience has taught me that though this kind of careful planning does save some original capital cost, it does not adequately take into account the factors of time and progress—or new requirements. It is not flexible enough to meet technical or style changes. For instance, the standard size of stoves was increased after we had started to build Radburn. When some original installations wore out there was not enough space for the new models. The same inflexible tightness has made many garages inadequate since some types of American autos were increased in size.

The time factor is not always sufficiently considered in economical planning. As residential financing is based on long-term amortization over the useful life of the house, and not on the immediate payment of all capital costs, there must be adequate space for change and for various arrangements of equipment. Good business sense, as well as a desire to make our homes as livable and attractive as possible over their long future life, requires not only enough space for now, but sufficient room to allow for growth and change.

Spacious planning of this kind is equally—perhaps even more—essential in site and group planning. Inadequate space for parking or garaging causes increasing difficulties in America as the proportion of automobiles to families goes up. Shopping districts without spacious parking areas

are losing trade to new centers, where the planners have foreseen the need for ample parking space to serve an increasing number of people using cars. In California, it is generally advocatd that car parks should be three times greater in area than selling space.

In many new housing developments there is a tendency to omit garages—and thus reduce building costs. This is understandable during a period of high construction costs. But where inadequate or inappropriate space is left for future garages, or for parking of many more cars for tenants and visitors than may be immediately needed, the development is likely ultimately to lose occupants and to be a poor paying investment.

Spaciousness in planning, with an eye to unforeseeable future needs and developments, is particularly important in public centers. None of us can actually prophesy just what activities will be required by a community as time goes on. The space requirements for recreation, education, and entertainment have a tendency to expand continuously. The number of community facilities that are first desirable, then essential, are increasing; there are, for example, health centers, youth centers, nurseries—and who knows what next?

All of this is an argument for openness—for leaving plenty of uncovered ground while the land is still cheap, and while it can be planned and developed at a minimum cost of utilities and highways. On the whole we did show this kind of foresight at Radburn, particularly in the interior parks and the recreation spaces.

The Building of Radburn

During the first few years at Radburn we were able to draw on the experience gained at Sunnyside, of large-scale building operations in which the installation of streets, parks and utilities keeps pace with the construction of houses.

The problems which faced us at Radburn were made more difficult as the main utility lines and framework of municipal services did not exist. We had to plan and construct a sewage disposal plant as well as main sewers. All had to be arranged within a long-term development program and in co-ordination with different governmental authorities and public utility corporations. The staff of

Fig. 35—A hedge-lined path leading from the houses to an inner park.

Fig. 36—The service lane to houses in Burnham Place. This is used for garages, parking, deliveries, the drying of laundry and as an outdoor workplace.

the City Housing Corporation included members with the many technical skills required.

Louis Brownlow, who had been the chief officer of the municipal government of Washington, was invaluable in all civic affairs and, particularly, in establishing diplomatic relations with the Borough of Fairlawn and the New Jersey State agencies.

Ralph Eberlin, who had been civil engineer at Sunnyside, grew and developed with his varied responsibilities at Radburn. He laid out and supervised the construction of roads and utilities as well as buildings, and he was responsible for site engineering in relation to all structures. Later, after Herbert Emmerich went to Washington, he became General Manager as well as Superintendent of Construction—a big job—but he was a doer, not merely an administrator.

In the busy days of construction, Ralph Eberlin would drive over to Radburn in his old Ford, the rear seat piled high with boots, surveying instruments and blue prints of architectural and engineering drawings. On the way we would discuss the next construction job, and would stop to search for the working drawings roughly filed in Ralph's office on wheels.

Eberlin in the Second World War was Colonel in charge of most U.S.A. construction in Eastern India and up to China. He is now the outstanding American site engineer—at least I think so. We have worked together on many jobs since Radburn.

Life in the Community

The early residents, approximately 400 families during the first few years, established the character of the town. They were mostly young people of medium income and almost exclusively from New York and New Jersey. They came to Radburn mainly because of their children. Seventy per cent of the men worked in New York City, and to live in Radburn meant commuting. But it was an economical place in which to live. It was suburban and it offered unusual advantages.

Although a few owned their own businesses, the great majority of men were employees with annual

Fig. 37—The private life of the family is in the home and private garden, close to, but independent of, the community life in the inner parks.

incomes between $2,000 and $5,000. Their occupations, in 1933, were mainly 'whitecollar'; salesmen, engineers, teachers, 'junior executives,' etc.

The educational and religious background was also more or less the same. About 86 per cent of the men and 75 per cent of the women had received their education in American colleges. Seventy-seven per cent belonged to Protestant churches and about 16 per cent were Roman Catholic.

These elements of similarity, added to the novel setting, promised a full community life. The promise was more than fulfilled. The formation of a citizen's organization was only the beginning of a close association of friends and neighbors. The community and what happened in it was soon the chief leisure interest of Radburn people.

Home and community as sources of recreation and culture became very important in America in the years, 1929 to 1935, when the family allowance for these interests was practically nil. At Radburn this partially accounts for the widespread, enthusiastic participation in community life that took place. Ninety-seven per cent of the adult population joined other members of the community in some form of activity. Approximately half the community worked in the Parent-Teacher Association, in Citizens' Association committees, or in the Radburn Citizens' Association.

By 1937 the depression was over but it had left its serious effects in Radburn. Numerous young families had to give up their homes. Some had gone away. Others remained as renters. Many bided the time when they might return and start over again.

Curtailment of expenditures had been exercised in the community program as well as the family budgets. The City Housing Corporation could no longer assist. The financial status of Radburn people called for elimination of those parts of their program which were not essential.

In November 1937, the Citizens' Association appointed a committee to re-evaluate the community program. This committee in its report reviewing the life and spirit of Radburn eight years after its inception, concluded: [13]

'We look forward with confidence to the future of Radburn as a desirable place in which to live and raise our children, not to a city of 25,000 people as originally conceived, but to a community assured of an orderly growth, retaining the virtues of smallness but at the same time reaching a size which will assist us to have the civic values we all desire.'

Then came World War II.

The great shifting of population throughout the country, affected by war industry, war preparation, and war itself, caused a tremendous turnover in Radburn families from 1939 to 1945. But stability has returned.

Wandering about the town today, one is conscious of a sense of the stability of an old community with a definite character and roots. But there is also a spirit of youth and a feeling of revived energy and ambition. Just below the surface, one finds all about the town an awareness of neighbors and their interests, of their abilities, their ambitions and their needs.

You are told about it by an elderly man who is a cripple and can't get about easily. According to him, after eleven years in the town, 'No one needs to be in a jam here—all he needs to do is to call for help.'

Doing things together is an everyday indication of happy family life. This grows out of the physical plan and the plan for living. Mother and children can spend the afternoon together at a swimming pool by strolling across their park; father and daughter can play tennis on Sunday morning—within easy call of the dinner bell. When the Players perform just down at the Plaza, and one of those glamorous people beyond the footlights is a member of the family, the whole clan turns out.

The twenty-five per cent of the population who are 'ol'timers' have weathered the almost overwhelming storms of eighteen difficult years and have carried on the traditions of friendliness, neighborliness, and civic responsibility.

The informal relationship of houses, the ease with which one can cross a couple of lawns and call out 'Who's home?' has affected the social and civic expression of the people. Neighbors can see each other frequently and with little effort. Pooling of interest and effort follows.

Radburn's plan has resulted in well-kept parks and common areas even through years of depression and war. The activity observed in yards and gardens, the friendly atmosphere, the relaxed tempo of the community, speak of pleasure in living. Moreover, the basic requirement at Radburn that residents share in the cost of the social program has resulted in continuing responsibility for what happens in the community. Inability of Radburn to expand after the depression created obstacles to the town's progress, but the physical layout and the original plan for sharing responsibility retained unity in the town.

Undesirable social tendencies as well as commendable ones are related to the physical plan. Experience at Radburn is a pretty convincing argument for the theory that it is not wise to undertake the development of a town until the fulfillment of the complete physical plan can be assured.

Radburn has never been a separate governmental entity, but from the start has been a part of the Borough of Fairlawn. Friction seems to have existed between Radburn and the rest of Fairlawn. The inability of Radburn to expand in an orderly fashion, as planned, created a very small town, with exceptional facilities, in the midst of people for whom the Borough could not afford similar advantages. Whether or not the attitudes were fair, it is understandable that the people of the new town were not popular with their less privileged neighbors and that a social chasm should develop very quickly. The matter of Fairlawn votes snowing under the projected high school in 1935 was the culminating episode of several years of friction between Fairlawn and Radburn residents. Almost before Radburn was built, Fairlawn people feared that the new community of 25,000 might control the old Borough of Fairlawn, with its 5,000 population.

Years of working together and real effort on the part of wise Radburn people and those from outside the town perhaps bridged the gap in time, but the bad situation of the early years planted seeds far from democratic in nature.

If a town cannot be large enough to include a normal cross-section of American people or to serve with its facilities the entire population of a political unit, the bad social effects might easily outweigh the benefits.

GOVERNMENTAL COMMUNITY ORGANIZATION.—Radburn was better planned for an integrated community life than Sunnyside. The wide-spread parks, the safe footpaths for pedestrians, giving easy access to the homes of neighbors, all led the way to friendliness and neighborliness.

The City Housing Corporation devised a plan for maintaining property and for a shared responsibility based on the experience gained at Sunnyside. This was developed under the able leadership of Louis Brownlow and Major John Walker. At Radburn restrictions to protect architectural harmony were made part of the purchase deed. These restrictive covenants provided for public services required in an urban community, but not yet adequately provided in the local semi-rural Borough of Fairlawn. These included sewage disposal, garbage collection, street lighting, policing and operation of the large park areas, playgrounds and recreation facilities.[14]

As the local tax rate of Fairlawn would not cover the cost of these extra services, the Radburn Association was empowered to impose an additional annual charge which could never exceed one-half the current Borough taxes.

RADBURN ASSOCIATION.—The Radburn Association was incorporated as a non-profit, non-stock corporation to fix, collect, and disburse the annual charges, to maintain the necessary community services, parks and recreation facilities, and to interpret and apply the protective restrictions.

The Association was governed by a self-perpetuating Board of Trustees. The first nine trustees were civic leaders of New Jersey or officers of the City Housing Corporation. The 1929 report of the City Housing Corporation stated:

'The powers and responsibilities of the Radburn Association will devolve upon the residents of Radburn, but we have not attempted to say in advance exactly when or in precisely what manner.'

In short, the Radburn Association was to have the power and functions of a municipal government, including taxation. An American government without public representation! Luckily it was well-administered for the good of the Radburn people by one of the ablest town managers in America, John Walker, chosen by the Trustees.

The Municipal services for the first few years consisted of sewerage, garbage and ash removal, and street cleaning, street lighting, police, fire and

Fig. 38—There is space for every kind of recreation within easy reach of every home.

health, as well as care of parks. Some of these functions have now been taken over by the Borough. Some were eliminated because of the decrease of financial resources. The only services of this type, now provided for by the Radburn Association, are the care of parks and walks, and the Radburn Volunteer Fire Department.

In the early years, the Radburn Association provided gymnasium instruction in the elementary school. But since the expense was all carried by Radburn people and this service was given to all children who attended the school, it was eliminated in 1941. The school now conducts its own physical education program with a Borough physical education supervisor visiting weekly.

THE FIRST RADBURN CITIZENS' ASSOCIATION.— The Radburn Citizens' Association was formed two months after the first family moved in. The purposes of the organization were to discuss questions of community interest, to formulate and express community opinion, and to co-operate in creating a community life. The Association had no real power.

The Citizens' Association was extremely active during the early years when enthusiasm was high and residents were getting acquainted. It then sponsored a great variety of activities through its numerous committees: educational and civic as well as recreational and religious.[15] Need for the association's participation decreased as the basic program of community activities became routine. Financial difficulties of the nineteen-thirties also caused curtailment. Throughout the war Radburn, like other American communities, was involved in a program of war work, and the Citizens' Association found little need either to supplement or implement the work of the Radburn Association. The Citizens' Association has continued to function to the present time, but mainly as a forum open to all Radburnites on matters of interest to the neighborhood.

As many Radburn people felt that the Radburn Association has not progressed sufficiently toward a democratic state, the Citizens' Association, after a thorough study in 1938, recommended plans for reorganization of the Radburn Association which would give the residents more direct representation,

Fig. 39—One of Radburn's two swimming pools, which form centers of outdoor life in the summer.

more democratic control, and more responsibility.

EDUCATION.—The general community plan of Radburn with three elementary schools and one combined junior and senior high school as the center of educational, cultural, and recreational life of the town, was destroyed by the depression. Only one school had been built. As Radburn and the surrounding area became more densely populated, in 1941 a wing was added, which includes a pleasant, large auditorium with a stage, dressing-room, lavatories, and a kitchen. However, the Radburn Players continue to use a small hall and stage in the Plaza building because of the inadequate stage lighting and make-up rooms, the small size of the stage and, above all, the fees for rental and janitor in the school auditorium.

In 1943 a high school was operated in Fairlawn. It is within walking distance of Radburn, but on the opposite side of the railroad; about 350 Radburn young people attend.

RECREATION.—Radburn was above all else planned for children. Facilities for their play are dispersed throughout the community. The two play-grounds, located in the north and south centers of Radburn, are primarily for the use of the elementary school children. They are supervised during the summer months, and instruction is given in a variety of sports and other playground activities. 'Tot-lots,' equipped for the little ones under four, and supervised by trained leaders, are also at either end of town and are open all summer. The two swimming pools and the wading pool, where there is instruction in swimming as well as safety assured by experienced life guards, are so popular that the guest privileges once possible for residents are increasingly difficult to grant. There is no fee for the use of the pools by residents. The operating expenses are paid by the Radburn Association.

The tennis courts are restricted to the use of residents and guests when accompanied by a resident. There is no charge for the use of the courts. Nearby is the athletic field, six and three-quarter acres in size—an extremely popular spot in summer and winter for football, softball and other games.

An existing small two-story building on the grounds, popularly known as 'The Grange,' was

Fig. 40—Children ride their bicycles on the park paths. There is no danger from automobiles. A further separation of functions should lead to the provision of separate bicycle paths. In recent years these have been added in Central Park, New York.

Fig. 41—The family at work on the house and in the garden.

Fig. 42—A first view of an inner park.

early equipped as a gymnasium. It also houses a large 'quiet' games room. In the absence of a real gymnasium in the Radburn school building, this has been used by men, women and children as the community gym. Here the children gather for music, drama, scouting, games, dancing, and other social activities.

The Plaza Building, opposite the railroad, accommodates all of Radburn's stores. Since this was built we have learned much about neighborhood shopping centers and their relation to the economic, social, and architectural plan of a community. A study of shopping centers, with particular reference to Radburn, was made by Catherine Bauer and myself, but too late to be of use there. It served later as basis of Greenbelt's delightful and successful commercial center.[16]

The upper floors of the Plaza building are used as Radburn's Community Center. Besides the offices of the Radburn Association, the study of the 'Church in Radburn' minister, and the Radburn Library, there are several rooms for recreation. One of these, with a stage and raised floor, has made the theater one of the popular interests of the community. Another large room, with a kitchen adjoining, has served a wide variety of social functions.

These rooms are all used daily by children and in the evenings by adults for educational, recreational, or civic gatherings. Saturday evening open forums are held. On Sunday the rooms accommodate religious classes.

The opportunities for the young people, in addition to the extensive parks and open areas, the paths safe for wheeled toys, the safety of access to school and play areas, have contributed in a large measure to the popularity of Radburn as a place for growing families. A survey among the new residents in 1937, made by the Radburn Citizens' Association, indicated that 85 per cent of them moved to Radburn because of the recreation facilities.

ADULT CULTURAL LIFE.—The energy of the early days at Radburn was spontaneous and tremendous and within the first year there were formed important cultural groups such as the Radburn Singers, the Radburn Players, the Friends of Music, and the Garden Club. A library was started and various sports were organized.

The combination of physical plan, community plan, and the youth of the residents—the majority of whom were college-graduates—offered an unusual opportunity for cultural and social activity. It led to experimentation in the field of Adult Education. With the aid of a grant from the Carnegie Foundation in 1931-33, Mr. Robert Hudson studied the activities of this lively young community and developed a broad program of Education and Recreation. His report was appropriately called 'Radburn —a Plan of Living.'

Forced leisure of the partially unemployed during the depression gave time for continued community activity. This gradually dried up as many of the 'old-timers' lost their homes and moved away—and as defense and war activities filled everyone's time.

The adult community activities of today are primarily recreational; golf, bowling, and softball— eight teams of it. The Garden Club continues, ending the season with its annual Flower Show.

A few cultural organizations carry on. The Radburn Players are still active on their 20th anniversary, and the Radburn Singers will probably be revived in the near future. The Community Forum, now in its 12th year, about ten times a year discusses vital problems of the day. Speakers and topics are liberal in character. The usual audience of 40 or 50 is entirely of Radburn people. Although all Fairlawn has been invited—in the hope of breaking the feeling of exclusion—few have come.

RADBURN REVISITED.—The impressive feature of Radburn superblocks are the inner parks (Fig. 31). You enter from the highway by a path between hedges (Fig. 35). These are of varied height. Some partially hide, others disclose, the gardens beyond; well-cared-for, very personal gardens, many of them gay with early flowers and shaded by varied trees—a quarter of a century old or more. They partly conceal the two-story houses of brick and wood (Fig. 37).

It is late spring; people are burning off old paint and putting on a new white coat, or trimming hedges or spading gardens (Fig. 41).

Then at the path's end the park opens up to you. An apparently endless grassy lawn, with groups of trees (Fig. 42). Around the edges are the paths, alive with children on bicycles and velocipedes (Fig. 40). Beyond the hedge's border are the private gardens of the end houses of the lanes. There is only limited composition of the buildings— their harmony comes mainly from similarity of materials —common brick and white clapboards (Fig. 32). They are unified also by the simple good taste of Fred Ackerman, the architect of this group. But above all it is the natural green that dominates and controls the picture. Your architecture cannot look bad when time makes it part of the bigger composition of landscape. Radburn has come of age architecturally because time has mellowed it into a oneness. Harsh lines are subdued and enveloped by the verdure. It is almost what happens in primeval forest to rock and tree bark when they have lived together for a long time—they seem to reflect each other's color and texture (Fig. 15).

The picture constantly goes through kaleidoscopic changes of planting and distant structures as one walks up the center of the broad lawn. It is so spaciously open that one thinks of a lordly estate, but it is filled with democratic life. Little girls playing tag; boys playing baseball or on their backs looking up through the leaves at the blue, their bicycles at their sides; and here comes a whole family in dripping bathing suits (Fig. 45).

The outdoor swimming pool is the real center of Radburn's summer life. During the long hours after work it is gay with youthful color and movement (Fig. 39). Next to it is the wading pool for the little ones (Fig. 51). Beyond is the large field for baseball or other big games, and enclosed nearby is the playground for the younger ones, with slides and other apparatus. On our way we have passed sand-boxes for the tots, at the end of each block, each enclosed by a little fence and hidden by bushes (Fig. 43). Beyond the pool and playground is the elementary school (Fig. 44).

We go through an underpass to the next superblock (Fig. 24). If we look up we may see an automobile against the sky. We had forgotten that our civilization is dominated by motors. Nowhere within the peaceful superblocks are you reminded of their existence. In early June the rosebushes dominate the landscape in the passage between the two superblocks (Fig. 45).

The second inner park is different in form, in topography, in planting. There is a small unobtrusive natural theater, and on the higher ground

a rustic pavilion. The lawns again are spacious and broad. The trees and bushes are massed so as to leave large open spaces, easy for machine mowing (Fig. 42).

At the end of the park are two low but massive apartment buildings (Fig. 46).

Another inner park was partially completed at the other side of Fairlawn Avenue. It was intended that it should be the center of the second neighborhood. Another swimming pool was built there— close to the playground which forms part of the inner park. The school which we proposed should be built at the further end of the park was never erected (Figs. 27, 47, 48 and 50).

The function of the auto side of the houses is the reverse of that facing parks and gardens. The two sides are as different as night and day. The dead-end lanes are some 400 feet in depth. On most of them houses stand out, perhaps too strongly, for lack of green foreground and hiding foliage. Some of the earlier buildings seem crowded: we architects had planned for short rows intermingled with single units. We were finally restricted to free-standing units. Our sense of economy in paving and utilities led to some tightness. It creates annoyance where there are semi-public paths connecting lanes and walks, and people pass close to windows. Later, with houses attached in twos or threes, as in Burnham Place, we achieved a greater sense of spaciousness (Fig. 34).

On the service side the washing is festooned— and I recollect that in the days when houses were first opened to public inspection the dominant problem was where to hang the laundry. Mr. Bing and his associates had gone with us in our American planning revolution; street and walk divorced, house faced round, superblocks. But here the salesmen rebelled. They could not sell houses to good Americans if the week's washing was to be displayed on the public side. So, on the days when the houses were first shown, we tried the drying lines on different sides of various houses. The public decided that laundry naturally belonged with other services, and not in the park or garden. And there it has remained (Fig. 36).

The garages are set back far enough to allow for a parked car for visitors between them and the road. Perhaps with the latest, longer machines they

Fig. 43—At the point where each group of houses joins the inner park, there are sand boxes.

Fig. 44—The formal playground in the inner park, between the swimming pool and the school.

are crowded now. As time goes on I am convinced that we architects must always plan spaciously—allowing for the growth and change of all equipment.

The ends of the lanes, where the cars must turn, are particularly tight. We planned for U-turns. Backing to turn, especially with big cars, is a clumsy process. It takes too much time—particularly when the delivery boy has entered the wrong lane. It leads to improper language!

We built some culs-de-sac with circles, which when large enough, make a turn and get-away easy. Burnham Place, which is illustrated, is an example (Figs. 33 and 34). And it shows how much more attractively attached or triple houses can be grouped.

Radburn: Success or Failure?

Radburn was never completed. Only a small portion of the new town was built before the operation was engulfed by the depression. On the surface Radburn may appear a failure. But essentially it was a great success. It was a splendid adventure: a voyage of discovery in search of a new and practical form of urban environment to meet the actual requirements of today. This exploration opened up and charted the way—no matter how limited the settlement that remains. The two superblocks that were built, and in which people have lived happily and safely for twenty years, have demonstrated the essentials of the new form of city, that is increasingly accepted as the basis of planning urban residential areas in Europe and America. With this in mind let us examine and evaluate its apparent shortcomings.

Radburn did not become a Garden City. It lacked a complete greenbelt. It did not succeed in securing industry. Its underlying land, excepting the inner block parks, was not retained in single ownership for or by the community. All this is true—but the fact remains that in spite of the avowed intention of the Corporation to create a Garden City, eventually the pressing need of demonstrating the Radburn Idea overshadowed the Garden City idea. In large part it superseded it. For instance, our thoughts, as planners, were concentrated on the value of the living green close to homes in the midst of the superblocks: it seemed more essential

than greenbelts. The retention of the ownership of
the underlying land was not part of the program of
Mr. Bing and his associates on the Board of the
City Housing Corporation. They considered this
impractical in the New York region at that time,
because of the difficulty of mortgaging leaseholds,
and of selling property when the ownership of the
land did not go with the house. As to industry: we
planned for it physically, but our timing was bad.
This was probably due less to bad judgment than to
the unforeseen breakdown of the national economy.

The financial vicissitudes of Radburn were due
to matters beyond the control of those who conceived, planned, developed or operated it. They
did not result from the novel form of the Radburn
plan. Nor were they caused by its community organization and operation, or the charges for these.
Why Radburn was not completed and the City
Housing Corporation went into bankruptcy is
shown on the diagram that faces page 19 (Fig.
1). The graphic indication of business failure,
unemployment, national deflation, which was reflected in the loss of jobs and the impoverishment
of the people of Radburn and ultimately in the
bankruptcy of the City Housing Corporation, came
from causes that could not be controlled by any
individual or private corporation. A depression,
when it comes, is like a tornado; no human being
can then stop it. It cuts down all in its path—
it leaves destruction behind.

When Radburn was conceived in 1928, all the
economic trends were upward—the sky was the
limit. But the first inhabitants had hardly put their
houses in order when the stock exchange broke:
the depression was under way. However, construction continued at Radburn as elsewhere in the
New York area for a while, though at a continuously decreasing rate. In 1933 only twelve houses
were erected at Radburn.

Continuous, large-scale development is essential
to the financial success of a new town such as
Radburn. Otherwise the carrying charges on land,
main highways, and utilities will soon devour possible profit and force the operating company deeper
and deeper into debt. This is what happened at
Radburn. At Sunnyside large-scale development
had been continued during five years, with the
construction of roads and the installation of utili-

Fig. 45—Rosebushes flank the footway to the underpass.

*Fig. 46—The apartment buildings overlook an inner
park. Andrew J. Thomas, Architect.*

*Fig. 47—The inner park which would have formed the
center of the second neighborhood had it been completed. The second swimming pool is beyond the
bicycles in the background.*

ties paralleling the building of complete blocks of houses, all of which were marketed as soon as they were finished. The Corporation was confident of equaling or bettering this record at Radburn. No one believed the deflation would last long. So the Corporation, advised by its planners, continued to buy land, until it had acquired some two square miles at a total cost of approximately three and a third million dollars. Most of this was purchased at a high price for rural land. Only a small portion of it was improved before the depression engulfed the Corporation. During the following ten years the land decreased in value until it reached a low of 10 per cent of the purchase price. Other investments that had been made on the presumption of a rapid and continuous growth of population were for many years carried at a loss. Examples are the large sewage disposal plant and the Radburn Building planned as a shopping and community center. To add to these financial difficulties, the returns from houses already sold decreased. Purchasers out of employment could no longer pay all —or, in many cases, any—of their monthly charges. The City Housing Corporation had the junior interest in the mortgages at Sunnyside and Radburn. Ultimately a good many of the houses were returned to the Corporation. They could not be resold—at that time; there was no market. The houses were gradually rented. But the return on them, as on all of the investment, was far too little to pay operation expenses and carrying charges. The City Housing Corporation which had guaranteed the Sunnyside notes as well as the Radburn bonds was forced into bankruptcy. As a result it had to give up or sell the greater part of the land. The reorganized Corporation later was able to continue building, but only at a slow rate on the small portion of the land that remained. The dream of a complete new town for 25,000 people had been destroyed by the depression.

The Radburn experience indicates that a private corporation has only a gambling chance to carry through to completion the building of a city. There are too many valleys, as well as hills, on those graphs—too many unforeseeable and uncontrollable factors (Fig. 1). If we are to build New Towns in America—or rather when we build them—for I am convinced we will—there must be a certain

Fig. 48—The reverse side of the houses shown in Fig. 50. The topography of the site with some judicious grading made it possible to place the garages below the living quarters.

Fig. 49 — Air view of Radburn. Photo taken in 1955.
(Litton Industries — Aero Service Division)

*Fig. 50—Row houses facing the park leading into the
second neighborhood, which was never completed. The
steps in the foreground are from the inner park. James
Renwick Thomson, Architect.*

amount of government co-operation. Of this I will speak later. None of the forms of governmental financial assistance that exist now in connection with housing or redevelopment was available in the nineteen-thirties. The City Housing Corporation was on its own when it started to build a new city. It did a good job—within the economic limitations. True, mistakes in judgment were made in timing and in other regards. But Alexander Bing's purpose and the method he chose of carrying it through were fundamentally sound: *large scale,* orderly and continuous building development according to a logical plan that met the requirements of sensible good living, individual and community, no matter how the plans and development might upset conventional method and form.

That was twenty years ago. The Radburn idea is now accepted as a fundamental basis of urban residential planning in many lands. I visited Sweden this summer. In Stockholm, I found that the basic form for the remainder of that beautiful city—which is to be completed in about ten years for an additional 100,000 people—will be derived in large part from the Radburn plan. It will consist of green communities, made up of superblocks with central parks, and the separation of walks and roads. Gothenburg's growth will follow a similar general pattern. Other countries are planning variations on the Radburn Idea. Warsaw intends to reconstruct on that basis. Radburn is influencing the plans for New Towns in England. Back in America, the Greenbelt Towns and wartime housing developments are direct or indirct descendants. The redevelopment plans for Los Angeles and other cities show similar derivation. And so, though the seeds that Alexander Bing and his associates planted in the Borough of Fairlawn had a limited growth at Radburn, they are germinating, developing and flowering in varied forms throughout the world.

Conclusions

I. THE RADBURN PLAN serves present day requirements of good living in a more practical and pleasant way than does the conventional American city pattern.

It is safer.

It is more orderly and convenient.

It is more spacious and peaceful.

Fig. 51—The wading pool for small children next to one of the swimming pools.

It brings people closer to nature.

It costs less than other types of development with an equivalent amount of open spaces.

Most people who live in Radburn prefer it. They enjoy the expansive nearby verdure; they appreciate the freedom from worry about their childrens' safety.

Radburn works in practice as it was intended to function when it was only the Radburn Idea, twenty years ago.

II. A PLAN FOR LIVING, in addition to an appropriate, flexible physical setting, requires an organization with vision, capable leaders and adequate finance for the operation of the physical plant.

Until there are competent and well-financed governmental agencies for this purpose, a private association is essential.

To be effective such an organization should:

1. Start to function when the New Town opens.
2. Include in its membership all families in the community—both tenants and home-owners. All must pay for its services just as they pay rent and taxes.
3. Be a single central organization rather than a group of separate sectional block associations.

III. A SEPARATE POLITICAL ENTITY is required by a New Town with a new form and advanced objectives, so that it may freely and clearly carry out its purposes.

A private government within the borders of a political entity, which gives special services and privileges to its members which are not available to the entire urban area, causes resentment and leads to disunion.

All services for which people are taxed should be directed and operated by their elected representatives.

IV. THE BUILDING OF A NEW TOWN requires large capital investment in land, utilities, highways and public buildings on which there can be little, if any, financial return for many years. Lacking governmental assistance, a private corporation (with the exception of organizations with large aggregates of capital such as insurance companies or endowed foundations) have small chance of more than temporary success under economic conditions such as those illustrated on the graph in Fig. 1.

Governmental co-operation is required, at least in the following:

1. Taking land—all the land that will be needed to complete the New Town.
2. Holding the land until needed for construction; or financing the land cost at low rates for long periods.
3. Financing the cost of main lines and central works of essential utilities and main highways, on low and long financial terms.
4. Assisting the local government authorities in the construction of essential public buildings such as schools.
5. Financial aid similar to that given to existing municipalities, including subsidies, for housing low income workers.

V. CONTINUOUS RAPID GROWTH of a New Town is imperative in the early years, so that overhead expenses do not devour all earnings.

VI. CONVENIENTLY PLACED AND VARIED INDUSTRY is an essential requirement of a New Town. Therefore industrial plans must be specific and realistic. Generalizations are valueless.

Timing of industrial development must be synchronized with that of the building of homes and community equipment.

Fig. 52—Air view after completion of the second unit in 1935. The public park is to the left, but the junior and senior playfields and the 25 acres of woodland are not shown.

3

CHATHAM VILLAGE

Ingham and Boyd, Architects

Clarence S. Stein and Henry Wright,

Site Planners and Consultant Architects

In 1929, when Henry Buhl, Jr., left 13 million dollars to a foundation for the welfare of the people of Pittsburgh, business was booming. At the proposal of the socially-minded director, Dr. Charles F. Lewis, the foundation determined to make some of this money do double service: 1st, pioneering in community housing for those of limited income; 2nd, demonstrating the security of 100 per cent investment in good large-scale housing development. In Chatham Village he did both. For 17 years it has been one of America's most attractive low-rental communities ($11.35 per room per month rental, during hard times reduced to $9). It blazed new trails in hillside site planning of row houses in America. There have been no vacancies except while one tenant replaced another. As investment it has paid as well as the Foundation's sound securities; 4.32 per cent net return in addition to a depreciation fund which, in 31 years (more than half of which have already passed), will pay back the whole original investment in buildings.

Preliminary Research and Study

The success of Chatham Village was in large part due to two years of preliminary study. First, in 1930, Dr. Lewis investigated the work of limited dividend companies such as the City Housing Corporation. Then a survey was made, by the Bureau of Business Research of the University of Pitts-

burgh, of housing needs and markets. Meanwhile a large low-cost site within easy transportation distance of the central business district was sought. Sociological, economic, and civic studies were made of the surroundings of the most desirable sites.

Henry Wright and I were then asked to make preliminary studies of houses to be sold to clerical workers as a safe investment. The houses were to be built according to a community plan and a hilly site was tentatively chosen.[17]

The Buhl Foundation desired to investigate the soundness of selling homes and, because of local habits, considered free-standing houses essential for sale. But we found that all our schemes using individual structures were too costly for those who were to be served. On the other hand, row houses, based on the Sunnyside experience, could be built for about two thousand dollars less per house. It was just cheap enough. This scheme was finally accepted on the basis that houses must be rented, not sold. That proved to be a fortunate decision— as Chatham Village has demonstrated the advantages, to both landlord and to occupants, of a rental policy (Fig. 53).

The Site and the Plan

THE SITE chosen was a wooded hillside of 45 acres looking down on a public park. It was two miles from the 'Golden Triangle,' where the clerical workers who were to be housed were working. The grounds had hardly been changed since William Penn retired it as a manor farm. Nearby were schools, churches, a library, and other facilities for the surrounding single-family houses.

GENERAL PLAN.—Only 16 (30 per cent) of the 45 acres have been used in the two developments for purely housing purposes. The rest are in open spaces that form a miniature greenbelt surrounding three sides: four acres are playground, 25 acres are forest with a picnic ground and two miles of pedestrian trails. The old manor house serves as a club (Fig. 55).

Chatham Village was naturally influenced by our experience at Radburn and Sunnyside, with superblocks, paths and roads separated, houses fronting on inner greens. The single superblock proposed in early studies of the first unit was ultimately divided in two by the purely local Sulgrave Road—because as a dead-end street it seemed too long. (Figs. 53, 55 and 59).

The garage compounds were used to group the garages for the houses that could not easily be arranged with basement garage. They were far better than the Sunnyside group garages, both in construction and in convenience. They have been found satisfactory in spite of the American habit of keeping a car in the house as some European farmers keep their cattle. The compound is unquestionably the economical solution of the garage problem in a closely-knit community.

SITE PLAN.—Chatham Village is one of the outstanding American examples of housing and site planning. I feel free to say this because the site plan was mainly the work of my associate Henry Wright. He had a feeling for the shape of the ground and what could be done to mold it to the practical needs of home and community that seemed superhuman. He appeared to sense the site possibilities long before surveys were made. Besides this he had an analytical mind that went to the roots of the basic problems of development costs.

The form of Chatham Village in relation to the ground gives one the pleasure that comes from visiting the best of the site planning work in England, such as Raymond Unwin's Hampstead Garden Suburb (Fig. 52).

SITE TOPOGRAPHY dominated the general plan far more than at Radburn and Sunnyside. Careful study, with builders' estimates, indicated that the hilly ground could be more economically molded to our need by using large-scale machinery, that would form a series of wide terraces, rather than by detailed handwork around individual houses. The large terraces were carefully graded, so there is a minimum of easy garden steps.

Row houses were found advantageous on the hillsides (Figs. 57, 60, 61 and 66). Their foundations served as economical retaining walls. By running most groups with the contours we were able to secure a well-lighted basement one-half above ground. Those basements which faced roads were

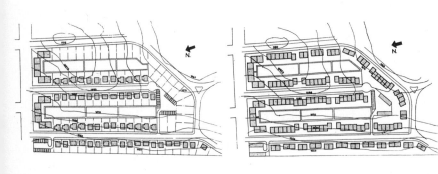

Fig. 53—Two of the preliminary studies made for part of the Chatham Village site. The one solution provided 80 six-room detached houses to sell, on the average, at about $10,500. The other provided 128 row houses to sell for prices between $7,860 and $9,042.

Fig. 54—The greenbelt surrounding Chatham Village has two miles of pedestrian trails.

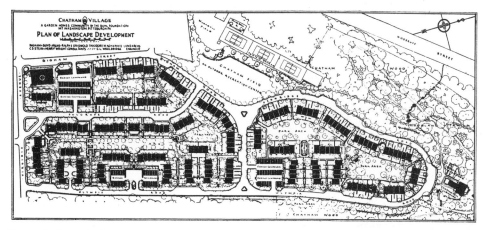

Fig. 55—General plan of the development showing the final layout, the landscape design and the club house.

used as garages, having direct stairs to livingroom and kitchen. On the other side where, thanks to topography, they faced west there were sunrooms for recreation (Fig. 57).

HOUSES are all two-story single-family dwellings. There are two basic types that have been developed out of the Sunnyside row houses as a result of the information derived from the detailed cost studies made there (Fig. 56).

The three-bedroom house has been widened to 20½ feet. These two extra feet added only moderately to th total cost on cheap land. As a result the smaller bedroom becomes more than an infant's room and the lower floor is no longer cramped. In the houses above garages there is space for a vestibule leading from both livingroom and kitchen by the stairs to laundry and garage.

The two-bedroom house is 26 feet deep, 2 feet less than the Sunnyside houses. It is also slightly narrower. There are two types of ground floor, one with typical kitchen and dining-nook, the other with compact kitchenette, purely working space, but with a larger eating place. Livingroom and diningroom in both cases form one space. These small houses were used instead of the two-family house, as at Sunnyside and elsewhere. The latter were objected to because the lower apartment was noisy and the upper floor tenants too far removed from the garden. The expense of two Chatham small units totalling 26-ft. x 35-ft. (910 sq. ft.) was only slightly more than the other 28-ft. x 25-ft. (700 sq. ft.).[18] Mechanical equipment was practically the same. Land was cheap. The Sunnyside two-family houses were more likely to have vacancies—as contrasted with 100 per cent use of the Chatham dwellings

Another matter in which our experience dictated building for time use, rather than on a basis of original cost, was in regard to exterior materials. At Chatham Village these were chosen as far as poslsible to save maintenance costs. Therefore stone doorways and slate roofs were used with brick exterior walls. The architectural richness and variety was achieved by Ingham and Boyd, the architects, by the use of very simple means: the massing of the buildings and the rhythmic location of unornamented doors, windows, balconies and stairs. The harmonious landscape was designed by Griswold and Kohankie, Landscape Architects.

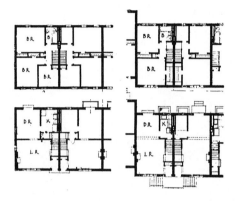

Fig. 56—The two basic type plans—the one for a six-room house. Both types were improvement of those built at Sunnyside.

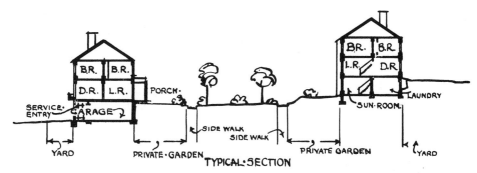

Fig. 57—Cross-section through a hillside block at Chatham Village. Garages in lower houses are at basement level. Upper houses have basement sun rooms facing the garden.

Fig. 58—Winter in Chatham Village.

Fig. 59—Final plan of the first unit of Chatham Village showing the interior park, the walk systems and streets with parking bays and the garage compounds.

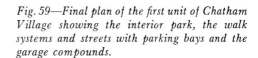

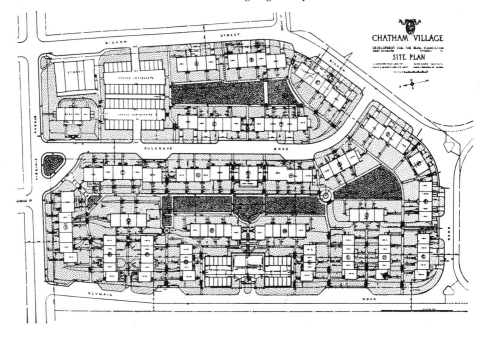

CHATHAM VILLAGE

Investment Financing

ECONOMICS.—The first decade in the history of Chatham Village was, economically, the hardest the U.S.A. has known. It included the depression, mortgage panic, readjustment, war, frozen rents and soaring operation costs. These did not affect the Foundation's 100 per cent investment, which was all their own funds, free and clear. The City Housing Corporation was ruined by the lending institutions and striking 'home-owners' of Sunnyside, who refused to pay. Meanwhile Chatham Village was over 99 per cent full of tenants who paid regularly. There has been less than 7/100 of 1 per cent uncollected rent. Although rentals were reduced temporarily during the hard years, from $11.35 to $9.65, net returns, after depreciation was taken into account, have dropped below 4 per cent for only one year—and have averaged over 4 per cent.

When building work reached a low ebb in 1932 the Foundation built the first 129 houses at near bottom costs. Prices were higher, but still low, in 1935 when the second unit of 68 houses was added.

Charles Lewis, who is primarily responsible for the conception and realization of Chatham Village, said of it:[19]

Fig. 60—*Approach up a hill to a central green in 1953.*

'A part of the success of the Village was in its timing. However, a greater element of success was the fact that the Village was based upon exceedingly thorough and careful social, economic, site planning, and architectural studies over a period of more than two years before ground was broken. Nor was the timing a greater factor, in our opinion, than the Foundation's financial policy with respect to management, based on faith to build well, confident in the soundness of the investment.'

Home Ownership or Rental

THE INHABITANTS.—Chatham Village was built for moderate-income clerical workers. Most of its inhabitants have come from the office buildings in Pittsburgh's 'Golden Triangle.' Some were from wealthier families. But young married people were all hard up during the depression. Some have risen to junior executive positions, but they stay on in Chatham Village. Teachers, research workers and other professionals form 20 per cent.

Apparently, they like Chatham Village. The

Fig. 61—A view of houses in the first unit of Chatham Village. Photo taken in the spring of 1938.

1955   *Figs. 62 and 63—Seasonal changes in Chatham Village.*   *1937*

Fig. 64—Air view of the first unit of Chatham Village. Photo taken soon after completion in 1932. (McLaughlin Aerial Surveys, New York)

Fig. 65—The William Penn Oak, which was growing when the Penn family owned the property, was preserved.

Fig. 66—Row houses at different levels, to fit the hillside site.

Fig. 67—A central green in 1955.

turnover of tenants is very low. The average tenancy was for 7 years during the first 15 years. At least half of those who moved did so because of business transfers to other cities.

Luckily for them they were tenants, not 'homeowners.' When they had to move the Foundation freed them of their lease as quickly as possible, sometimes in 24 hours. There was always a long waiting list.

The American people are still pioneering. A great many of them are nomads and tend to migrate, particularly in their youth. Families expand and then disperse. So a house seldom serves the family for the mortgage period.

Experience at Chatham Village demonstrated, as compared with Sunnyside, the fallacy of the American faith, almost a religious belief, in what is called 'home ownership.'

The Sunnyside people—and a good many of those at Radburn—found that when they could no longer pay interest on their mortgage, owning your own home was merely another form of tenancy. They had the minority holding in their dwelling; voting power was held by the lending institutions. They discovered that they had actually been the janitor, caring for the mortgagee's property. They found that all their savings which had gone into the maintenance of their home, the years of payment to reduce the mortgage, the interest they had regularly paid, were cancelled when the depression deprived them of job, income, and savings. They rebelled. They attacked the City Housing Corporation with whom they had direct dealings. But this Corporation, as far as mortgages were concerned, had become by this time only the agent of the lending institutions. Mr. Bing and his associates gave the owners as much time as they could to pay. But they were powerless; the lending institutions were in command. Ultimately a great many of the Sunnyside 'owners' lost their homes. The City Housing Corporation went bankrupt. Alexander Bing, who had made such a valiant and unselfish fight for constructive housing and community planning, was vehemently attacked.

A well-managed rental policy in a large-scale, planned community appears to pay the landlord better than does a sales policy—10 per cent down and collect the rest if—! The City Housing Corporation made a return on its rental apartments and lost on most that it sold at both Sunnyside and Radburn. The 4.2 per cent average net return on investment, with half that investment paid off out of earnings in 15 years at Chatham Village, seems adequate evidence of the advantage in renting to the proprietor of a well-planned and well-operated housing community.

Conclusions

Chatham Village, with less than 200 homes, has made an astoundingly large contribution to American community housing. A community such as Chatham Village demonstrated:

1. *The security of 100 per cent investment.* Charles Lewis said:[20]

'The secret of the investment success of any large-scale neighborhood held in one ownership is that it is planned, that it is managed as an investment, and that it is large-scale.'

Insurance companies in America are tending to follow this policy, particularly the Metropolitan Life and the New York Life Insurance Company.

2. *A greenbelt,* even one as small as that of Chatham, insulates a community from neighborhood depreciation and external annoyance.

3. *A rental* rather than sale policy is likely to be a better long-time investment. It also offers more security and freedom to most American families of moderate means.

4. *A hillside site* is a challenging problem for economical planning, but it offers unique possibilities for beauty, variety and convenience.

5. *Time*—plenty of it—for the study of economic, social, civic, and above all physical planning is well invested in a project that may live a half-century.

6. *Row houses and group garages* in a community have many advantages, aesthetic as well as economic. They can be made very livable.

Fig. 68—The great central court of the first unit (1930) of Phipps Garden Apartments.

4

PHIPPS GARDEN APARTMENTS (I)

Clarence S. Stein, Architect

The Phipps Garden Apartments were erected on a portion of the property originally purchased for Sunnyside (Fig. 3).

The Society of Phipps Houses, the promoter, was no more affected by the depression than was the Buhl Foundation. Formed by the steel magnate Henry Phipps 'to provide . . . housing accommodation for the working classes,' it built new projects when it had accumulated adequate earnings for the 4 per cent or so net return on its past developments to make a 100 per cent capital investment. It proposed at Sunnyside to house white-collar clerical workers in place of the lower-income manual workers it cared for in its compact Manhattan tenements. Therefore more spacious rooms and courts were required.

THE SITE was one of those few at Sunnyside near the railroad where we had succeeded in having useless streets closed. Therefore it was 460 feet wide. It was practically square, with a depth of 400 feet. The location was some 600 yards from the rapid transit and other means of transportation. Too far, we had thought, when we were completing Sunnyside, for anything but small houses. So we had made a number of studies of row house groups, taking advantage of the unusually broad square block. By 1931 a large number of apartment buildings had been built around Sunnyside.

The new owner decided that apartments were required to give adequate return on the valuation of the land, which had increased between the time the City Housing Corporation bought the land in 1924 and sold it to Phipps Houses. Because of the distance from transportation it seemed the development must be made unusually attractive.

Planned Around a Great Court

THE ARCHITECT'S PROBLEM was to (1) plan buildings with enough families to distribute the land cost sufficiently to keep down rents, at the same time (2) preserve attractive openness and spaciousness so as to minimize vacancies, and (3) minimize as far as possible depreciation from obsolescence, structural, functional, or economic. All studies of plan and mass we tested by comparative estimate, not only of capital but also of maintenance costs.

The Phipps family were liberal clients. They wanted a sound job—and an attractive one. Although they required a certain yet limited monetary return, they were liberal in expenditures that served to make the buildings sound in construction and attractive in appearance. They wanted exteriors less severe in appearance than the Sunnyside houses. So I am afraid I was somewhat too exuberant in the use of brick pattern. The vari-colored special brick was attractive, but my puritanical sense of economy has since led me back to our local common Hudson River brick.

One thing for which I am everlastingly thankful —the Phipps family loved rich foliage, and approved of the expenditure of $2,900 on six large elm trees. These made the great court a living green place from the beginning.

The southern 250-ft. portion of the plot was studied to see how many families could be well housed without losing the sense of spacious openness. The advantages of four-story walkups and six-story elevator buildings was compared in various arrangements around a single central court.

The final group plan consisted of six six-story units and sixteen walk-up units (Fig. 73). In spite of the fact that 43 per cent of the site was covered with building and the central open area was divided into four bays, there is a real sense of openness. The contrast of height of the buildings adds greatly to its interest, but I would have preferred to have a still more spacious foreground from which to view them (Fig. 68).

The site work was studied with care and affection. The landscape gardening by Marjorie S. Cautley was rich, varied, and imaginative. The planting has been well cared for by the able manager, Ernest Schofield. We even sank a private well so as to be sure the gardens would be watered in case the city's supply should be inadequate at any time.

The life of the community focuses on the great court or central park. (Fig. 68). All units are en-

tered from it, most livingrooms face it, balconies are turned toward it. Careful grading of the sloping terrain permitted the use of some space, below the first floor but above the ground, as apartments with their own private terraces and enclosed gardens (Fig. 70).

The great court was intended as a place of restful natural beauty, as a park, not a playground. Arrangements were made to give the tenants the privileges of the Sunnyside Park, with its playground, across the street. At first they made little use of it, as they did not consider themselves a part of the existing Sunnyside Community. But time has changed that. Now, 259 of the Phipps families belong to the Park Association and, during the last few years all of the elected officers have been Phipps tenants. For the young children, a playground was set up in a large lot purchased by Phipps Houses, across Middleburg Avenue. This is attended by most of the 150 children between 8 and 14 years old. In addition, the Social Hall and other basement space serves for the activities of boys in the groups of 6 to 9 and 9 to 11 years of age, as well as for Girl Scouts, Brownies and two groups of dancers. There is a nursery school and

Fig. 69—Two units combined in a six-story elevator apartment building. Because of the semi-fireproof construction, each apartment was required to have access to two stairways. In this design there is a fire stair well between the central apartments and indented stair wells at the bottom of the T's.

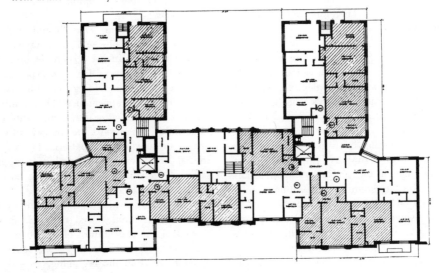

Fig. 70—There are public and private gardens in the great court; a private garden is behind the hedge.

89

a large community room in the basement, in the space above ground but not available for apartments. But the architect must admit that the nursery was not perfectly orientated: that at Hillside was much better (Fig. 73).

Walk-up or Elevator Apartment Buildings

UNIT PLANS.—A further development of the simple, compact, I-shaped unit of Sunnyside was used for most of the four-story walk-up apartments (Fig. 97). To increase room sizes the depth of the structure was deepened but the width remained 50-ft. as it had been through the history of Sunnyside. It continued all the good qualities of directness, simplicity, good light and ventilation. Also it repeated the defect of access to other rooms through the livingroom. This still seemed the most economical way of securing maximum livable space. That it has been acceptable is indicated by the fact that the Phipps Apartments have been almost 100 per cent occupied for nineteen years (Fig. 72).

The apartments in the taller buildings were far less satisfactory from the point of view of ventilation, directness of circulation, and economical use of space. This was in spite of endless study. It was because we calculated that an elevator in a moderate rental apartment requires about 100 rooms to pay for installation and maintenance costs. Self-service elevators were the type chosen. Seventeen rooms to a floor demands a complicated plan form —at least a T with dark centers and long wings (Fig. 69).

I think it is safe to generalize from our experience. The elevator apartment building cannot economically be made as livable as the walk-up. Without wastefulness, which is unacceptable in public housing and inexcusable in housing for those of moderate means, the taller apartment building must sacrifice the best ventilation, limit sunlight, and restrict privacy.

In the Phipps Apartments the costs of the elevator units were greater than those of the walk-ups. According to our estimates the former were approximately 42 cents, the other 39 cents per cubic foot. As there was more usable space and less corridor and foyer in the walk-ups, the actual difference for equivalent rooms was still greater.

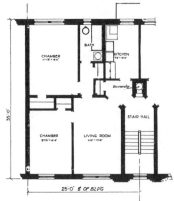

Fig. 71—The four-room walk-up apartment is the element from which the other units were developed.

Fig. 72—Balconies leading to a fire-escape required by law. The balconies were painted light green, the fire-escapes brick color.

Operation and maintenance of elevators adds to the cost of the taller buildings. The addition for this factor in 1938 was about 75 cents per room per month.

The rents charged in the four-room apartments are one to two dollars more per room for the elevator buildings, making a difference of about 8 per cent—more for the small-sized apartments.

The tendency in New York at present is toward apartment buildings of 12 to 14 stories, even for those of limited income. The law requires these tall buildings to have two elevators and two stairs for each unit. This requires the organization of about 40 rooms per floor, and results in long public or private corridors or lack of privacy. Cross-ventilation is at a minimum and there are other sacrifices of comfort, convenience or livability.

The 12 to 14 story apartment buildings which are being erected in large numbers in New York by the Municipal Housing Authority, and by insurance companies as investments, are ingeniously planned and in many cases elaborately equipped. None the less, practically all are far more deficient from the point of view of livability than if they were less high. The principal excuse given for crowding of over 300 persons per acre in these skyscrapers is the so-called 'land value.' But the present tendency in America is to try to wipe out this artificial or imaginary dam to sensible housing progress by governmental subsidy under the redevelopment laws.

Building Technology

TECHNOLOGICAL PROGRESS affected the plan of Phipps Apartments in various ways. Push-button elevators, during the planning, had been made completely safe after a few serious accidents to children. Their installation eliminated the cost of attendants.

Dumb-waiters had been used in all our Sunnyside apartment buildings. These were objectionable because of the space required and the dangers of a service passage in the basement, and they also transmitted domestic noises and conversation. They had been needed for deliveries, particularly of ice, and for the disposal of refuse. Mechanical refrigera-

Fig. 73—Plot plan of Phipps Garden Apartmnts (I) showing general arrangement at basement level. Included are management offices, nursery, community social room, perambulator stores (note ramps to these). Stippled buildings are six stories high, all others are four stories. There are six private gardens to basement apartments, as well as an enclosed play space for the nursery. Two units on ground level, in buildings N and Q, have terraces.

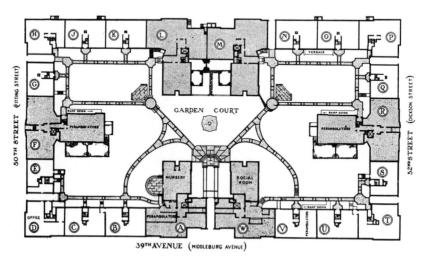

tion was to be installed in Phipps, and incinerators with access at each floor were just coming into use. Therefore, I advised against dumb-waiters.

Although the directors of Phipps Houses approved my suggestion to install incinerators they at first decided to play safe and also have dumb-waiters. These ultimately were eliminated — they have not been missed. However, in the case of fuel for the boilers, the directors insisted, in addition to oil tanks, that a large bin for coal be installed. This was good judgment as war conditions made oil difficult to secure, and the use of coal was advisable, if not essential.

CONSTRUCTION was sound because the owner was going to manage the development, which was built as a long term investment, and not as a commercial speculation. Exterior walls and fire walls separating apartments are of solid brick masonry. Salt-glazed brick walls were used around stairways, wood-trim on exteriors and public interiors was minimized. Door frames are of metal. The roofs are slated instead of the typical tar and gravel finish.

Staircases, fire-walls, and the slabs under the lower floors are the only parts of the buildings completely fireproof. This is in accordance with building law requirements. At Hillside we were to learn the financial advantages of complete fire protection that led to its use in the second part of Phipps to be built in 1935.

Conclusions

I. *Walk-up apartment buildings* compared with equivalent unit-plan elevator buildings are:

1. Cheaper to construct.

2. Less costly to operate and maintain.

3. More livable: they have better ventilation, more sunshine, less reflection of noise and heat from walls at right angles, and they are more accessible to the ground.

II. *Good landscaping,* including the planting of well grown trees in the beginning, is a sound investment—financially as well as in good living.

III. *Private gardens* or terraces are desirable for tenants on the ground floor of apartment houses.

Fig. 74—A typical apartment building entrance seen through an archway on the main axis.

5 HILLSIDE HOMES

Clarence S. Stein, Architect

In 1932, at the depth of the depression, the idea that was to be realized in Hillside took shape. In the beginning it was only an architect's abstract conception. There was no site, no client, no local precedent, no available financing—just an idea.

The Idea

Direct governmental housing, or credit for housing, did not exist in the U.S.A. Most of the building industry had been unemployed for years. President Roosevelt's New Deal promised large scale financing. How could that be used to build a complete, integrated neighborhood within the larger framework of our cities? In New York City, custom dictated mostly communities of apartment houses. These could not then be built for the very poor—housing subsidies were still in the future. However, an untried New York State law offered partial tax exemption to dwellings renting from $11 a room per month.

I decided to develop diagrammatically the basic conception of a self-contained, integrated residential neighborhood in New York, for desirable community living in apartment buildings at $11 per room rental (Fig. 75).

Phipps Garden Apartments was the basis of the first studies. The object was to secure the same advantages of apartments with cross-ventilation, surrounding garden courts, but at a third less rental.

Continued study, with comparative estimates by the builders, Starrett Brothers and Eken, indicated that the required result necessitated:

1. Land costing one dollar per square foot or less.
2. A building operation four times as large as the one at Phipps.
3. The use of over one-half of the basements for apartments.
4. A simplification of exterior and of interior equipment, and smaller room sizes than Phipps.
5. Financing at low interest and with long amortization.
6. Tax exemption of the buildings.

Meanwhile the city was combed for large low-cost sites fitting the following requirements:

1. Adequate for a community of 5,000 (at 250 persons per acre, about 20 acres).
2. Improved land at one dollar per square foot or less.
3. Possibility of closing streets to eliminate through traffic.
4. Adjacent to an elementary school.
5. Attractive site without undue construction difficulties such as rocks and swamps.

The Site

The property finally selected was a 26-acre undeveloped piece of land owned by Nathan Straus. Fortunately, he was deeply interested in housing those with limited incomes, and later, he was to become Administrator of the U. S. Housing Authority. The price of the land was 70 cents per square foot, exclusive of the area mapped for streets. This site, by reason of its slope, permitted

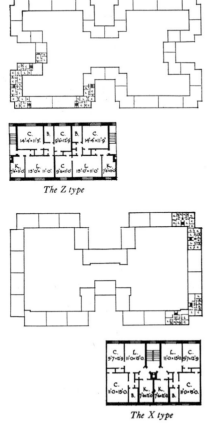

The Z type

The X type

Fig. 75—Above are two plot plans which were in the early studies. A plot of 460 feet by 260 feet was assumed for convenience in comparison with the Phipps Garden Apartments. Various apartment type plans were developed in the studies. The X type uses the same layout as the Phipps scheme, but with smaller rooms. In the Z type the span was decreased to 29 feet, as compared with 33 feet for the X type and 35 feet for Phipps Garden Apartments (I).

maximum utilization of the basements for apartments (Fig. 78).

Planning Hillside

Once the site was determined, we applied our theoretical buildings and courts to it (Fig. 79). Every change in the drawing was paralleled by study on the three-dimensional model, in relation to the site and topography (Fig. 83). Finally, a full-sized four-room unit was built and furnished. Thus various construction methods and materials were tested. Here the two-inch solid plaster partitions which we afterwards used were tried out. Complete units of plumbing and other mechanical equipment were studied in detail to find ways of cutting costs, securing greater efficiency, and saving time in erection. And here I discovered that by moving one closet it would be possible to reach all rooms in the apartment without passing through the livingroom.

As a result of judicious grading of the hilly site we were able to utilize one half of the basement area for apartments. They could be placed one step above grade on the garden court side and thus have a door leading directly out to a private terrace—on the other side they are entered from the public stairs by going down a half flight, and they have cross ventilation. I had experimented with this arrangement at Phipps. At Hillside we were able to secure 188 garden apartments. They have been very popular and particularly convenient for old people, who are thus saved the necessity of climbing stairs. They can have a good view of the life going on in the court and can be near, without always being with, their family (Fig. 92).

But if one-half of the basement was to be utilized for rental apartments it was necessary to find out the space requirements of all other essential demands upon basement space: storage space for trunks, screens, perambulators, rooms for gas and electric meters; administration and maintenance of buildings and grounds; community social facilities such as nursery school, assembly room, clubrooms; boiler room and fuel storage (Figs. 76 and 77). So during the year in which we waited for governmental loans, a detailed survey of the adequacy and size of these facilities in existing hous-

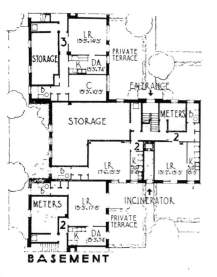

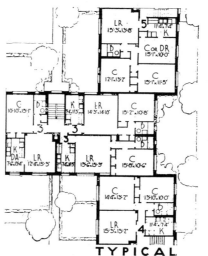

BASEMENT

TYPICAL

Fig. 76—Typical apartments in I units arranged as a T, and characteristic basement plan showing a combination of apartments and utility rooms. Although typical units were used throughout (without variation), the basement layouts were varied according to site conditions and the requirements for utilities, storage, and communal facilities.

ing developments was made for our office by Catherine Bauer and Margaret Morgan.

Meanwhile, so as to encourage building, Federal financing was offered at increasingly easy terms (Fig. 85). Finally, in September, 1933, the Public Works Administration approved a loan of 85 per cent of the cost at 4 per cent interest (Fig. 81). A long amortization was allowed on the basis of fireproof construction.

The general plan, as approved, was carried out. It included the central playground and the grouping of standard units around great courts (Figs. 80 and 86).

Only one main feature of the earlier plans was lost; and this, to me, was an important one. Hillside had been designed as a neighborhood within a superblock. Only one street was to have cut through—and the central pedestrian way was to have passed under it. After a fight lasting two years we were unable to eliminate mapped streets.

The elderly Superintendent of Highways said that he had devoted a lifetime to planning the streets on the map—and there they must stay! And there they are, even those that go nowhere. As a result of children hit by autos, Seymour Avenue has been made a 'play-street' and so closed to through traffic.

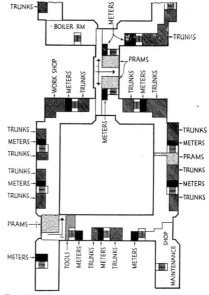

Fig. 77—Diagram showing carefully determined and conveniently located basement services. White portions indicate spaces used for garden court apartments.

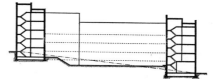

Fig. 78—A section showing how the natural slope was used to create garden court apartments at different levels.

HILLSIDE HOMES

The stores and movie theater that fringe Boston Road would, I believe, have served the community better and been more successful financially and as civic design, if they had been unified in a group around a green, as was afterwards done at Greenbelt.

UNIT PLANS.—The unit plans of Hillside grew out of experience at Sunnyside and Phipps (Fig. 97). The predominating type of apartment with two bedrooms added greatly to privacy and efficiency. All rooms are accessible from a small central entrance passage. Despite the need of economizing to remain within the $11 rental, the room sizes were increased and proportions improved. This and the change to fireproof construction, which has lessened maintenance costs, were the results of continuous united study and research by builder and architect.

The advantage of the simple I unit, for economy of space and cost as well as increased light and ventilation, the development of the T composed of three I units, led to the elimination of L, T, or U forms in walk-up apartments (Figs. 76 and 82). Livability is therefore superior in these as compared with the six-story elevator buildings in which the construction and maintenance costs of elevators required many rooms around each elevator shaft. On the other hand, the taller buildings, located on the crest of the Hillside site, have certain advantages. From them one gets a broad view in every direction and, in the general composition, the larger mass adds interest and variety.

Most American housing reformers claim that walk-up apartments of more than three stories are objectionable. Tenants at Phipps and Hillside seem to disagree. There have been practically no vacancies in the top floor at either place. Perhaps this is partially due to the fact that we put our balconies on the upper story, and the management charges about one dollar less per room each month (Figs. 80 and 86).

Building Hillside

When construction started on Hillside, most of the building industry had been out of employment for two years or more. There was a long queue of bricklayers waiting outside the enclosure. They were hungry for work: but they were out of the habit.

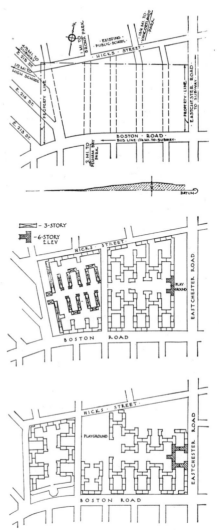

Fig. 79—The site selected was a 26-acre undeveloped piece of land. Its section facilitated the development of garden apartments one-half story below street entrance level. Two of a series of preliminary layouts are shown. The first included some three-story two-family buildings. The second has a 2½-acre playground for elementary school children. This was later moved to the southern side of the plot.

Fig. 80—Air view of the Hillside Homes development. The main traffic artery, the Boston Post Road, is on the right, the public school on the left. The distant part of the site is 55-ft. above the nearer.

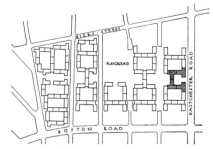

Fig. 81—In September, 1933, the new Public Works Administration approved a loan of 85 per cent, subject to a satisfactory contract, based on this plan. This loan allowed a 4 per cent interest rate as compared with the 5 per cent required by R.F.C. A change to fireproof construction throughout ensured a longer period of

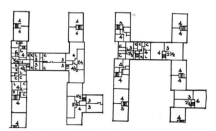

Fig. 82—A further step forward in the architectural studies was made when it was decided to replace the old T units (left) by I units joined together in T form (right) with less waste and cost.

amortization. At this stage it was apparent that closing streets would be a lengthy business. So no buildings were shown covering mapped streets.

HILLSIDE HOMES

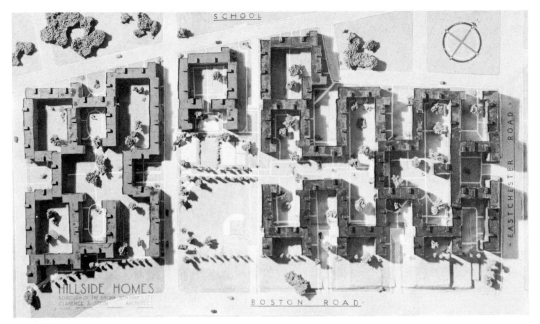

Fig. 83—The model used for three-dimensional studies.

Fig. 84—A court on the central axis.

At first they each laid only some 750 bricks a day. But as they got the swing of the work their pace increased; and, before long, they were laying 1,100 a day. It was a lovely sight to see the long line of men in rhythmic motion on the scaffolds, following the gang leaders. They seemed to draw a curtain of beautifully textured brick up from the ground toward the sky. It was good to see homes being erected once more.

Starrett Brothers and Eken had the great job completely and superbly organized. One trade methodically followed another from footings to roof—and then moved on to the next block. The strong competition of the trades, as building started again, along with the organization of the work, did much to keep down costs. This made it possible to build larger rooms than those of Phipps, and still keep within the limits of the maximum $11 average room rental. But much of the economy of construction was due to the long period devoted to the study of plans and construction in which the staff of architect and builder co-operated. I wish I could give credit to the various talented people who worked with me and Andrew Eken, the builder, in the production of Hillside. One I cannot neglect, my associate Frank Vitolo, because of the outstanding part he played at Hillside and Phipps. He formed the essential link between architect and builder. For Frank was an architect who understood the ways and the nature of the various construction trades as thoroughly as a builder did. Moreover, he knew all the intricacies of the complicated legal framework of building and housing laws, more thoroughly even than the building department officials. What is more they knew he knew. So therefore, when Frank Vitolo presented one of my unorthodox plan arrangements, they felt sure that Frank was on sound legal ground. The unorthodox plans were generally approved. Frank Vitolo got things done, not only because he so completely understood the practice and law of building, but because he understood the people he dealt with. He was a fine person, and we all respected and loved him.

Life in Hillside

The 1400 families that moved into Hillside in 1935 came mainly from the surrounding Borough of the Bronx. The wage-earners were white-collar workers, predominantly salesmen, with average annual salaries of about $2500.

The playground, nursery school, clubrooms, and the safe green courts drew families with children. Almost a third of the population was below 21 years (3,000 adults, 1,430 children). A good many of those children, now grown up, have returned from the war to bring up their own youngsters in Hillside.

In the typical Bronx apartment, from which the tenants of Hillside came, there is no sense of community ties or neighborliness. You may live for years on the same floor with families who remain strangers. Not so in Hillside. Hillside for twelve years has been a neighborly community, buzzing with activity. This was the result of the combination of the physical plan and the development of community activities.

The two and a half acre playground is the central feature (Fig. 89). Here, for all ages, is everything from ballgames to wading pool. Here, on summer evenings, the whole community, some 4,500 strong, gather, or lean out of surrounding windows, to enjoy pageants, festivals, or dramatic productions. A shelter built in the hillside offers protection from sun and rain, with toilets at either side.

The main community rooms are in the basement of the building to the north. This space, as a result of the natural slope, is above ground level. Here are the office of the community consultant (note: in the democracy of Hillside, 'consultant,' not director), various club and game rooms, and finally the assembly room. Here dance and music classes, calisthenics, plays, women's clubs, and festivals follow each other from early morning to late night.

The main community rooms have served well in their present central location. However, I think it would have been better to put them in a separate structure. This could have very well been an enlargement of the shelter in the park, with rooms on both upper and playground level. Apart from other advantages it would separate the meeting-rooms exit from the apartment houses, where it is sometimes disturbing at night when crowds depart.

The Assembly Room, of some 375 seats, is too

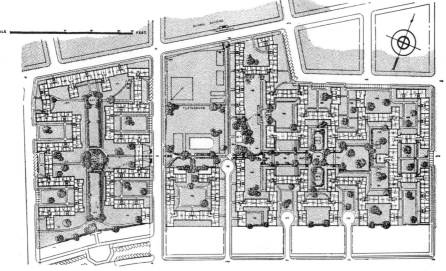

Fig. 85—Preliminary site plan, dated July 1932. All the mapped through streets had been eliminated with one exception. This was used as the basis for the application made to the Reconstruction Finance Corporation, a Federal government agency. By this time the owner had decided to retain a 100-ft. strip along the main traffic road; incidentally, this decreased the cost of the land by eliminating the part that would be most heavily taxed, and the project lost merely that portion of land least desirable for residential purposes because of its proximity to noisy traffic. On November 1, 1932, the R.F.C. approved a loan on this layout, which had been previously approved by the New York State Housing Board. The loan was to consist of two-thirds of the estimated cost of land and buildings at 5 per cent interest, with an amortization of 2 per cent. 5,378 rooms were provided in semi-fireproof construction.

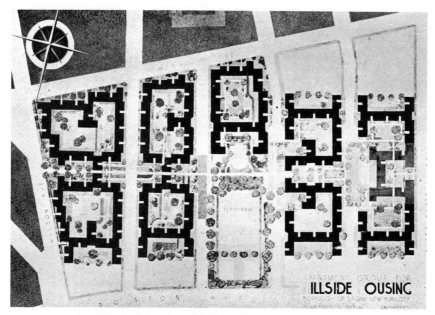

Fig. 86—The final site plan of Hillside Homes, dated September 1933.

Fig. 87—The interior of one of the workshops, in which both children and adults may pursue their hobbies in groups.

Fig. 88—One of the two nursery school rooms.

Fig. 89—The two-and-half-acre playground forms the central feature of Hillside Homes.

Fig. 90—The central axis showing the rising ground.

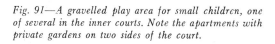

Fig. 91—A gravelled play area for small children, one of several in the inner courts. Note the apartments with private gardens on two sides of the court.

Fig. 92—Garden apartments are particularly convenient for old people.

small for gatherings of the whole Hillside Community. But the public school across the street has an auditorium large enough to serve such assemblies, although the Hillside residents feel freer and more at home in their own large community room. There they can sit around after meetings, talk, eat and drink, and, if they like, dance.

The workshops were distributed one in each court, where we found well-lighted space in basements not practicable for apartments. They are spacious, unplastered but painted, with a sink and toilet in each. No specific use was determined in advance. As those interested in a special activity such as painting, handicrafts, modeling, or other hobby, got together, these rooms were made available (Fig. 87). Some activities were temporary, such as painting and sculpture. Others were longer-lived, such as the camera club, which equipped its own workshop with darkroom, elaborate lighting, and a comfortable clubroom in which to discuss its techniques and carry on an educational program.

In the beginning most of the Hillside tenants were young parents. Their first activity was organization of a nursery school. The management offered free space and basic equipment for the carefully-planned nursery school facilities, and guidance of an expert teacher (Fig. 88). Teachers' College, Columbia University, provided student teachers. The mothers whose children did not attend the nursery, either because of the expense or because of its limited space, organized group care in each court. They took turns supervising the gravelled play areas, each of which included a sandbox, under the guidance of the nursery school director, and so actually served as an extension of the nursery school into the community as a whole (Fig. 91).

In the same way there were requests from groups of residents who had like interests to use all available space. The management gave heat and a limited amount of janitorial service free, as well as help and guidance, when it was required, from one of America's ables recreation leaders, Louise P. Blackham.

A community council, representing all clubs, developed in time, and has assumed sponsorship of projects of general community-wide interest.

The setting and the social organization of Hillside have for over twelve years created a real neighborhood community in which at least half the families have actively participated. As a result, the potentialities of personality and citizenship, too often stifled by city apartment life, here grew through association and experience in civic life.

Vacancy figures provide a good indication of what people think of home and community life. In most New York City apartment buildings, the number of vacant dwelling units increases as time goes on—and rises to between 10 and 15 per cent in hard times. This is not so at Hillside. In fourteen years there has never at any time been more than one quarter of one per cent vacancy or bad debt. Buildings which are more than ninety-nine per cent occupied make possible low rentals and an adequate return on the investment.

For eleven years Hillside Homes paid its full six per cent interest on the capital investment and, in addition, all operation and maintenance costs and the amortization of mortgages were fully covered. The greatly increased costs of operation, and the freezing of rents due to the war and its after effects, made it necessary to postpone the payment of interest on the capital investment for a period of two years. Since then, permission has been secured to raise rentals from $11 a room per month to $12.32. This has allowed the payment not merely of current dividends but also the paying up of previous unpaid dividends. So, for many years to come, Hillside Homes promises to continue its success as a financial investment. Its success as a neighborhood community has always been well assured.

*Fig. 93—The large inner court showing the facade fac-
ing the earlier development.*

6

PHIPPS GARDEN APARTMENTS (II)

Clarence S. Stein, Architect

By 1935 Phipps Houses had put aside sufficient from earnings to complete that development. The addition was to use the remaining portion of the site—460 x 200 ft. (Fig. 95). Its design was influenced both by management experience in the first Phipps Apartments and my experience at Hillside Homes. It was therefore decided that:

1. Fireproof construction should be used throughout. The owner expected to operate the building throughout its life, which we hoped and expected would be long. The expenses were therefore figured on a time basis, that is, operation and maintenance expense had more weight than original capital costs. There was an additional advantage that fireproof apartments in New York do not require exterior fire-escapes, which made design easier and more attractive.

2. Four-story walk-up buildings rather than elevator apartment structures should be used for reasons I gave in discussing the first construction. Lengthy study of Hillside Homes had confirmed my opinion that far more livable dwellings, and somewhat lower costs, could be attained in the walk-up buildings. After figuring the difference in costs and returns on buildings of three usable floors instead of four, it was decided that we would stick to the taller buildings. This was because tenants had shown their satisfaction by keeping the upper floor apartments full most of the time. We

estimated that the three-story building would have cost $1,186 instead of $1,149 per room for the four-story one.

A large number of small units that might serve for bachelors or newly-weds or, on the lower floors, for old folks, were used. These single large rooms, with a special niche for dining near the compact kitchenette and with windows on two sides, have been found very comfortable. The single bedroom apartment, with all rooms directly accessible to the compact entrance corridor, has worked very well.

Further development of these two types of units for small families would be useful in some future building of towns in which families with children would be housed in single family dwellings with gardens, and newcomers, or those without youngsters, might have the convenience of apartments cared for by the management.

A further development of the T composed of three I buildings, tried at Hillside, gives all apartments windows on two or three sides (Fig. 98). In the four-room unit, as a result of moving the kitchen to the end, the livingroom has been arranged with its long side parallel to the outer wall. This is an improvement that Wright and I had long desired—but we had not wanted to unduly increase street frontage.

Exteriors are less elaborate than in the first

Fig. 94—A typical entrance to an apartment stair hall. The lighting fixture indicates the particular stairhall at night as well as in the daytime.

Phipps. Harmony was secured by use of the same brick and similar but simpler patterns (Fig. 94).

There were advantages and economies in adding to the size of the Phipps development. The manager, Ernest Schofield, needed little addition to the staff for operating the buildings. The heating plant in the old building was connected to the new structure.

The general plan was determined somewhat by the long narrow form of the remaining plot. It was affected by my desire to continue the use of the effective T-grouping of buildings. The result was a series of open courts facing the older structure (Fig. 93). The greater part of the apartments face it rather than the outside. Each court has an individual type of garden (Fig. 96).

These courts with one side open appear on plan to have great advantages over the completely enclosed central green. They work well here because they turn toward and form part of the group building. There is no traffic between the buildings, excepting on the few occasions when deliveries of oil and other supplies must be made. If the open courts had faced toward a street they might have been objectionable because of traffic noises and their echo. The court enclosed on four sides, as in the first section, has, if it is large enough, a sense of spacious privacy and unity. Large entrance passages and the low buildings let in the summer breezes (Figs. 73 and 95).

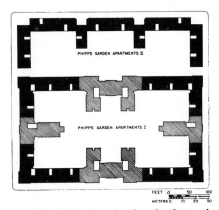

Fig. 95—Block plan showing the first and second units of development. The hatched portions are six-story elevator apartments; the solid portions are four-story walk-up apartments.

Fig. 96—The gardens in each court are varied in detail. This is known as the Dutch Garden.

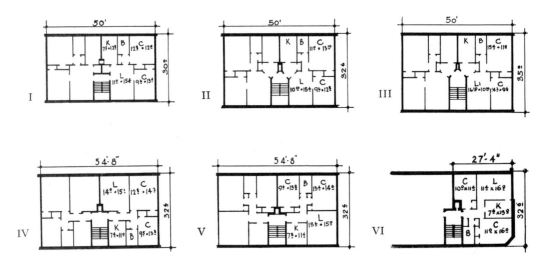

Fig. 97—EVOLUTION OF THE FOUR-ROOM APARTMENT 1926-36. The first apartments built at Sunnyside were similar to the two-family houses erected at the some time in 1924. Two apartments were behind a facade fifty feet in length. This length was used in each development until 1931, when the first unit of Phipps Garden Apartments was constructed. But the depth was increased from year to year. The gross area per room was increased from 181 square feet in 1924 to 219 square feet in 1931.

I. 1926, SUNNYSIDE, MONROE COURT, 187 SQ. FT. GROSS PER ROOM. The compact Sunnyside plan has little corridor and no foyer. All other rooms are entered from the living room. Plumbing is concentrated and the location of structural walls is determined by the length of standard wooden joists. In spite of the lack of privacy in the living room, this type has always been popular. There is good cross-ventilation and the plan is most economical.

II. 1927, SUNNYSIDE, 203 SQ. FT. GROSS PER ROOM. The convenience of the plan was greatly increased by adding a foyer with direct access from it to the kitchen.

III. 1931, PHIPPS GARDEN APART-MENTS (I), 187 SQ. FT. GROSS PER ROOM. The plan and method of construction were similar but the depth of the apartments was increased.

IV and V. 1932, HILLSIDE HOMES, 223 SQ. FT. GROSS PER ROOM. At Hillside there was direct access from the entrance hall to every room. This was secured by moving a closet. The additional 4-ft. 8-in. in the length permitted great internal flexibility and, in particular, it allowed an arrangement with the kitchen and bathroom on the same side. There were two alternative plans. The living room could be placed on either side to face a garden court or the sun. Where an apartment was on a corner, it was possible to have windows on two sides of the living room. The additional cost of fireproof construction (employing reinforced concrete) was balanced by the lower interest rates on the mortgage and the longer life allowed for in the amortization.

VI. 1935, PHIPPS GARDEN APART-MENTS (II), 223 SQ. FT. GROSS PER ROOM. In the second unit of Phipps Garden Apartments, fireproof construction was again employed and the four-room apartment units had a third external wall. Together, they allowed greater freedom in design. The long side of the living room is on the main external wall and there is a door from it to the kitchen. The extra cost involved in the separation of bathroom and kitchen is fully recompensed by the advantage of having direct access between the kitchen and living room, and a kitchen deep enough to allow a comfortable dining space.

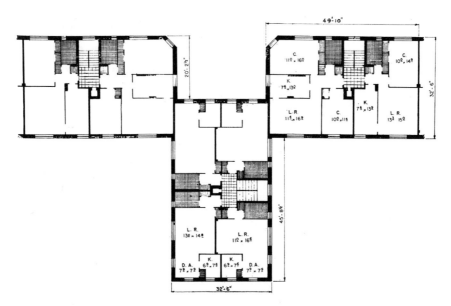

Fig. 98—*Typical apartment plans in three I units arranged as a T. This is a further improvement of the Hillside Homes arrangement. The four-room apartment has light and ventilation on three sides, the smaller apartments on two sides. The smallest apartments can be grouped four to a stair.*

VALLEY STREAM PROJECT

and Clarence S. Stein, Charles Butler, Frank Vitolo, Architects Associated

By 1935 a vast number of workers in the United States were unemployed and receiving assistance from the government. Building had practically ceased. Housing construction around New York, for instance, declined 95 per cent between 1928 and 1932—and 85 per cent of the building workers were unemployed.

The construction industry is one of the largest in the country. Its activity affects not only structural work but numerous other occupations in factories, forests and mines, and also, indirectly, many services and commerce. Therefore much thought was given at Washington to ending the depression by getting the building industry going again. This came to be called 'priming the pump.' Everyone talked about it—but nobody did anything about it. Valley Stream and a group of other communities, planned to be built throughout the country near industrial or business centers, were intended as a first step toward 'priming the industrial pump.'

Dwellings for 18,000

Valley Stream was to provide dwellings for 18,000 people and it was to be built, together with the other large, integrated communities, to fulfil a primary objective of giving employment.

Secondly, families were to live in these towns in sound and decent houses at low rentals, and there were to be community facilities to provide oppor-

tunities for the advantageous use of leisure time. The low rentals were to be maintained not only in times of depression, but at all times.

Thirdly, the towns were to demonstrate to the whole country a better way to design, build and manage communities to serve contemporary needs in an economical manner.

The proposal was made by a group, which besides having an interest in the purposes above, had individual interest. The heads of three of the largest corporations manufacturing building materials and apparatus were on the Board. They wanted to get their factories going again. The president of a large building company naturally desired to revive the dormant construction industry. Even one of the great airlines was represented. Here was an opportunity to dispose of airfields in various parts of the country which were being replaced by larger municipal fields.

We architects wanted to carry the Radburn Idea further—to see complete, modern, integrated communities planned, built and operated. We hoped this would be the next move toward New Towns.

CHOICE OF LOCATION. The first step was to choose the sites. Airfields throughout the country were examined from the point of view of physical conditions, including the availability of essential utilities, and future regional work opportunities. After a first selection had been made, a more detailed, but still a quick, study was made of social, economic, and governmental (including educational) conditions in nearby communities. This was carried out by Catherine Bauer and others. I went out to Los Angeles and San Francisco to investigate conditions there. It is interesting that the site on which we afterwards developed Baldwin Hills Village was suggested to me at that time. Its advantages were apparent although it, and the vast area around, were still vacant and undeveloped.

It was finally decided that the preliminary drawings and estimates be prepared for developments in or near Milwaukee, Wisconsin; Los Angeles and San Francisco, California; and Valley Stream in Nassau County—just outside New York City.

In the end these projects were not built. A large government is slow of action and its machinery complicated. So the building of communities was postponed until, to relieve unemployment, the Greenbelt Towns were constructed by workers mainly unskilled in building. The opportunity to use the vast number of unemployed building craftsmen to create economical homes at low rentals in pleasant modern communities was lost in 1933. At that time work was most needed in the construction industry (see frontispiece).

I will speak of one of the developments only, Valley Stream, which is characteristic in general of the design of all four. Even though it was only a project, I think its plans formed an important step toward the development of the Greenbelt Towns, and ultimately toward New Towns in America.

THE SITE consisted of 350 acres of flat land just beyond the New York City border. It was well drained, and its sand and gravel soil could be economically used for large-scale building. The property was surrounded on three sides by well built-up areas.

THE TOWN PLAN followed the Radburn pattern with superblocks, underpasses, central parks, and an even more complete separation of pedestrian and auto (Fig. 99). We proposed that the groups of houses be protected from the noises and odors of passing motor cars by placing them, in general, sixty feet away from the highways. This space was to be used for garages, grouped in this location for the following reasons:

1. So as to concentrate the paved surfaces and thus cut down the cost of highways, and
2. to make practical use of the space along the highways, and screen the houses in the group from dust and noise (Figs. 100 and 101).

This arrangement, as is apparent, would give utmost economy in roads and walks. It was open to the criticism that an American wants to leave his auto just outside his door. But, as many of the

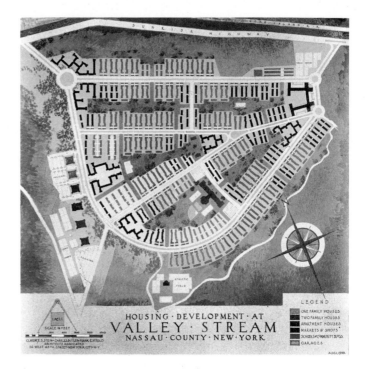

Fig. 99—General plan of Valley Stream Project.

Fig. 100—A service and garden court study showing proposed planting.

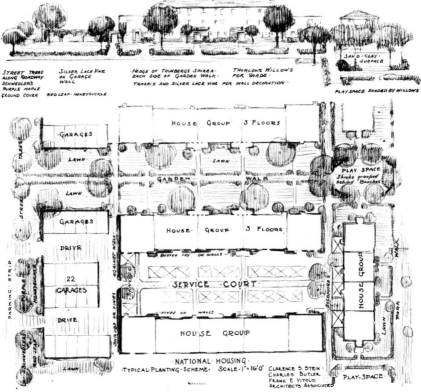

tenants in Phipps Garden Apartments walked 200 feet or more to their stair entrance, I believed that they would do it in row houses or flats if the inducement of low rentals were great enough. Although we were not able to try out this idea at Valley Stream, we used it successfully at Greenbelt, Md. Since then it has been further developed at various places—finally at Baldwin Hills Village.

HOUSES were to be built in rows for economy, and thus to assure low rentals. In addition to two-family houses two stories in height, we proposed three-floor buildings with one family using the lower and another the two upper floors. There was to be housing for 4,500 families, at thirteen to the acre.

COMMUNITY FACILITIES. A greenbelt of limited width was proposed to surround the development. In this was to be the athletic field. Seven acres in the center of the development were to be given to Nassau County for school and playground. The existing hangars were to have been turned into markets and garages with surrounding parking space.

COST STUDIES which our office made included, in addition to estimates of construction and utilities made by the builder, a financial statement of annual income and expenses. We had learned from experience that the costs which counted in the long run were the operation-maintenance costs and carrying charges, rather than the original capital costs. In this connection there was a new problem. Valley Stream we proposed as an independent municipality. Therefore, the costs of government would have to be calculated as part of the annual expenses of the inhabitants. Whether it was charged to them as taxes or as rent did not matter in determining their living costs.

The cost of government must be added to that of operating, maintaining and financing buildings and grounds. So I made a study of the costs of government of small communities in this part of America as a basis for the budget of Valley Stream. I was aided by one of America's ablest town managers, John Walker, who had managd Radburn and other places. Our studies for Valley Stream served as basis for my future recommendations to the Resettlement Administration that were to be used in the Greenbelt Towns.

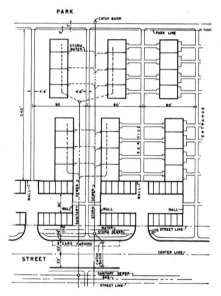

Fig. 101—Proposed layout of utilities by Ralph Eberlin.

Fig. 102—Children using the inner block paths on the way home from school in the Resettlement Development.

8 GREENBELT

**Douglas D. Ellington and R. J. Wadsworth,
Chief Architects
Hale Walker, Town Planner**

When Franklin D. Roosevelt became President of the United States in March, 1933, ten million American workers were unemployed. The summer before a demonstration 'Bonus Army' of veterans had marched on Washington. Some of the unemployed settled down at the capital and built 'Hoovervilles.' The New Deal's first attempts to reverse Hoover's policy of leaving the jobless to local care succeeded in giving employment, but were in the main unproductive 'boondoggling.'

There were two outstanding exceptions: the first was the Tennessee Valley Authority, the fame of which is world-wide. Only second in importance as a demonstration of future possibilities was the building of the so-called Greenbelt Towns. Here the seed of future city development was planted. For in these towns for the first time were amalgamated the three basic conceptions from which new towns are being evolved: the Garden City, the Radburn Idea, and the Neighborhood Unit.

THE PURPOSES as officially stated were:

1. To give useful work to men on unemployment relief.
2. To demonstrate in practice the soundness of planning and operating towns according to certain garden city principles.
3. To provide low-rent housing in healthful surroundings, both physical and social, for

families that are in the low-income bracket.

The creation of the Greenbelt Towns was made possible by the Emergency Relief Appropriation Act and the National Industrial Recovery Act, both of 1935. By executive order of September of that year the President established the Resettlement Administration and prescribed its functions in regard to the Greenbelt Towns. Since then the administration of these communities has been successively transferred to various federal agencies: in December 1936 to the Secretary of Agriculture, under whom it operated as a separate unit of the Department, the name of which was afterwards changed to Farm Security Administration; in February 1942 the President transferred all housing developments which did not relate chiefly to farming to the National Housing Agency, afterward the National Public Housing Authority, and now the Public Housing Administration. In 1949, as a result of special legislation for that purpose (Senate No. 351), the towns were to be disposed of by sale, with first preference to veterans' and present tenants' groups organized on a non-profit basis. Negotiations were put under way for that purpose.

Organization for Production of the Towns

To return to that 'Never-Never' land of the New Deal: President Roosevelt appointed Rexford

Guy Tugwell, one of his brain-trusters who fervently believed in Ebenezer Howard's Garden City, as Administrator of the Resettlement Administration. To produce the proposed new communities Tugwell set up, as part of the administration, the Suburban Resettlement Division under John Lansill as Director.

The Federal Governmental officials and employees multiplied and multiplied during 1935. All office buildings in Washington were overcrowded. The Suburban Division of Resettlement was finally lodged in the extravagant mansion of a former multi-millionaire, Senator MacLane. The drafting rooms, in which the homes of the poor were to be designed, surrounded a monumental marble stairway which was said to simulate the *rococo* central hall of the Atlantic liner on which the Senator had made his first trip abroad. On the landing half-way up the stairs one collided with a monstrous sculptural group of naked figures, so bulky and heavy that the government could not afford to resettle it.

In these surroundings the architects, engineers and other technicians planned homes and communities for families with incomes of $1,250 a year. It was no easy task for designers, to whom residential architecture had meant individually tailored mansions for those who could afford conspicuous waste, to limit themselves to bare essentials. Some of the early studies looked as though they were meant for the Westchester villas of young bankers. But, ultimately, the architects created a great and unified beauty out of essential requirements and simple designs.

The technicians were wisely divided into teams, each responsible for a single town—and working as though they were separate and distinct offices. Each group was headed by one or two senior planners, architects, engineers and a co-ordinator. Assisting were a staff of younger technicians and draftsmen. The Chief of the Planning Staff, Frederick Bigger, under whom the groups worked, was broadminded. He had no decided formulas. He believed that each town should be a distinct experiment—that new ideas and new approaches should be given the maximum possible opportunity to develop. This method is in sharp contrast with that which afterwards developed in the various governmental housing agencies. They so regulate and standardize housing that the essential abilities of the architects—imagination, invention and ingenuity—are dried up and negated.

Fred Bigger decided to let the technicians be on their own as far as possible, so that they would take risks, so that they would explore and experiment. As a result they worked with enthusiasm, and gave their utmost. All the towns consequently have characterful individuality.

However, so that the planners and architects should not lose sight of the objective, this statement of the functions of the organization was given them as guide:

'To obtain a large tract of land, and thus avoid the complications due to diverse ownerships; in this tract to create a community, protected by an encircling green belt; the community to be designed for families of predominantly modest income, and arranged and administered (managed) so as to encourage that kind of family and community life which will be better than they now enjoy, but which will not involve subjecting them to coercion or theoretical and untested discipline; the dwellings and the land upon which they are located to be held in one ownership, preferably a corporated entity to which the federal government will transfer title, and which entity or corporation will rent or lease the dwellings but will not sell them; a municipal government to be set up, in character with such governments now existing or possible in that region; co-ordination to be established, in relation to the local and state governments, so that there may be provided those public services of educational and other character which the community will require; and finally, to accomplish these purposes in such a way that the community may be a taxpaying participant in the region, that extravagant outlays from the individual family income will not be a necessity, and that the rent will be suitable to families of modest income.

'To develop a land-use plan for the entire tract; to devise, under the direction of the Administrator, a system of rural economy co-ordinated with the land-use plan for the rural portions of the tract surrounding the suburban community; and to integrate both the physical plans and the economies of the rural area and the suburban community.'

Among the first problems of the new agency were how many new communities to build and where to place them. The number would be limited by the funds available and the fact that, because unskilled labor must in large part be used, costs would be very high. On the other hand unemployment was nation-wide; work was needed everywhere and at once.

The location of the limited number of towns that could be built must be determined on the basis of the above-stated purposes that they were 'to demonstrate . . . garden city principles.' That, among other things, meant that the towns be placed convenient to industrial opportunity — in fact that the towns be planned both for work and living, as had been advocated by Ebenezer Howard. Therefore Warren Vinton, the chief economist, devoted himself to a painstaking study of the probable future industrial opportunities near various large cities.

Without waiting for the completion of this research an acute emergency — or, should I say, political embarrassment — led to the immediate locating of the first community near Washington. The 'Hoovervilles' left by the 'Bonus Army' on the doorstep of Congress was too much like hanging the nation's wash in the front yard of the Capitol. It had to be removed. And so plans and specifications for Greenbelt, Maryland, 13 miles from the center of the Capitol were rushed.

In the end only two other towns were constructed: Greendale, Wisconsin, seven miles from the business center of Milwaukee; and Greenhills, Ohio, five miles north of Cincinnati.

Although these three were among America's outstanding demonstrations of New Towns, it must be admitted that they all missed out on the score of industry. Cincinnati, Milwaukee, and Washington have grown as centers of industry, business or government. But the Greenbelt Towns have not yet drawn in factories or offices. They have continued in the role of suburbs, near but yet too expensively far from employment. All this shows the difficulty and the importance of co-ordinating broad physical planning with industrial planning.

In the location of the fourth project, Warren Vinton did prove to be an industrial prophet; the New Brunswick area of New Jersey has of late had a fantastic industrial growth. The town of Greenbrook, of which Henry Wright was planner and Albert Mayer and Henry Churchill the architects, would probably have been a complete garden city. But it was never built because of local opposition and the threat of court action.

John Lansill, Director of the Suburban Division, asked me to offer constructive criticism of the plans that were being developed. After studying them, I felt that the greatest danger was unnecessary wastefulness, not only in capital expenditure, but what was even more important in this case, in operation and maintenance. I therefore prepared a series of studies of the effect on both capital and operation-maintenance costs of various manners of grouping as well as planning houses. Finally I decided that to find the most economical means of securing good living in these new towns we would have to consider other elements than those that formed part of housing developments in an existing urban area. The Greenbelt Towns were to be independent municipalities. Therefore, economy of town management was quite as important as in housing development operation in making them financially successful. By financially successful I here mean run so that their operation and maintenance would be covered by their rentals. To do more—that is to pay off the exorbitant cost of their building or to pay interest on the federal government's investment—seemed hardly possible as the tenants were all to be chosen from low income groups. The effect of size of community on operation-maintenance costs therefore became a real, and in fact, a basic element in their success.

It was apparent that the construction cost of the Greenbelt Towns would be high because of use of unskilled labor: these capital costs therefore could and in fact must be written off as unemployment relief. But on the other hand I felt certain that Congress would not annually appropriate monies to pay for deficit. Therefore it was essential to plan and build and to organize management so as to minimize the operation-maintenance expenses. This does not mean that the original costs could be wasted on unnecessarily large, elaborate, or complicated construction or equipment. On the contrary, as the capital expenditure voted by Congress would be limited, it was important that it be used to house as many families as possible.

To assist the planners in determining their plan in such a manner as to minimize capital costs as well as operation-maintenance expenditures 'without jeopardizing the popularity, social success, and future influence of the development' I made two studies:

1. *A Report of Method of Appraising House*

Plans.[21] This did not use the customary method of allowing a given number of square feet for each type of room. Such procedure only by good luck produces livable homes with flexible use. The method followed stated—or rather illustrated in diagrams—the minimum requirements in terms of requisite furniture, space for human activity and movement, and varied possible location of doors, windows and clothes-closets. As far as possible the attempt was made to allow for a number of desirable arrangements, to serve as a method of developing or appraising plans on the basis of minimum cost for adequate and varied use.

2. *Studies of the Relative Improvement Costs of House Grouping.*[22] To appraise different arrangements of houses in relation to·access from paths, roads, parking areas and parks, diagrammatic plans of 11 different groupings were made. The cost of each was carefully estimated as under normal conditions of construction as they existed at the time we were actively building Radburn.

The studies showed a difference of 100 per cent per family for its proportions of roads, walks, local utilities and landscaping between the normal method of placing houses along a main highway and an arrangement similar to the earlier studies for Valley Stream (See Fig. 100). This latter arrangement was tried out in various forms at Greenbelt, and I will report later as to their success.

Two studies were made that dealt primarily with cost of operation and maintenance. The one had to do with the projects as rental housing developments.[23] This followed the usual method of cost accounting to which we had become accustomed in making preliminary studies for Chatham Village, Hillside Homes, and other large-scale housing.

The other report, which dealt with local government cost, had less precedent.[24] The costs of government generally come to the house-owner or landlord in a package or lump sum as taxes—and as far as the tenant is concerned these costs are lost or hidden in his rent. The proposed Resettlement projects were to be unified, self-supporting communities in which a tenant's monthly charges must cover *all* costs of operation and maintenance, both as a town and as a housing operation.

I attempted to organize this study in such a way as to show the relative effect of change of policy or of cost of any single factor such as education, type of house, grouping of houses, manner of disposing of waste, income group to be housed, portion of income that can be afforded for rent, distance and cost of transportation, etc. Primarily, I was interested in finding out the effect of the change of the number of family units on the costs of both housing operation and government.

This study was restricted to municipalities of 3,000 to 7,000 population; these were the probable limits of the proposed towns, at least in the first stage of construction.

The comparative study of Operation-Maintenance Costs of Government and Housing indicated not only that the cost per unit (family or person) grew increasingly less as the population grew in size, but also that the charges required to pay these operation and maintenance costs, even without allowance for interest or amortization, were too high in the 3,000-population projects to be possible for the $1,250-income group that was to be housed. Both of these conclusions have been verified by the experience in the three towns during the past ten years. At Greenbelt the unit cost decreased very much in the proportion we had indicated when the number of inhabitants increased from about 3,000 to 7,000.

SHOPPING CENTERS. The final study dealt with shopping centers.[25] It attempted to determine the different requirements of towns of 3,000 to 7,000 population. It estimated the probable local expenditures if shops were properly designed; the types and size of stores that could be successfully supported; and the incomes that could be derived from the shopkeeper and by the landlord in the towns of various sizes. The actual experience at Greenbelt has in general tendency confirmed these predictions as explained later. (See p. 217).

Three Basic Planning Ideas

The Greenbelt Towns are the first experiments in the combined development of the three basic ideas of the modern community: the Garden City, the Radburn Idea, and the Neighborhood Unit. These three conceptions in greater or less degree form the essential basis of the plans for New Towns that are being discussed, planned, or constructed in various parts of the Western World.

In Sweden, in Poland, in Great Britain, the planners are starting out on the great voyage of discovery of the form and operation of new communities that will fit today's living, practically, economically, and at the same time spaciously, safely, and beautifully.

For over a decade Greendale, Greenhills, and Greenbelt have in embryo form been trying out the various elements of the evolving city. All too little is known of how these ideas really work. New conceptions of planning of communities are constantly discussed as pure theories, long after they have been tested in the solid form of actual building and community living. Again and again the same experiments are carried out at vast expense, without study or analysis of past experience. It is true that dissimilar places, peoples, times, customs and politics require different settings and forms of communities. It is true that we cannot take, in every detail, a type of community that fitted English life at the beginning of the century, or even one that fits it now, and expect it to operate successfully in America or Russia. But we should study the basic conceptions wherever they have had the test of time.

The analysis of the 11 to 12 years' experience in the Greenbelt Towns can be of the greatest practical value to planners, architects, and engineers, as well as to administrators, sociologists, economists, and leaders in recreation, education, and various other fields, if we can discover just to what extent and how the three basic conceptions have worked in practice. To what degree were the Garden City, the Radburn and the Neighborhood Ideas developed and carried out? How were they limited in application—by the size or the operation of the development; by its relations to the federal government; by costs or financial policy; by regional or local customs or by the nature of its inhabitants? How did its form or operation differ from the original conception of the idea, or its application elsewhere (The Garden City in England, the Radburn Idea where first tried out at Radburn, New Jersey, for example)? How did it differ from the manner in which the idea is now being used in creating New Communities in other countries? Finally, what do the people who have lived in the community think of the elements of

the ideas in practice? In short how do they work?

This last, an analysis of the human reactions to these new forms and conceptions, is of course the hardest to get at. The evolution of the form of the Garden City is too incomplete. The Neighborhood Idea is still somewhat nebulous. It is difficult to separate the elements. But it is important, even on the basis of a limited study or information, to try to analyze the application of the Garden City, Radburn and Neighborhood Ideas.

The three Greenbelt Towns all followed these basic conceptions—but they did so differently, in varying degrees, and often with contrasting emphases. This was due in part to the fact that the design and development of the three towns was wisely given into the hands of three separate teams of planners, architects, engineers and administrators, rather than being standardized by a single centralized office. Therefore there were three different conceptions of desirability for good living and broad economy, and of the extent to which Garden City, Radburn or Neighborhood Unit Ideas should be applied. The form these took was influenced not only by the planners' taste or experience, but also by the distinctive qualities of the site; the topography, soil, and climate; the regional character of the population, local customs and regulations, and politics. In operation and realization all of these elements have modified the application of the three basic conceptions. Their effectiveness has also been limited by the small size and gradual growth of the towns.

For these reasons a study or analysis of the elements of the three towns is of greater value if made separately for each. It would be too complicated for the reader—as well as the analyst—to describe the elements of the three at the same time. A more thorough investigation of one place with limited comparison with the others should be more valuable and more understandable.

Why Greenbelt, Maryland, Is Chosen as a Subject

I have selected Greenbelt, Maryland, as the principal subject of this study, rather than Greendale or Greenhills, for a number of reasons:

1. Greenbelt has grown from a town of less than 3,000 to about 7,500 population. Thus we can study the relation of size and distance as elements

To High School and Washington-Baltimore Blvd.

Transformer
Station

Recreational Area

Recreational
Association
Clubhouse

Greenbelt Lake

Tennis
Courts

Dam

Crescent
Road

Ridge
Road

Westway

Trail to High School

American
Legion
Post

Community Gardens

Southway

To High School and Washington-Baltimore Blvd.

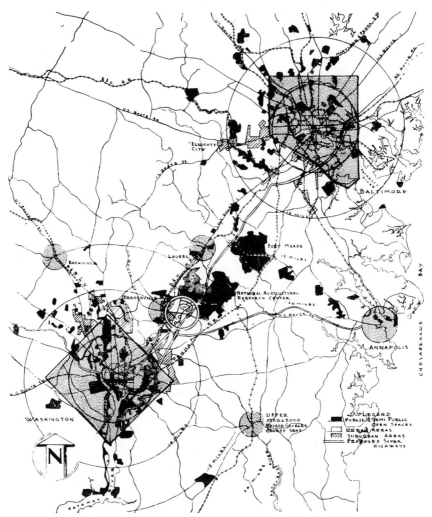

Fig. 104—Regional map showing relation of Greenbelt to outside urban influences, and proximity of National Agricultural Research Center.

Fig. 103 (previous spread)—Aerial view of Greenbelt compiled by G. T. Marts and G. Nichols.

of a neighborhood. Also we are able to compare two different methods of realizing the Radburn Idea in planning for a similar population and local conditions, but with a different approach on the part of the planners and builders.

2. Greenbelt, for various reasons, carried out and developed the Radburn Idea more fully and completely than either of the other towns. It applied all the elements full-heartedly and with fresh approach rather than partially as at the other towns. It revealed its possibilities in some ways more clearly than Radburn.

3. Greenbelt also allows one to compare the effect of two sizes of community on the cost of government and management and the various elements of these. Although this may not seem to relate directly to the three basic ideas, it is of great importance as indicating one of the means of determining the desirable size of a Garden City or New Town.

Before analyzing Greenbelt in relation to the three basic ideas, let us consider its site, the people for whom it was created, and the general plan that was dictated by these.

The Greenbelt Site

The site of Greenbelt is about 13 miles from the center of the National Capital (Fig. 104). When it was chosen in 1935, Prince George's County, Maryland, in which it was situated, was sparsely settled. Up to that time most of the overflow from the limiting ten-mile square of the District of Columbia had streamed toward Virginia, where standards of education were higher. But since the war there has been a building boom in Prince George's County— a boom of a disorderly, unorganized character. The main access from the north to Washington, U. S. Route No. 1, which passes through the Greenbelt property, is now a continuous strip development of ugly, unrelated stores and houses. The nearby municipalities of Hyattsville, Riverdale and Berwyn have been sprawling rapidly over the landscape toward Washington. But the 3,300 acres or so which the government purchased for this great experiment in city building in 1935 is still mainly open country.

The land for Greenbelt was gradually acquired from numerous owners, the family titles to the property of some going back to the original grants from the King of England. It was no longer of much agricultural value. It had been overworked as farm-land, especially for tobacco-growing, and had ceased to be used for this purpose. Therefore it was bought for an average of $90 an acre. Little if any of the extensive open land that surrounds the development has been used for agriculture since its purchase.

The southern 1,200 acres, separated by the Branchville-Glendale Road from the northern area in which the present development is located, is of a rougher topography, with pine-wood ravines and plateaus of oak and other hardwoods. In this section there are about 300 acres of pasture and grainfields. This might make an excellent and much needed National or State Park, and thus serve as an additional permanent protective greenbelt.

The General Plan

If you are fortunate you will first see Greenbelt from the air while flying between New York and Washington (Fig. 103). The town is formed in the shape of a graceful crescent set on a vast background of green. For a moment its attractive flowing curves remind you of the Crescent at Bath, England. But the Greenbelt crescent is much bigger and bolder; it is much freer — though no less rhythmic. It is not so monumentally formal. The Bath crescent is a closed wall of masonry with landscape foreground and background; at Greenbelt most of the principal buildings are at right angles rather than parallel to the great curve.

The Greenbelt crescent is marked mainly by the graceful sweep of the two main highways, and the shadow of lower land that surrounds the natural plateau that suggested and give it its form.

The essential shape of the Greenbelt town plan was indicated by nature. Here, as in many other great plans, the planners' job was primarily to discover, not invent. As Benton MacKaye says:

'Planning is a scientific charting and picturing of the thing . . . which man desires and which the eternal forces will permit. The basic achievement of planning is to make potentialities visible . . . Planning is revelation.'26

The planners of Greenbelt revealed the potentialities of the great curved plateau as a beautiful place for good living. The plateau was roughly a

GREENBELT

thousand feet wide, more or less, at various places. The two main cross-town highways, Crescent and Ridge Road, although almost parallel, gradually open up the central area for some 5,000 feet then, to the north, they separate rapidly to take in the broadening of the plateau. They follow the curve of this highland but not always at the very ridge. The land in many places rises gradually and gracefully at one or both sides of the highways to form tree-clad backgrounds to the house groups, or to allow of their location at varying levels. The arched swings of the highways have great enough radii to permit safe visibility for auto driving. The driver's view is increased by the fact that buildings are either widely spaced and at right angles to the road, or have a liberal set-back.

The inner crescent sweeps round the spacious community center, some 1,500 feet wide and, including the athletic field, quite as deep. This forms the heart of Greenbelt. Here is the focus for the common life of the town, and here, in its physical center, are located in logical and beautiful arrangement the various elements for community activities. Here is the seat of government and management; the focus of cultural, religious, and educational life; the main recreational and entertainment center; and the market place.

The area between Crescent Road and Ridge Road is cut about every 1,000 feet by connecting traffic ways. The space is thus divided into superblocks of about 14 acres each.

The five superblocks south of Northway formed the main site of the houses built between the winter of 1935-36 and autumn of 1937 by the Resettlement Administration. In addition to this inner superblock area a few groups on the outside of Crescent Road and Ridge Road were completed, along with the apartment buildings on Parkway Road (Figs. 103 and 105). The other houses were built as part of the Defense Homes Development.

The People

The first settlers of Greenbelt moved in as the homes were completed between October 1937 and the summer of 1938. The demand for living places in the Washington area was limitless. It was therefore necessary for the government to set artificial limitation in choosing its tenants. Preference was given to poorly housed families whose incomes were limited but who could however afford the rentals which were set at $21.75 to $45.85 per month. In the row houses first choice was given to young married families with children. There was place for the smaller families, and even for bachelors, in the three-story apartment buildings. These small units were built to increase the number of families as much as possible when it was discovered that the $14 million or so—including $570,000 for land—that was being spent, would be insufficient, because of the use of unskilled labor, to build the 1,000 houses that had been set as a minimum. The apartment units consisted of one or two rooms and kitchenette (Fig. 118, E1-6). Thus of the first 885 families many were small in size and lived in apartments. Altogether there was a population of 2,831: an average of only 3.2 per family.

Greenbelt started as a young community in every way; fathers and mothers were practically all under 30, and most of the children, although two or three to a family, were still under school age.

An effort was made to populate the town with an average cross-section of residents. Proportions found in the nearby District of Columbia were applied. Among the first residents, therefore, 70 per cent of the wage-earners were government workers, 30 per cent non-government; 30 per cent were Catholic, 7 per cent Jewish, and 63 per cent Protestant.

The families were fairly homogeneous in respect to education. Most were high-school graduates, a small percentage professionally trained, and a small proportion had had little schooling. The government workers represented the white-collar clerical group; the other 30 per cent were professional or manual workers.

During over a decade of life Greenbelt, Maryland, is the only one of the Towns that had any decided increase in population. The original construction was undertaken in an emergency, and the second was again the result of an emergency. As a prelude to America's entry into the Second World War, during the so-called Defense period, factories again opened wide their doors, industrial employment shot up, and Washington became a beehive filled with administrative and clerical paper-work. Congress, through the Lanham Act, set aside funds to

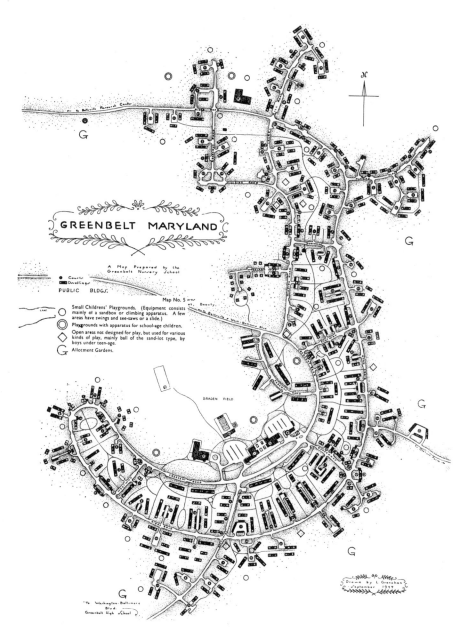

Fig. 105—General plan of Greenbelt prepared to show outdoor recreational facilities in housing areas. Note the location of play areas for groups of various ages.

build homes and finance community facilities for workers in 'essential defense industry.' As a result 1,000 homes were added to Greenbelt at the end of 1941.

The make-up of the new group was different from that of the original Greenbelt people. Families were older and larger. The average family size, which had been 3.2 in 1941, before Defense Homes were built, was 3.7 in 1943. War-time incomes were higher. No income limits could be established, since essential workers had to be housed. In 1940 the median family income was $1,599, in 1943 it was about $2,900.

By and large the groups merged. They meet at the stores; they work and play together in varied social and recreational activities; they are represented on the council and, at election time, they vote on the same local issues.

Greenbelt as a Garden City

Rex Tugwell and his associates were apparently more deeply influenced by Ebenezer Howard's Garden City than any other idea in their conception of the New Towns they proposed to create. To what extent was Howard's program realized? What were the causes and what the effects of the variations from Howard's conception?

The accepted definition of a Garden City is:

'A garden city is a town planned for industry and healthy living, of a size that makes possible a full measure of social life, but no larger, surrounded by a permanent rural belt, the whole of the land being in public ownership, or held in trust for the community.'

PLANNED FOR LIVING. All of the Greenbelt Towns are exceptionally well planned for healthy living. They meet the requirements of good living in these days, and they do it at a moderate cost, so that people of limited means can secure these advantages. That they enjoy them is attested by the inquiry that we made at Greenbelt and by similar investigations in the other two towns.

PLANNED FOR INDUSTRY they have not been— and none of the three towns have had any industry worth considering within its boundaries. Although all of them were located in regions in which employment has grown, they have all had serious difficulties because of travel to work—caused by time consumed and the cost of transportation.

Let us consider Greenbelt. It is true that there is about 2,500 feet frontage on the Baltimore and Ohio Railroad toward the western boundaries of Greenbelt which would not require much grading or fill to prepare it for industry. But there are many and various considerations other than railroad frontage that determine the location of new factories in a district that has little heavy or related industries. They might or might not be induced to come. The Washington area is not an industrial region in the usual sense—even though George Washington in locating the Capital thought it would be. The predominating occupation is government: most Greenbelt workers are employed by the Federal Government. The basic problem is not to find new types of employment but to bring some of the predominating work closer to or within the boundaries of Greenbelt.

Federal agencies are crowded in Washington; their employees are forced to make long, tiresome journeys to and from work; the streets of the capital are congested; traffic is blocked, parking space scarce; if there is danger from atomic warfare anywhere in this country it is the concentrated governmental focus of federal administration. If agencies, or those portions of agencies which need not be in the executive nerve center in Washington, should be decentralized, no better nearby place than Greenbelt could be found. There is plenty of space for office or laboratory buildings and for outdoor experimentation, as at the Agricultural Research Center, as well as for a largely increased number of homes in Greenbelt, with all its combined country and city attractions.

The Census Bureau has already started to decentralize by setting up a branch at Suitland in Maryland. But this was apparently chosen without adequate investigation as to possibilities of securing housing for employees. Most of them must travel to and from Washington or beyond.

Greenbelt has had at its very door from the beginning what on the surface appears a natural source of employment. That is the National Agricultural Research Center at Beltsville[27] (see Fig. 104). This is the largest experimental station of the kind in the U.S.A., occupying 12,000 acres. It borders Greenbelt to the north, and employs over 2,100 workers (including 875 in the Plant Industry Section). These workers, a great part of them scientific specialists and other technicians, would make ideal inhabitants of Greenbelt. And yet up to a short time ago none of them lived in the town; even now there are only 83 of the 1,236 employees of the Center itself who are inhabitants of Greenbelt, and most of these lived in the town before they got their jobs.

C. A. Logan, the Chief of the Center, had a careful survey made some time ago and found that the average distance travelled was 10 to 15 miles each way. Many of the employees lived at the other side of Washington, in Arlington, Virginia. Twice a day in their travel they passed the Greenbelt inhabitants bound for Washington, and quite a number of them who work in the colossal Pentagon Building near Arlington.

Now a good many of the Agricultural Center workers have moved out to the houses built since the war at Beltsville, Silvertown, and other Maryland towns. But a great many still spend 50 minutes each way on the special buses to and from Washington.

Workers at the Center have not lived in Greenbelt for two different reasons. In the beginning only low-income workers were admitted to the Development, and most employees of the Research Center earned too much. Second, although there was no income limit in the Defense Homes, eligibility was restricted to workers who came to metropolitan Washington after July, 1941, and who were employed by agencies having priority ratings as essential war work. Most Agricultural Center work was not considered essential. This excluded some 95 per cent of the employees of the center.

Because Greenbelt is purely a dormitory city serving Washington, its workers are forced to make lengthy trips back and forth daily, many of them slowly through congested Washington streets. The majority, who travel by buses and streetcars, must change once or twice and spend about an hour each way. Weekly passes are $2.25. That means $117 for yearly transportation, or, with allowance for the travel of members of the family, about $140 per family. In budgeting cost of family living in the studies for the Resettlement Administration I allowed $45 to $60 a year for travel.

Cost of transportation by automobile, even when used by a group cooperatively, costs even more

than by buses and streetcars. The trip to Washington can be made in half an hour or so. But during the rush hours at the beginning and end of the day the main highways are blocked by traffic—and this is just when the Greenbelt workers use them.

The proposed express highway between Baltimore and Washington will cut travel time from Greenbelt. There will be a clover-leaf permitting entrance to the superhighways at the eastern border of Greenbelt. It is uncertain whether public buses will be permitted on the highway. If not, most of the Greenbelt workers will still devote the equivalent of over a tenth of their working hours to the journey to and from work.

PERMANENT GREENBELT. Greenbelts have continued to form an essential part of the three towns since the beginning. ' . . . In this tract to create a community, protected by an encircling greenbelt . . . ' formed part of the statement of the objectives of the Resettlement program, which also proposed 'a system of rural economy co-ordinate with the land use plan for the rural portions of the tract surrounding the suburban community.' The importance of the greenbelts was accentuated by the names of the towns. In all three towns there is still a predominance of open land; the developed areas form a very small part of the total tracts.

In Greenbelt the land has not been used for agricultural purposes, unless you call the allotment gardens agriculture. These have been located in five places, more or less near the residential areas. Here 500 families have grown food on 50-feet x 50-feet plots. Up to a short time ago these were ploughed and fertilized by the town for a charge of $1 each (Fig. 103).

The two other towns have been much more successful in using their open land for farming. At Greenhills about 4,000 acres are in agricultural use. There are 34 old farms used as suburban residences with one to 20 acres each, but the greater part of the land is occupied by 28 full-time farmers, whose products are chiefly dairy. Although a farmers' market was originally proposed, the dairymen have tended almost entirely to market their milk, eggs, poultry, and vegetables in the bigger center at Cincinnati.

At Greendale there are about 3,000 acres in 18 farms or dairies of 100 to 240 acres each, as well

Fig. 106—An aerial view showing the Resettlement Development at Greenbelt.

Fig. 107—Greenbelt from the air, showing the Resettlement Development shortly after completion. Left center is the community center, community-school, swimming pool, shopping center with parking area at either end, and the underpass below Crescent Road. (Library of Congress photo by Fairchild Aerial Surveys Inc., New York)

as rural homes and 25 acres of allotment gardens.

In Greendale and Greenhills the unity of town and country has been of mutual advantage to the urban and rural population. Farms, dairies, and forests form a familiar part of the daily life of the town children and their parents. Town and farm folks have come to know each other as neighbors, friends and associates. They gather together in town meetings, at church, social parties, and lectures, at the movies, the co-operative stores, or, in Greendale, at the tavern. This association has broken down barriers of misunderstanding between farmer and factory workers at Greendale, and in Greenhills.

At Greenbelt the great open area that surrounds it has served for recreation and free contact with the out-of-doors, rather than agriculture. Groups of little ones explore it without restraint; they are pioneers and Indians in their own wilderness. In the picturesque rugged section to the south, areas have been set aside for both Boy Scouts and Girl Scouts. On weekends the whole family is united in hiking and picnicking in the woods. At the side of the lake are picnic tables and benches as well as fireplaces on which to prepare hot meals. At the lake, young and old fish for striped bass. From the lake can be heard the crack of rifles from nearby Greenbelt Gun Club. Although swimming in the lake has been temporarily prohibited because of lack of sufficient town funds to pay guards, sunbathing and boating are favorite forms of relaxation. There is horseback riding also, for a more limited number who rent their horses from nearby stables.

Large portions of the surrounding greenbelt at Greendale and Greenhills have been dedicated to permanent use as parks and recreation areas, by putting them in the hands of the County Park Departments. At Greenbelt this method of perpetuating the protection is not yet accomplished. However, the National Capital Park and Planning Commission is considering a large tract in the southern portion as a regional park. This land, which is in large part rough and well-wooded, and cut by a meandering brook some 50 feet below the higher plateaus, would make an excellent semi-wilderness recreation area. As a public park it would be a permanent protective greenbelt to the

south, as the National Agricultural Center is along the northern boundary. The narrow green natural wall along the future Washington-Baltimore Superhighway, with only one point of access to Greenbelt, will protect the eastern boundary. Only a park to the west is required to complete the greenbelt.

The Congress, when it passed legislation at a recent session for the purpose of disposing of the three towns, signified its desire to preserve the greenbelt by authorizing the Public Housing Commissioner to transfer 'streets, roads, public buildings, federally owned utilities, playgrounds, swimming pools, and parks, including adequate open land surrounding or adjacent to each project, to the appropriate non-Federal governmental agency.'[28]

To clarify the meaning of this section, the report of the Senate Subcommittee, written by Senator Paul H. Douglas, stated:

'The particular portion of the amendment relating to adequate open land is intended to preserve as far as practicable the original design of having each of these projects protected by a green belt of park and forest land surrounding such a community. In fact the committee deems it desirable that the Commissioner exercise his authority in such a manner as to retain the essential character of the entire original development in any disposal of these projects.'[29]

PUBLIC OWNERSHIP. 'The whole of the land being in public ownership, or held in trust for the community'—this last section of the definition of a Garden City has been followed—at least up to the present. The Federal Government has remained in possession of all of the three towns, with the exception of comparatively small areas. For example, in the three towns churches have lately purchased plots, and in Greenhills, two moderate-sized groups of houses for sale have been developed by private builders: the latter cannot, in my opinion, be called 'an improvement.' On a smaller scale a limited number of lots at Greendale have been sold and covered with inharmonious houses.

Of the future I cannot as yet report.[30] In the sale of the towns, which will be consummated in the near future, Congress has stated that preference be given to 'veteran groups organized on a nonprofit basis (provided that any such group shall accept as a member . . . any tenant occupying a

Fig. 108—An airview of Greenbelt. In the center East-way crosses from Ridge Road to Crescent Road. Photographed before the Defense Homes to the east of Ridge Road were built. (Fairchild Aerial Surveys Inc., New York)

Fig. 109—The shores and the lake are used for picnicking and play. Swimming, which was popular, is not permitted now because of the lack of funds to pay guards.

dwelling unit) . . .' But whether this will serve as a means of preserving single ownership for the good of the community is questionable: the 'home ownership' idea has been well sold in America in spite of its apparent weaknesses.

LIMITED SIZE. 'Of a size that makes possible a full measure of social life, but no larger'—this is the only section of the Garden City definition that remains. Unquestionably the people of Greenbelt have had a very full measure of community life. There are features that can be added as the population of Greenbelt grows.

The important element concerning size, about which we know altogether too little, is its effect on the cost of operating government. We do know that when a town grows beyond a certain size the cost per family or per person tends to augment for many services. This may be due to the increased complexity or increased administrative expenses of operating a gigantic undertaking of any kind— whether commercial, industrial or governmental. We have also judged that the costs of operating government in a smaller municipality decreased as the town increased in size up to a certain point. However, there has been very little definite study of this subject that is of much value. At Greenbelt we have been able, I think, to gather some important facts in this almost unexplored field. Of this later.

The Radburn Idea

Although the Garden City was the inspiration for the general conception of Greenbelt, in detailed form it followed the elements of the Radburn Idea. So here is another opportunity to find out how it works, with its superblocks with central greens, and streets and paths insulated from each other, and with different kinds of roads for different purposes. Here again is a chance to see what the people think of it; people who had been accustomed to living in a conventional type of American city with houses facing on busy thoroughfares, and with schools, parks, playgrounds and stores accessible only by crossing one or many streets. So from time to time during this last 10 years I have visited the town and community managers, the director of the stores and various other friends at Greenbelt. I learnt much from O. Kline Fulmer, the architect,

who after working on the plans and helping to supervise the construction was assistant manager. I saw his three children grow up happily and freely at Greenbelt, and Mrs. Fulmer told me about the busy life one spent at Greenbelt keeping up with its many activities. To get an up-to-date impression of the reaction of the people who live there now, a short time ago with the aid of Kate Edelman, we questioned some 21 of the inhabitants in regard to their attitude toward certain features of the plan—and particularly those that were influenced by the Radburn Idea. The people interviewed lived in different sections of the town; some in the older, some in the newer development; some dwelt in apartments, the others in houses of various sizes. Some of them had had homes in Greenbelt ever since it was started; most had been there over three years. The majority had lived previously on the outskirts of a large city; a few had never before lived outside a big city. All those interviewed were married, and with two exceptions had one to four children. Six were men; all of the women did their own housework, although several had other employment.

The attitude of the people interviewed was favorable on most points, but opinions ranged from uncritical enthusiasm to the unqualified disapproval of 'everything about Greenbelt' on the part of one woman.

STREET AND PARKING PATTERN. Everyone—including the woman who dislikes Greenbelt—agreed that the street lay-out is convenient for traffic. As to convenience for various kinds of deliveries: no one reported any complaint from milkmen, grocery-truck men, drivers of furniture trucks, moving-vans, expressmen or anyone making deliveries of any kind.

The original Resettlement Development carried out the theories and practices evolved at Radburn more thoroughly than the later Defense Homes Development. This included superblocks with parks as backbone; specialized means of circulation, each planned and built for one and only one special purpose; complete separation of pedestrian and automobile; houses with two fronts, one for service, the other for reposeful living. In fact in some ways the Radburn Idea was carried a step further, for instance, in experimentation in various ways of relating and distinguishing automobile and pedestrian access and also, of the greatest importance, in the complete separation of pedestrians and motor vehicles in the Community Center.

Although the Radburn Idea served as model for the plans of the Defense Homes as well as for the earlier development, the actual execution was quite different. This seems to have been due in part to the financial limitations in the latter development. The cost of the 1,000 units was only $4,500,000 excluding the land, which had already been paid for.

The difference, I believe, was mainly the result of the manner in which the work was carried out. I have spoken of the spirit of enthusiastic dedication to the discovery and development of new communities, with which the groups of architects and planners worked in the MacLane residence in the Resettlement days.

The job of producing the required drawings and specifications for the Defense addition was dumped into the factory-like office of the Public Works Agency along with innumerable other projects, and supervision was from the center. Work was shot through the draftingroom efficiently and speedily, and was followed by economical and quick construction.

Fortunately, the general plan for the location of the new houses had been in the main determined in the inspired days of the Resettlement Administration. As you see them from the sky the two developments seem to be a single united design. The Defense Development in the main was intended to follow the principles of the Radburn Idea in harmony with the early Greenbelt plan. Advantage was taken of the existing main utility lines by constructing some groups to the south and east of Ridge Road. But the greater part of the addition was constructed beyond Northway, where the earlier development ended.

GARAGES. For the earlier development of 885 dwelling units, 475 garages were built. As no garages were added for the Defense Development these 475 garages are all there are now for the 1,885 Greenbelt families, who in 1949 had 1,374 passenger automobiles. There is a strong competition for the existing garages, and a continued demand for more garages. Although in the original

development more garages were planned for than were built, not enough space was set aside there or in the Defense Homes to meet the present need. This is another example of the need for allowing plenty of land for future change and growth.

PARKING. According to people questioned, parking space at the town center is adequate and accessible. Parking arrangements for cars of residents themselves are generally found convenient. But parking space for the cars of visitors is too limited, according to several residents who have found their own spaces taken up by people visiting in the neighborhood and who have been forced to leave their own cars on the street. In the Defense Homes sections, however, where overnight parking in the street is allowed, many of the residents prefer to leave their cars on the street rather than in the parking lot, in order to avoid the danger of running into the children who use these parking areas for play.

In the Resettlement Development the auto approach to houses is, in most cases, from paved areas permitting no through passage. Some of these are dead-end lanes leading to all the houses served. But, in the main, the cul-de-sac went through a logical change, resulting in a service court. This, which was further developed at Baldwin Hills Village in all its various forms, differed distinctly from the Radburn service road, which gives direct motor access to all houses. The best of these were arranged so that the automobiles maneuvered and in many cases remained in a forecourt, and the houses faced on and are served from a path, some at a hundred feet or so distance from the forecourt. Others are separated from the paved area by rows of garages. This disposition permits easier use of sloping land. It gives greater privacy. It completely protects the entrance and the surroundings of the houses from the annoyance of automobiles. It is safer than the Raburn type of cul-de-sac or the paved courts surrounded by and directly accessible to dwellings as used in the later Defense Development at Greenbelt (Fig. 108).

The original purpose in using this type of service forecourt, similar to that suggested for Valley Stream (See Fig. 100) was primarily economy. The studies which I made of the relative improvement costs of various schemes of house grouping for the

Fig. 110—Typical row house built of cinderblocks and painted. Brick is used as a decoration.

Fig. 111—Bungalow forming end of row of houses; most of these so-called "Honeymoon Cottages" are inhabited by elderly couples.

Resettlement Administration, before the final planning of the towns, had shown that the normal cost per family of utilities, roads and paths, as well as grading and planting of house lots for the typical American arrangement of houses facing a traffic street could be decreased to a minimum by use of such garage and parking compounds. Thus a saving of approximately 54 per cent in the improvement costs could be made. This I noted in my report to Mr. John Lansill on November 19, 1935:

'The cheapest arrangement as affecting improvement costs, is that of row houses on lanes without vehicular roads in the lanes, but with garages grouped at the entrance to lanes. This arrangement has great advantages from the point of view of good living. It offers increased safety and quiet on the service side of the houses and at the same time it permits complete privacy on the garden side. On the other hand, some planners may prefer to sacrifice these advantages for the convenience of direct access to each house by automobile and greater ease in the delivery of bulky goods and fuel, and easier fire protection.'

The automobile access to the Defense Homes follows the same general planning as did the earlier development. It was based on stereotyped formulae that had the general objective of concentrating the parking of, and the servicing by, automobiles in a compact court off the street. But it was done crudely, without adequate consideration of appearance, either from the inside or the outside of houses, and—what is more important—without sufficient precaution against danger to children.

As in the Resettlement Development, the Defense Homes consisted of simple row houses grouped around dead-end automobile lanes or courts. All principal rooms looked away from the service side. The unit plans were particularly good for use in connection with the Radburn Idea of livingroom and bedroom facing and opening out to safe and peaceful green (Figs. 118 and 119). The main doorways were properly located. But they are seldom used—for they lead to unfinished open spaces. The paths on the 'garden' side were never constructed. In fact there is not only no incentive to planting a garden, but sufficient top soil was never supplied to make gardening successful. There are few trees and therefore little shade. Not enough trees were

planted around the houses to invite the use of these open spaces for playing or loafing. The members of the families or their friends seldom approach this side, for most of the inner block connections of the main framework of paths were never realized. Even where they exist, the houses are separated from them by barren fields or mud. Underpasses were entirely omitted. So at most places the roads are used by the pedestrians. In a few of the more used or dangerous places the sidewalks have since been added.

The outstanding difference between the two developments is in the location and surroundings of the automobile courts. The typical Defense houses face directly on the dreary concrete pavement of the courts. In many cases the service door, which is by necessity used also as the main entrance, is but a short distance away (Fig. 115). No hedges or fences were included in the original work. None have been added since, except a few rough fences built by tenants, in spite of regulations forbidding such variations in the prevailing monotony. The uninspired design of the wooden houses would not have been objectionable in a setting of trees and gardens. The external environment of the Defense Homes is illkept and disorderly. In these slumlike surroundings there is little incentive to exercise the loving care that the earlier tenants give to gardens and hedges.

The difference goes deeper than appearance. Safety for children has been decreased as has outdoor comfort and repose for adults. Underpasses near schools have been replaced by policing of road crossings (Figs. 112 and 113); the inner block paths are missing; the park play areas were not developed on the safer side of the house. The little child has no choice but the paved court, with the constant danger of moving vehicles, as children's playground. In questioning tenants in regard to their observations on the safety of the plan it was mainly those living in the Defense Homes that were apprehensive of danger. And rightly, as illustrated by a tragic incident that occurred lately. A child was killed by an automobile in one of the service courts in the Defense Development. I went out to Greenbelt from Washington as soon as I heard of it, to see how it happened. The City Manager showed me

Fig. 112—A Greenbelt underpass leading directly to the community-school.

Fig. 113—Because of lack of inner block paths and underpasses, children must be policed at road crossings in the Greenbelt Defense Development.

where the municipal refuse-collecting truck had turned to drive out of the court, and how the little girl had run out from the house and directly under the rear wheel of the truck. The yard between the paved auto space and the house was narrow; there was no fence or hedge to enclose the yard; the other side, where there should have been a garden and a walk, was uninviting.

The probability of a fatal accident of the kind described above is less in most of the courts of the Resettlement Development. In a great number of these the houses do not open directly on the paved court; they are served by forecourts such as I have described above, or the house rows do not run parallel with the court but are at an angle to it, or the residences are separated from the courts by garages. It is true that some of the groups face the paved lanes. They are the exception. Moreover, in most of the Resettlement houses, the yards are enclosed by hedges (Figs. 114 and 116) and the other side of the house is attractive for playing. Danger has been greatly lessened by thoughtful planning and planting in the early development. But even these are by no means 100 per cent effective for keeping children out of danger.

Parents in all parts of the town report that small children play in the parking courts. The paved surface is a little uneven for wheeltoys, but handy, being so near the house. Mothers dislike the use of the parking areas for play for all of the reasons that attract the children: they do not like the sand or the mud the children track into the house. They worry, too, about the danger from cars entering or backing out of the parking lots.

People living in houses adjoining the courts do not like the noise. Car-owners also complained that cars were scratched and dented by the play of the children.

The problem of parking-lot play in the original part of the town is very minor, compared with that in the Defense Homes sections. Here many of the parking lots were said to have been given over almost entirely to the children, who find these the only sizeable areas for play in the immediate vicinity. 'My heart is in my mouth every time I drive into one of these areas,' said one woman, who parks her car on the street a hundred feet away, rather than take the risk of running over a child on the parking area.

In an attempt to lure the children away from the parking areas, a number of pieces of play equipment have been installed this past summer in areas between groups of buildings. Apparently children play in the auto courts first for easy use of their wheeled toys and vehicles, and secondly, to get out of the damp and muddy soil after it has rained. In connection with Radburn, I observed that there should be adequate paved area solely for play—completely separated from the paved areas for vehicles, and therefore on the opposite side of the house. A number of the house plans are arranged so that the livingroom and sometimes also the kitchen-dining-room and the main bedroom run through the house (Fig. 118, C2-2 and C3-6). Thus the mother can more easily keep an eye on the youngsters at either side of the house.

Several people reported that some children—not their own— play in the streets. The principal reason for this is the lack of open space in which the little ones can play ball. The only other important recreational use made of the streets is for sledding in winter; the children prefer the streets to sledruns provided for their use away from the street.

No one mentioned the use of the streets for bicycling, which is evidently considered quite safe even for small children seven or eight years of age along the side of the streets. Except for bicycling, the number of children found playing on the street

Fig. 114—Garage court on service side of Resettlement Development houses. Note protection of hedges.

Fig. 115—Parking court on service side of Defense Development houses. There is no protection for children leaving the house. They play mostly on these courts, as paths and gardens are lacking on the other side of the houses.

Fig. 116—Laundry on the service side of Resettlement Development houses. Orderly separation of play and work.

Fig. 117—Laundry on the service side of Greenbelt Defense Development houses. Disorderly use of same space for drying, auto parking, and children's play.

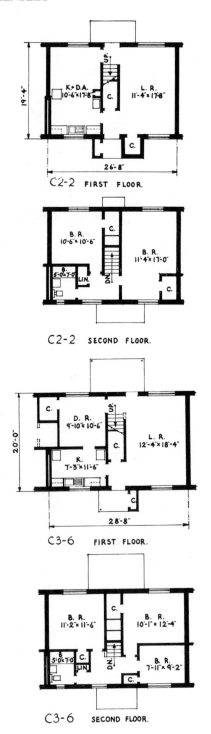

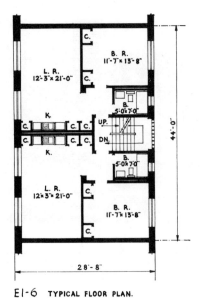

Fig. 118—Some Resettlement Development living units. C2 and C3 are typical two-story houses with living rooms from front to rear. The maximum amount of living space is on the garden side. E1 is one of the apartment types for small families in three-story walk-ups. A1 is a three-room bungalow. These are mainly occupied by old folk but were known as "Honeymoon Homes."

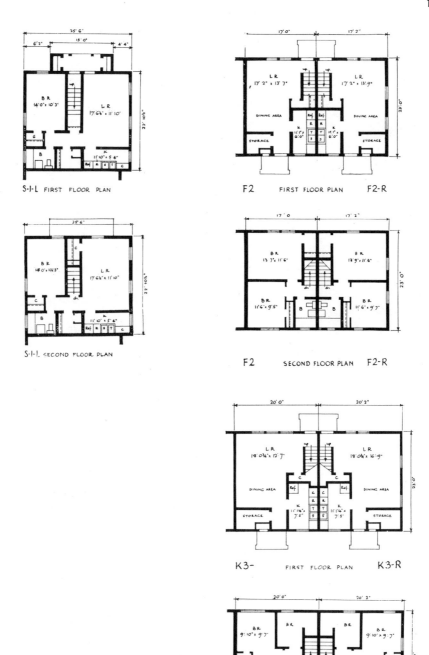

Fig. 119—Greenbelt. Some Defense Homes living units. S1 shows typical small flats which occur one above the other as end units. F2 and K3 are two- and three-bedroom two-story houses. Tenants find there is a shortage of storage space despite provision made. The houses were planned to face garden side, but paths were never built and there are few gardens.

Fig. 120—Family life at Greenbelt.

Fig. 121—Life in the open around apartment houses.

Fig. 122—Private gardens along a path leading to the woods.

Fig. 123—Everyone trims his own hedge.

at any time is negligible, compared with the number that can be seen in almost any conventionally-planned suburban development.

WALK SYSTEM AT GREENBELT. The main framework of walks is completely separated from roads The backbone of pedestrian circulation passes through the center of the superblocks, gracefully following the crescent dictated by the form of the land. Through each garden court it is connected to the highways by collecting paths. From these the private walks sprout. It is all like the orderly growth of a tree—or the human nerve system.

This describes the walk pattern in the Resettlement Section where the system was completed There it works very well and is generally satisfactory. Everyone we interviewed there agreed that the routes to the town center and to the various parts of the village were direct and convenient It is quite a different matter in the Defense Section where some one told us 'It's a wonderful system—or would be if we had it.' Not only were the paths to the garden side of the house omitted there, but also many of the main paths. Here if the paths are indirect or steeply sloped people sometimes make a short-cut by crossing or following roads. This is particularly apparent where, because of economy, walks which tenants really need were sometimes omitted. In some cases their persistent direct promenading makes a path where it should have been planned.

No one can claim that the 'Safety System' of separating pedestrians and autos works 100 per cent, even where the planning is carefully and sanely carried out. Humans are human. They will take the short cut when in a hurry to save time. Excepting where youngsters consistently crossed traffic there are no sidewalks along the edges of the streets. Outsiders and newcomers miss these, and sometimes walk in the roads. Even old inhabitants do so if they find it more direct. Two women said they occasionally use the street instead of the walks when pushing a load of groceries plus a baby, because the connecting walk to their homes is difficult to climb. The highways are used more at night than in daytime, particularly in the Defense Section where the walks often follow circuitous routes. Even in the older parts some said they followed the road because of lack of sufficient central lighting on the inner block

paths. The lights, which were placed low, are attractive and economical in original cost, but have not proved practical (see Fig. 102). This is because ingenious children who delight in destroying bulbs can easily get at them.

Despite the corner-cutting indulged in by most of the people interviewed, all of them prefer the center-block walk plan to the conventional scheme. They appreciate particularly the added safety for children, and even the elders, who admitted taking short-cuts along the streets, instruct their small children to use the center-block paths on their way to and from school, just as the parents do at Radburn.

UNDERPASSES. Parents take particular care to train the little ones to walk through the underpasses connecting the main central walk system with the shopping center and school. Most of them do so, even when it takes longer than if they crossed the highways. Use by adults and older children depends on comparative convenience. Where access is direct and by easy sloping paths practically everyone goes through the underpass. The underpass leading to the center of the marketplace is almost always used by women on the way to the center, but on their return they sometimes use the highway, as I have said, to avoid the grade. Where grades do not gradually and easily lead to the underpass, or where the path as it approaches the road is at its level, older children and others in a hurry by-pass it and cut across streets. But even at such places I have noted that shoppers with full bags or loaded baby-carriages take the longer way passing below the highway. One under-pass is found hazardous by pedestrians because children on bicycles use its long curving walk and grade as a speedway. As a whole the people of Greenbelt find that the underpasses serve their purpose. They strongly favor them.

THE USE OF OPEN SPACES in a logical way is one of the basic innovations of the Greenbelt, as of the Radburn plan.

A *Service yard* on the street or lane side is strange to tenants at first, but ultimately most of them see its advantages. 'Now that I'm used to it,' said one woman, 'I don't mind it a bit. And one thing that is nice about it is that you can sit out in your garden and not have the cars whizzing by.'

As long as they can hang their laundry out to dry, they are not fussy about its location—or its visibility. Sunshine directly on the clothes is considered important. 'Trees in the yard are nice, but they do interfere with drying clothes.' Several women who lived in the apartments referred to the lack of space for drying as a serious disadvantage— and felt that it should be provided.

INDIVIDUAL GARDENS. In the Resettlement Development, individual gardens are separated from each other and from the public paths and open areas by hedges. These enclosures are low. They do not give that complete privacy that the English require and secure by walls or tall hedges. But the Greenbelt hedges are sufficient to mark the limits of each family's own terrain, its little kingdom. This bounding seems to engender a proprietary pride in spite of the lack of actual ownership. You can observe its effect by comparing these earlier homes with the later Defense Homes which not only had no hedges or other lot enclosure, but also had inadequate top soil and planting in the beginning.

Many of the earlier settlers took full advantage of the fine natural background of varied trees and the careful initial landscape planting. A great number of the gardens are thoughtfully planted and well cared for—many, but not all, of course.

The interest in gardens in Greenbelt varies, as it does in all communities, so it was wise to differentiate the size of lots under tenants' care. I remember years ago, as I walked around Welwyn with Ebenezer Howard, the father of Garden Cities, that he pointed out how the large plots went to the tenants who wanted to do small-scale farming. Here in Greenbelt, it is to those who love floriculture. One end house is occupied by a worker whose every minute of spare time is devoted to making his surroundings an ever-changing prospect of brilliantly colored flowers. The interior of this house, planned for the utmost economy in space, might be criticized as tight, if it were not for the gay vistas of his own cultivated terrain that broaden his outlook on life.

ADVANTAGES OF OPEN SPACES. Since a bench or two or three chairs can be seen in practically every garden, one can assume that most of the people living in Greenbelt like to sit out in their yards at some time. Everyone interviewed said they enjoyed it. On a sunny day in summer almost every tree in the central part of the town is used as shelter for a resting place. A number said they like to sit and gossip in the Town Center.

SPACES USED FOR PLAY. In the original part of the town, where yards are clearly defined by hedges, children of all ages use their yards for some kinds of play. Usually a playpen is provided for the baby, and several families have built a little fenced enclosure within the larger hedged area for youngsters just beginning to walk. A good many parents have put up swings, installed sandboxes and provided other attractions to encourage their children to play in their own yards. A few yards have trees well adapted for climbing. Shrubs in some make good hiding-places for traditional games.

In the Defense Homes sections, it is difficult to distinguish between play in their own yards and play in the neighbors' yards, but a good deal of play, especially by the small children up to say seven years, centers around the area close to their homes; this may be in green courts, in parking areas, in their own or neighbors' yards.

Children of all ages get together in small groups in each others' yards—some irritation was reported in connection with such gatherings, primarily from nearby families with no noisy children of their own.

Play areas within the superblocks are used, parents told us, only intermittently; the children tend to use them consistently only during the hours of supervision in the summer. However, a good many of them serve as centers for informal group play, as well as for activities involving the use of the equipment.

Shopping Center

The most important forward step made at Greenbelt toward the evolution of New Towns that fit the special problems of these times was in the creation of the shopping center and the related community center (Fig. 124). Here at last the modern market square was integrated into the plan for complete separation of walkers and motors. At Radburn, although educational and recreational places could be safely reached by foot from all homes, the commercial buildings were built on an island cut off by streaming auto traffic. At Hillside the stores were an unrelated piece-meal addition that turned its back on the residential community. Baldwin Hills Village shops later were also dissociated from the Village.

Here, at Greenbelt, even more than in the characteristic European medieval marketplaces, there is a definite exclusion of active flow of traffic from the areas for peaceful shopping. Around the quiet square are grouped the varied functions of one of the finest small town centers of these days. It is both thoroughly functional and architecturally of a simple, attractive unity.

The market place is set back from the main traffic way, Crescent Road, and is on a one-way service road, which leads to the end of, but not through, the shopping plaza. This is for pedestrians only; a place for leisurely marketing, for resting on the park benches and gossiping. There is direct access to the square for walkers by the underpass under Crescent Road. This ties into the main path system of the inner blocks.

At the further end of the plaza the ground falls abruptly to an old wood that shades a playground for young boys and girls. Beyond, past the swimming pool, is the recreation field for the older ones and their dads—for everyone. The broad view is but slightly hidden by the somewhat too massive statue that was left from the WPA days when we were all so hard up that even a sculptor could get a job in connection with public housing. The same sculptress did some excellent panels on the exterior of the school-community building.

The Co-op's splendid new food supermarket built in 1948 was fortunately prevented from cutting the view of open countryside because building costs necessitated cutting down the length of the structure. At its side, stairs lead down to the lower floor which is to house the bowling alleys, and a restaurant which will look out on broad views of open country. From here are convenient walks to the little ones' playground and to the Youth Center.

At the other end of the plaza, paths lead to the Elementary School-Community Building, to the Swimming Pool—the center of summer community life, and beyond it to the Braden Athletic Field for baseball, tennis, and other sports of the grown boys and their parents; still further through the woods and picnic grounds is Greenbelt Lake. This is a half-mile stroll from the market-place, a peaceful hike with no danger or disturbance from motor vehicles.

The automobiles of visitors to the shopping center are parked off the roads on areas to the light and left, well screened from the market square. These serve not only shoppers and visitors to the movies; they are also convenient to the Swimming Pool, to the Community School and its Library. At the same time they are close to the various municipal offices; those of the City Manager and his staff at the west end, and the Police-Fire-Department to the east; also that of the Community Manager, who represents the Federal Landlord, PHA, and that of the Greenbelt Consumer Services, Inc., the co-operative the organization that runs the stores and the moving-picture house. These offices are on the second floor at either side of the Square. The Bank and the Post Office complete the community facilities of the central group that forms the focal point for the nerve system of walks and roads that circulate through the whole town (Fig. 103).

The Neighborhood Unit

At the present time the neighborhood unit is generally accepted as a basis for the purposeful design of new communities. But the Neighborhood less consciously influenced the planning of the Greenbelt Towns than the Garden City or the Radburn Idea. Yet the three towns are among the best applications of the principles laid down by Clarence Perry, which we would have carried out at Radburn, had its growth not been stunted.

Each Greenbelt Town in the beginning was, in effect, a single neighborhood. The focus of each is a planned neighborhood center consisting of school, community buildings, shopping center, government and management offices, and principal recreation activities. They are each built around such a planned center. However, only in Greenbelt have we an opportunity to study the effect of growth and changing size on the neighborhood. Here we can get some idea of how many people form a neighborhood community for different activities of various age or interest groups, and how the size of neighborhood is affected not only by distance, topography, and means of getting to and from a center, but also by many special factors that can

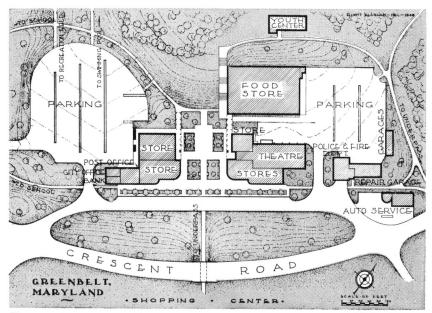

Fig. 124—Plan of the shopping center at Greenbelt showing the new food store and youth center.

Fig. 125—The movie theater and new supermarket in Greenbelt shopping center.

Fig. 126—The shopping center, looking towards the swimming pool.

not be broken down and classified quite so easily.

Greenbelt in the beginning had a population of 885 families, consisting of 2,831 people. All of the principal common activities were centered in a single well-planned and well-related group. Community center, elementary school, shopping center, town and management offices, police and fire station, automobile gas and service station, movie theater, swimming pool, recreation field: all these have a common related location that was central and was easily and safely reached by foot and by car.

The shopping center is the informal gathering place. Here is where one hears the news, discusses town politics, and here in the middle of the square or in the shade near the theater entrance, tickets are sold for town gatherings, dances, or lectures to support common town activities such as the Day Care Center. Townspeople of all ages come here. In the arcades at either side of the square, baby carriages are parked, and the youngsters, with little carts, waiting for their mothers, dart and play. Mothers with babies gossip in the sun; school children rush homeward; older boys and girls from the swimming pool are gaily bound for a five cent drink at the drug store (Figs. 125, 126).

The shopping center was so placed that all the residences built in 1936-37 by the Resettlement Administration were within one-half mile distance. The paths approaching this as well as the community-school building, all connected with the garden entrance of the houses, were as direct as the nature of the terrain and its park-like character permitted. They were protected from through auto traffic by underpasses (Figs. 103, 127, 128).

A neighborhood community is a group of people with common interests in which they actively participate. Greenbelt from the beginning was such a community. The children all went to the same school, with the exception of the few high school students and those who travelled to outside Catholic parochial institutions. At Greenbelt, school is an exciting place for the children, where they do things for the town as well as the school; in fact school is fun.

The elders gathered at the community building to attend the many and various social, cultural, or adult educational meetings. They came either in

special groups to clubs or classes or as a community to the Auditorium-Gymnasium to attend lectures or basketball games, to the holiday festivals, or the country fair at which they exhibited the products of their allotment gardens in the autumn. The swimming pool and the athletic field and the movies were meeting-places for everyone. So were the stores. The fact that these stores were a co-operative undertaking was another bond of union. The fact that they were well run, and had an adequate supply and variety to fill daily needs at reasonable cost, added to their general popularity. But above all everyone bought at the Shopping Center because it was convenient, easily and safely reached and adjacent to the other facilities that drew the people of Greenbelt together.

The planning theorists differ vehemently not only in regard to the validity of the Neighborhood Unit but even as to its proper size. Let us see what really happened when the population of Greenbelt was increased from 885 to 1,885 families—and from 2,831 persons to a population of 7,000 and more.

THE SHOPPING CENTER. When the town was expanded, the shopping center increased its total sales from roughly $450,000 to over a million, but the sales per person decreased from $158.90 in 1941 to $143.10 in 1943. It is true that the purchases of the average family, which had increased in size, did rise from $508 in 1941 to $531 per year. But this was small in proportion to the increase in the average income of the new (Defense) families, which was not necessarily low, so that their purchasing power was greater than that of the earlier settlers. Apparently a larger part of the purchasing power was used elsewhere—possibly by the workers at Washington, or at some store on the way back. The maximum walking distance to the shopping center, which had been no more than a half-mile, was in the case of the more northern of the Defense homes almost a mile. This quite apparently had much to do with the fact that sales did not show a greater increase. But topography also affected the business of the center. The ground mounted up from the stores toward the north. Women objected to carrying heavy bundles or pushing carts filled with purchases and babies up the slope.

When the Defense Homes were built a site was

Fig. 127—Greenbelt shopping center is safe for pedestrians. Beyond the arcade automobiles are parked.

Fig. 128—The path from the shopping center to the swimming pool and the school beyond.

set aside about three-quarters of a mile from the main market center for a North End Shopping Center. But there were no funds available for these or other needed community facilities. Ultimately the Co-op set up a temporary grocery store, because of the demand of the more northern inhabitants to have at least these essentials nearby.

However, so as to bind the increased population to the old center, the Greenbelt Consumers Service Inc. has met the difficulties growing out of distance by:

1. *The Co-op Pantry* or travelling market—a store on wheels that makes the rounds of the town daily with a varied stock of groceries, fruits and other supplies, conveniently displayed for customers who walk through the truck. Refrigerators and deep-freezers carry a choice supply of meats and other cold or frozen foods. The driver also collects clothing for pressing or cleaning.

2. *The Bus Line,* established in 1945 by the Co-op, brings passengers from all parts of the town to the center. The bus-driver delivers prescriptions from the drug store.

3. The great *Food Super-Market,* two and a half times the size of the old food store, that was added to the shopping center in 1948, offers increased variety, service and attractions. The space vacated by the old food store made possible the expansion of the Variety Store into a so-called Junior Department Store.

4. Plans for the addition, when financing is available, of a ten-alley *Bowling Center.* (Bowling is one of the favorite sports of Greenbelt. There were 77 teams in the Town in 1949 which were forced to drive several miles to play.) Bowling is to be in the basement under the super-market, along with a bakery and restaurant. As a result of the sloping terrain the latter will be above ground, well-lighted, and have a delightful view toward the woods.

5. *A Nursery* for the children of parents who are shopping is also part of the co-operative's proposed program.

All this expansion promises to make Greenbelt's principal market-place more than a local affair. The exceptionally fine and commodious super-market along with the other facilities and attractions — of which the peaceful, harmonious architectural and natural setting is an important factor, should draw customers from a wider area, outside Greenbelt's boundaries. It is true that other large super-markets with other shops and amusements are appearing along the main highways to Washington. But they are of the obsolete strip type without any natural setting and—what is more important from the point of view of lasting success—with utterly inadequate space for parking automobiles. The Greenbelt shopping center was supplied with two conveniently placed parking lots in the beginning. These were adequate before the construction of the new super-market. Unfortunately, some of this area has been taken over by the new building. However, there is additional open ground adjacent that can be added to the parking grounds, and that this be done is essential to the success of the stores if it is to be more than a purely local or neighborhood marketplace.

Education

THE SCHOOL COMMUNITY BUILDING, built as part of the Resettlement Development, was centrally located within a half-mile distance of all houses, and close to the stores. It can also be reached directly by paths and underpasses protected from auto dangers. In the beginning the average family's size was only slightly over three as a result of the large percentage of small apartments. In 1939 there were only 385 children in the elementary grades, financed and run by the County. The Kindergarten, of 80 children, in the same building, is supported and its teachers are employed by the Town, but is under the supervision of the County.

In the School Community Building there are 12 classrooms as well as a music room, homemaking room, arts and crafts workshop, health room, social room, and a large combined gymnasium-auditorium, and also the Town Library.

Without the high school children, 115 of them, the total of 465 did not crowd the schoolhouse. Up to the time the additional Defense Houses were built in 1941 the total number of children in the Elementary School remained much the same, although those in High School increased from 115 to 227. In 1943, after the new houses were constructed, there were 785 in the Elementary School,

175 in the kindergarten, and 283 in the High School.

No additional educational facilities were constructed with the 1,000 new houses in 1941, although a site was reserved opposite that for the North Shopping Center and about three-quarters of a mile from the old school. As a temporary measure classes were held, to the inconvenience of everybody, in residential buildings. It was not until 1946, after over three years of congestion and double sessions, that the North End Elementary School was opened with room for 500 children of the first to sixth grade, and for about 100 in the kindergarten. There is, in addition to the 12 classrooms, a multi-purpose assembly room.

The experience of Greenbelt's elementary schools' development seems to confirm the accepted neighborhood theory of one-half mile radius—at least for a community with houses at about seven or eight to the acre. The building of a new school was accepted as the practical thing to do when the town grew so that children would have to walk or be driven to the first school, a distance of three-quarters to one mile away. This in spite of the fact that ground space had been left so that the central building's size might be doubled.

In the Neighborhood Unit theory the high school building is generally considered the logical place for the district community center. But at Greenbelt the original central School Community Building has remained the unquestionable focus of community life. This was due to (1) its superior facilities for community purposes, (2) its more central location for Greenbelt people, (3) the fact that it is so closely related to the shopping and recreation-entertainment center and finally (4) habit on the part of the older inhabitants, and the fact that the later comers were absorbed into the established community life, whether they lived in the older section or the new north end portion of the town.

THE JUNIOR-SENIOR HIGH SCHOOL was placed near the western edge of the property, so that it might serve not only Greenbelt but also a surrounding area. It is about a mile and a half from the Community School. The High School building, in strong contrast to the older educational center, lacks any attraction architecturally or in regard to choice and treatment of site. The appropriation for the building was apparently cut to the bone—the architects had no opportunity to supply more than bare necessities. This is true both of the earlier structure, built in 1937, and the addition by the Federal Works Agency when they built the Defense Houses. There is accommodation for about 600 pupils in the six high school grades.

Prince George's County has for years been considering the erection of a large and adequately equipped senior high school that would care for a much greater area, and would probably be located near the University. Lack of funds, or rather increasing educational demands from various parts of the county, has led to the continuous postponement of this much needed improvement. Meanwhile, the Junior and Senior branches of the Greenbelt High School are forced to get along without adequate staff or modern equipment, which can only be afforded in a large institution. For a high school such facilities are naturally of far more importance than the distance that grown boys and girls must travel. This would indicate the advantage of solving education at high school level on a broad regional basis.

THE UNIVERSITY OF MARYLAND is within four miles of Greenbelt on the road to Washington. It can easily be reached by bus from the shopping center and by street-car. This makes higher education more convenient than it is in most parts of our larger cities. Residents of the State pay a very low tuition rate and veterans during the last few years received financial assistance under the G.I. Bill of Rights. Three hundred and twenty-five of the young people from Greenbelt were enrolled as regular students last year. In addition many of the townspeople take advantage of the University Extension Courses, not only cultural but practical. For instance, emergency or 'volunteer' fire fighters are obliged by the Protection Department of Greenbelt to take courses in fire protection at the University.

Community Activities

The school and the activities of the community are closely bound together at Greenbelt. It is not merely that the same building in the main center is used by all ages, all day and evening, and for all kinds of activity from dance to religion, from studying science or art to exhibiting one's own farming products in a country fair. There is no hard line between the use of the community-school as part of the regular County educational system and its service as town gathering place. The spirit of the town influences the school and the school plays an important part in forming that spirit.

The enthusiastic participation of parents in the school's work reflects the informal atmosphere of the town. The teachers and the building are as familiar to the parents as to the children, and so also is the program of the schools. The school program is difficult to label: no fashion of education is held up as a model of perfection, but rather a few basic purposes are kept in mind. At the Greenbelt schools the important thing is living—living successfully with others, rather than merely the individual himself—and the program grows out of this.

The children obviously love to go to school. They arrive on time and are happy while there. There is a contagious atmosphere, in the classrooms and out, of eagerness to learn and do things. Truancy is practically unheard of. The schools have enjoyed continuity of leadership, and their philosophy of education has had wide-spread influence on education in the surrounding community, and even throughout the county. The county is taking a leading position in the State in developing a more modern approach to education. The former principal of the school, Mrs. Reed, who made good use of the superior equipment of the Central School to influence the whole life of the community, is now supervisor of Prince George's County schools. As a result the other schools of the county are catching up to the higher standards of Greenbelt.

Community activities have not decentralized or started branches. This may be due to the fact that distance from the newly developed area is not too great, or that easy transportation is available by the Co-op bus which connects the whole town with the old center. It may also be because of the superior facilities of the Community-School Building which was planned and is operated to act as a Community Center. The North End School was not, and is not arranged or equipped to serve in this way. Only a very few special local activities

are held in its assembly rooms. The Boy and Girl Scouts meet there, and the Parents-Teachers group. The Community-School is an outstanding demonstration of what can be done through the multiple use of community facilities, and the cooperation of various agencies and different levels of government.

The Community Building is owned and operated by the Federal Public Housing Authority. The U.S. Government through FPHA merely loans the use of the building to Prince George's County as an elementary school. The County's Board of Education operates the school, furnishes textbooks and other supplies, and pays the teachers. Until 1949, the program of social activities was arranged through the office of the FPHA, but it now comes under the office of the City Manager. The town operates a public library and several kindergartens in the building. It also houses the town recreation department, which provides the physical education instruction for the elementary schools as part of the town recreation program. The Town Public Safety Officer promotes the program for safety, assisted by 40 school boys. Janitorial services, heat, water, light and maintenance of the building have been supplied under the direction of the FPHA Community Manager. They have been charged in part to the Town and in part to the Board of Education. By this means it has been possible to continue effectively the use of the building for the varied purposes for which it was designed.

In the North End Elementary School, where janitorial services and utilities are charged to the Board of Education only, it would be much more difficult to carry on a broad community program. School janitors are proverbially unco-operative, and County School Boards have inflexible rules that apply to all schools.

Adult Education is officially under the County School Board, which supplies teachers and pays most expenses. The program varies from year to year and includes classes in languages, arts and crafts, sewing, interior decorating, typing and shorthand, commercial law, public speaking, consumer education, and lectures and discussions on matters of general interest.

Facilities included in the original school that serve the general community, in addition to the classrooms and gym-auditorium, are the studios for arts and crafts, a music room, a social room—used also as a cafeteria—and the library. The social room is equipped with pingpong tables, radio-phonograph and games donated by the Town Council. The library although operated by the Town is used freely by the school.

RELIGION. For 11 years people have used the auditorium-gymnasium, social room and class-rooms of the Center School for religious services, their church organizations joining with all the other groups in the struggle for dates on the busy calendar.

On Sunday morning the large hall has been given over to the religious services of the Community Church, which represents in its congregation 14 Protestant denominations. Lutherans and the Church of Jesus Christ of the Latter Day Saints hold their services in other rooms of the building. The Hebrews take over on Friday evening. Mass is celebrated for Catholics in the moving-picture theater.

In the fall of 1946 all church congregations joined in an effort to find out what the religious situation actually was in the Town so that they might proceed to provide appropriate facilities. A very careful survey gave the basis of facts needed for planning. Building campaigns were started. The Town Council approved the sites selected. Land has been purchased by three different churches. The construction of the Protestant Community Church is under way and the Catholic Church will probably soon be built.

The sites chosen seem attractive. They are, however, widely distributed and have little relation, that I can see, to the community center or the general plan. In these days when so many people go to church by automobile, it would seem wise to locate a church, if possible, near enough to parking areas used on weekdays to serve the other buildings, or else to group two or more churches close enough togther to use common auto parking.

The experience of the Greenbelt Towns is valuable not only in showing the uses of multi-purpose educational-cultural buildings. It also indicates that, although some rooms serve adults as well as children, it is not always practical to use the same spaces and equipment for quite dissimilar purposes The County Colleges of Cambridgeshire, England,

have pointed the way to a fuller solution. Here under the brilliant leadership of the Educational Director, Henry Morris, buildings have been functionally designed for use not only as secondary schools, but also as community centers for all ages and varied groups; farmers as well as villagers and townspeople. The classrooms, studios, and laboratories serve day and night for young or old, and so in various ways does the auditorium-theater-gymnasium. But in addition there are special club and meeting rooms that were specially designed for community gatherings rather than teaching. The billiards and games room, and lounges, for instance, are available to the oldsters at all hours.

The desire of groups to have a place of their own is indicated at Greenbelt by various organizations. The American Legion has its own building, an old farmhouse which has been rebuilt for its many and varied activities. The veterans even use the allotment gardens near the Legion's house, although there are others nearer their own homes. The Youth Center is provided in a separate building, acquired through the efforts of Greenbelt people young and old. It consists of a large social room, kitchen and snack bar, and is a general headquarters for young peoples' activities.

GROUP CARE FOR SMALL CHILDREN. Although not housed in a school building, the nursery schools are both near the main community center. A cooperative nursery school was opened very early in Greenbelt's history. The federal government gave the use of a basement room in one of the apartment houses and some equipment. The parents engaged a director and the mothers shared responsibility for running the school, serving as assistants to the director. The school is still open.

Child care on a much larger scale was undertaken during the war when many Greenbelt mothers were employed. Under a special bill (The Lanham Act) the federal government provided funds to assist local communities in the care of children so that mothers might be released for war industry. Greenbelt received such assistance, and a large child care center was operated.

FPHA provided a whole building consisting of 11 bachelor apartments and an enclosed playground for the exclusive use of the center. They also provided maintenance, light, and the original

Fig. 129—Children leaving the community-school building.

Fig. 130—Play starts in the sandbox.

equipment. Parents of children cared for at the center paid $3.00 per week for all the services rendered.

Since the Lanham Act funds were withdrawn in 1946, a number of Greenbelt mothers have continued to keep the center in operation on a smaller scale. The management has continued to co-operate in this.

OUTDOOR RECREATION at Greenbelt is the one activity in which the community unit is not limited to the town as a whole or to the neighborhood. For play in the open the unit of population and area is broken down to a variety of sizes to fit the needs and above all the traveling capacity of different ages. Greenbelt is particularly well supplied with play spaces convenient to the needs of everyone from babyhood to old age (Figs. 103 and 105). For the infant there is the private yard within hearing and sight of the mother. For the smaller children there are the enclosed equipped playspaces and sand-boxes and climbing apparatus. These are generally located so as to serve a number of groups of houses, in the superblock center or in the green beyond the groups on the outer edge of the town. They are supervised by high school girls during the summer months. For children of school age playgrounds with apparatus are limited to five, more widely spaced. They are in open areas not designated for any particular type of play but used for various kinds of sport, and mainly for ball games on a diminutive scale by boys under teen age. For big games of baseball or football the older boys use Braden Field, as do their fathers. Here the town as a whole gathers as audience. Close by are the various outdoor facilities, forming part of the town center, in which all ages participate. At one end is the 25-acre lake, at the other the outdoor swimming pool—which forms the principal summertime community center. The swimming pool is not only a great success from the point of view of health and fun; it actually pays its own way (Fig. 132).

Cooperation and the Shopping Centers

GREENBELT CONSUMER SERVICES INC. has had a greater influence in molding the life of Greenbelt and its people than anything but the federal landlord, PHA, and the American democratic process as exemplified by their City Council and Town or City Manager.

When the town and the shopping center were ready in 1937, the Consumer Distribution Corporation,[31] a national organization, at first operated the stores, until the people of Greenbelt could determine whether they wanted to own their own business co-operatively. The 1946 Annual Report of Greenbelt Consumer Services, Inc., gives their decision. 'By the end of 1939 about 500 Greenbelt citizens had set aside $4,000 as initial payment for purchasing the local enterprises. On January 9, 1940, Greenbelt took over the operation of the stores through their own newly organized co-operative, Greenbelt Consumer Services, Inc. In spite of the war, every year has been a successful one for the Co-operative.'

Two-thirds of the Greenbelt families now hold stock; a number of them have taken the limit of $1,000 per person. Those who do not hold stock are Greenbelt people (a) who feel that residence in Greenbelt is a very temporary arrangement with them and buying stocks suggests something too permanent or (b) who feel that Co-ops interfere with free enterprise and therefore do not wish to co-operate.

There are some who object to the monopoly of commercial facilities and to the dominant leadership of the Consumer Services. This has been an important issue not only at many Council meetings but at hard-fought elections. From these it is apparent that the majority of the people of Greenbelt are in favor of the Co-operative and of its very able general manager, Samuel F. Ashelman, Jr.

A new lease was entered into in 1946 by the Greenbelt Consumer Services, Inc. for the facilities it had been using, that is, the food store, variety store, general merchandise, drug store, beauty shop, barber shop, movie theater, filling station, valet shop, tobacco and news stand. The lease stipulates that until November 1956, the federal government will not permit its property within a one-half mile radius of the shopping center to be used for any of the purposes outlined above. In addition, the Greenbelt Consumer Services, Inc. had a long term lease on about 40,000 square feet of vacant area in the present commercial center upon which it has constructed the supermarket.

Fig. 131—There are many equipped play spaces for younger children in Greenbelt's inner blocks.

Fig. 132—In summer the swimming pool is the real social center of Greenbelt.

GREENBELT

Therefore the first neighborhood will have a unified and a restricted shopping center until the end of 1956, no matter what may be the terms of sale of the residential buildings. Whether new stores built outside the half-mile limit will be able to compete with the well-entrenched and efficient Consumer Services is to be seen.

The central shopping center was planned on the basis of the requirements set up by the Special Report of 1935 to the Resettlement Administration.[32] This followed the method of determining commercial needs which had been developed in 'Store Buildings and Neighborhood Shopping Centers' by Cathrine Bauer and me in 1934.[33]

The fact that the principles and requirements formulated in the report to Mr. Lansill were followed in building and operating the Shopping Center with results very similar to those we predicted has convinced me that:

1. Shopping centers can be located and laid out to meet definite factual requirements in an orderly or attractive manner with every prospect—if not assurance—of financial success.

2. Commercial development, if left to the land speculators or individual shopkeepers, has a poor gambler's chance of success, financial or otherwise.

3. Limiting the number of and size of stores to the definite requirements best serves the interest of all concerned: the landlord, the shopkeepers, the buying public and finally the municipality.

4. The municipality can find one of its surest sources of income (either in taxes or rent) if development is properly limited, located and planned.

The basic principles followed in the planning of the commercial area of the three towns and particularly of Greenbelt are so concisely and succinctly stated in the Resettlement Report that I am going to copy it here:

SHOPPING CENTERS

The shopping centers of new towns built by the Suburban Resettlment Administration should be designed to give the inhabitants low prices, good quality, and convenient facilities, and at the same time, bring in the maximum possible revenue to the town.

For purposes of this preliminary study, we have assumed:

1. An average family income of $1,250 and an average family of four persons.
2. Rental of stores to commercial companies. (We are able to secure more definite information in regard to incomes and rentals paid by chain stores.) If the stores should be efficiently operated as co-operatives, lower living costs might be possible. The comparative advantage of such a step should be given further study.

The problem of providing adequate store facilities is affected by:

1. The degree to which the town will be used as a shopping center of the area.
2. The proportion of family expenditures made locally.
3. The family incomes.

1. *The town as a shopping center.*
It is unlikely that much outside business will be drawn to the new towns, since they will be off the main highways and the existing nearby industrial towns have established shopping centers.

2. *The proportion of family expenditures made locally.*
This is affected by the income group, the family size and family composition. Higher income groups are inclined to go to larger shopping centers for clothing, house furnishings, and certain other items which the low-income families must do without. The needs of small children will be met locally, whereas the needs of grown children are met better in the large center, where it is possible to shop for style and quality.

3. *The family income.*
Analysis of expenditure for various income groups, when related to local family expenditure and annual sales of different types of stores, gives us a fairly definite indication of the number and types of stores that might be supported.

The accompanying tables indicate—

1. Estimated local expenditures.
2. The types of stores that could be supported.
3. The income that could be derived from stores in towns of 3,000, 4,000, 6,000 and 7,000 population.

We are estimating rentals at 3 per cent of gross sales. These we believe are conservative as the number of stores will be restricted so as to increase as far as possible the gross sales of each store.

It is apparent that in towns of 1,000 families having incomes of $1,250, the estimated expenditure will provide adequately for food stores. One variety store which carries apparel and all sorts of household needs could exist on the expenditures for such items. There does not seem to be sufficient expenditure to maintain a typical chain drug store. However, independent stores are often operated on smaller margin and a drug store carrying on other types of business might be operated successfully.

Recreation needs outside of those supplied as part of the community facilities should be limited to a small movie house. A careful study should be made in regard to the possibility of successful operation in a small community and of the probability of increasing the patronage from outside of the town.

A combined filling station and auto accessory and repair shop could operate within the town independently of transient trade.

Expenditures for fuel would not maintain a commercial coal company. This could be bought through outside dealers or by setting up a co-operative.

A laundry service would probably be from a nearby town, although an agent might have space in the shopping center.

4. *General Policy in regard to stores.*

Store properties will be owned by the town and income from stores will be used to decrease dwelling rentals. The stores must therefore be efficient units, prices must be low and service at least as good as in neighboring communities. This will guarantee a large proportion of residents' expenditures to the local shopping center.

5. *Planning Requirements.*

One shopping center is sufficient for a 4,000 population town. This center ought to be within one-half mile of all dwellings. In larger towns of 6,000 or 7,000 population, there should either be two separate complete centers, or better still, one major center and several neighborhood food stores. The number of centers may be affected by topographical conditions.

6. *Location of shopping center.*

Locations are affected by the contours and the relation to the residence areas and the main approaches to the town—it is desirable that residents pass the center on the way in or out of the town. However, it is even more important that shopping centers be placed within easy and safe walking distance of all dwellings. As the approach usually should be through the park areas, access should be possible from park walks, without crossing vehicular roads. Adequate parking space for cars should also be provided.

7. *Store Areas and Layout.*

The layout and size of the stores is affected by the method of merchandising. The following estimates of space requirements for towns of 3,000—4,000 population are based on the experience of certain chain stores:

Store Areas.

Grocery and Meat (2 or 3 stores)	3,000-3,500 sq. ft.
Variety	6,000 sq. ft.
Drug	2,500 sq. ft.
Movie House	500-600 seats
Gas station and minor repairs	

So as to assist in determining the amount that low-income families would spend for various items the Bureau of Home Economics of the U.S. Department of Agriculture set up tentative budgets for families of four persons in annual income groups of $900, $1,250 and $1,600.

Item	Level A $900 yearly income	Level B $1,250 yearly income	Level C $1,600 yearly income
Food	400-475	475-520	560
Clothing	100-125	135-165	165-200
Housing	180	280	330
House operation (fuel, light, household supplies)	70-80	90-115	125-155
Furnishings and equipment (replacements)	20-35	35-55	35-75
Transportation	35-40	40-50	45-60
Recreation and education	20-30	35-60	55-75
Personal	10-25	20-30	30-45
Medical care	25-45	30-65	45-100
Community welfare (church, gifts, charity)	0-15	10-35	25-75
Savings	0-10	50-100	75-125
Total	860-1,060	1,200-1,475	1,490-1,800

TENTATIVE BUDGETS FOR A YEAR FOR FAMILIES OF FOUR PERSONS IN A SUBURBAN RESETTLEMENT COMMUNITY NOTE.—These budgets are based upon prevalent ways of spending as shown by studies of family expenditures. For food, adequacy as measured by nutritional standards is used as a basis for the suggested budget. For the remaining items of the budget, adequacy can be determined only by studies of the consumption habits and needs of families in each of the localities. These budgets suggest what may be the broad spending patterns of a group of families at each of the three income levels: they are not presented as examples of desirable spending plans for all families. A family budget, to be suited to a specific family, must be planned to meet its needs and desires under existing conditions. Each budget is set up with a range in expenditures for most items. Since the low total is in each case somewhat less than the suggested income level, there can be a little leeway in spending on some items. Obviously, a family cannot spend the top figure for many items without spending less than the bottom figure for others, if it is to keep within its income.

Family includes: husband, wife, boy aged 10, girl aged 8.

Suggestions for expenditure are based upon 1935 price levels.

GREENBELT

On the basis of this study we then estimated local store family expenditures.

ESTIMATED LOCAL STORE FAMILY EXPENDITURES

Based on $1,250 income budget for a family of 4 persons
NOTE on Transportation Expenditures. Amounts provided are only adequate where 5 cent fare transportation is available. The $45 transportation allowance plus the $50 provided for savings will be necessary to meet the extra costs of transportation in Suburban Resettlement Towns. Local conditions will have to be studied carefully in relation to this item. Further data on automobile expenditures is being prepared.

NOTE on Motion Picture Expenditures. Most of the recreation item will probably be spent in the local movie house. However this item is not included in the estimate of store expenditures as our shopping facilities are not affected by it. A town of 4,000 population can support a 500-600 seat movie house.

Then using the experience of chain stores as basis of the average sales required for a successful store in various categories we estimated the number of stores that might be supported by 1,000 families of four, with $1,250 incomes.

ESTIMATED ANNUAL STORE EXPENDITURES BY TYPES OF STORE

NUMBER OF STORES SUPPORTED BY 1,000 FAMILIES

Based on $1,250 income budget for a family of 4 persons
NOTE.—As the town grows and/or as higher income groups are accommodated, there will be need for other types as well as more stores. These would include service stores, e.g , tailor, laundry and cleaner, barber and beauty shop and, also such retail stores as shoe, millinery, electrical supply, hardware.

ESTIMATED LOCAL STORE FAMILY EXPENDITURES

Item		Total Annual Expenditure	Local Store Expenditure	Per Capita Expenditure
Food		$475-520	$475	$118.75
Clothing		145	50	12.50
House Operation		90	17	4.25
Coal	$53			
Oil	8			
Electricity	12			
Household Supplies	8			
Ice	9			
Furnishings and Equipment		35-55	45	11.25
Recreation and Education		35-60	10 (not inc. movies)	2.50
School supplies	5			
Newspapers, etc.	8-10			
Recreation (movies, trips, children's toys)	22-45			
Personal		22.50	11	2.75
Tobacco, soft drinks, etc.	10			
Barber shop, toilet needs	12.50			
Medical Care		30-65	10	2.50
First aid supplies, medicines	15			
Services	15-35			
			$618	$154.50

ESTIMATED ANNUAL STORE EXPENDITURES BY TYPES OF STORE

Store	Item	Per Family	Per 1,000 Families	Average Sales per Chain Store 1921-1930 (Varies irregularly with size of Chain)	Approximate Number of Stores
Grocery and Meat	Food	$475	$483	$483,000	$45,000-$170,000	3 large stores
	Household sup.	8			
Variety Dry Goods & Apparel	Clothing	50	100	100,000	50,000-250,000	1 combination
	Furnishings and Equipment	40			30,000-150,000
	Barbering	4			
	Personal Care	1			
	School Supplies	5			
Drug	Medical care	10	26	26,000	60,000-150,000	A small independent drug store could operate
	Books, newspapers, etc.	5			
	Household appliances	5			
	Tobacco	3			
	Soft Drinks	3			
Filling Stations Accessories Repairs	Automobile		25	25,000		Would depend on number using autos for transportation to work.
Coal, oil	Fuel	40	49	49,000		Would depend on policy.
	Ice	9			
Movie, etc.	Recreation		20	20,000		Further study required to determine if town can support a small theater.

Viewed from the angle of the community and its people I was particularly interested to see how the increase in size of purchasing public would affect the returns to the town or to the individual purchasers and citizens. This return might be in—

1. *taxes* under normal form of tenancy
2. *rent* to the municipality or other public agent such as the PHA
3. *dividends* if co-operative stores were set up
4. a combination of these

ESTIMATED STORE INCOME
assuming $1,250 median income group
and local expenditures at $155, per capita
and local food expenditures at $118, per capita

Population	3,000	4,000	6,000	7,000
Gross annual income of stores at $155 per person	$465,000	$620,000	$930,000	$1,085,000
Rentals at 3% of gross income (all stores)	13,950	18,600	27,900	32,550
Maintenance cost of all stores	2,000	2,000	2,000	2,000
Net income from all stores	11,950	16,600	25,900	30,550
Gross annual income of food stores at $118 per person	354,000	472,000	708,000	826,000
Rentals of food stores at 2.5% of gross income	8,850	11,800	17,700	20,650
Maintenance cost of food stores	1,200	1,200	1,200	1,200
Net income from food stores	7,650	10,600	16,500	19,450
Per capita net income from all stores	4	4.15	4.30	4.35

The indication of the probable effect of size on the return to community or individual purchases is in the last line, the per capita net income from stores. Our estimates showed an increase from $4 per year for 3,000 population to $4.35 for the 7,000 population.

Let us compare what actually happened at Greenbelt, Maryland, with these generalized estimates. The store income at Greenbelt is shown below. In 1941 the population was approximately 3,000; and in 1943 and 1946 about 7,000.

INCOMES for the 1935 estimate were based on $1,250 median per family. Actually the incomes have always been higher than this; even in the beginning the average was between $1,800 and $2,000; and the limit of incomes was set at $2,100. By July 1947 the average in the Resettlement section had risen to over $3,674, with 35 per cent over $4,000. No records have been taken of the incomes of the Defense Homes occupants. There was no income limit. They were housed not because of their need, but the national need. However, their median income was somewhat higher than that of the earlier inhabitants. Therefore the average spending power of the 7,000 population town was greater than that of the 3,000. The decreased value of the dollar since this study was made must naturally be considered.

SIZE OF FAMILIES was estimated at four (based on husband, wife, and children of eight and ten years). The average was much smaller in the beginning—3.2 increasing to 3.7 when the Defense Homes were built.

SIZE OF STORES proposed in the report for 3,000-4,000 population was 11,500 to 12,000 square feet. Slightly over 13,000 square feet was built. (This does not include office space.)

The supermarket later added 10,000 square feet of main floor selling space and the equivalent in semi-basement to the main center.

The table Greenbelt Store Incomes should be compared with estimated Store Income (see page 216). The estimate was made in 1935. The records were made in 1941, with 3,000 population, in 1943, soon after the increase of the town to a population of 7,000, and then in 1946 before the new store was built, with population only slightly increased. The gross income of stores for the 3,000 town was estimated at $465,000 (page 216). In 1941 it was $499,867.91. For the 7,000 population the estimate was $1,085,000. In 1943 it came to $1,001,668.94.

RENTALS which we estimated conservatively at 3 per cent of gross income, were 4.2 per cent in

Greenbelt Store Sales and Rentals

Year		Gross	Per-centage	Per Family	Per Person
1941	SALES	$449,867.91	100	$508.35	$158.90
	RENTS	19,078.13	4.2	21.55	6.74
1943	SALES	1,001,668.94	100	531.34	143.10
	RENTS	35,320.85	3.5	18.74	5.10
1946	SALES	1,414,741.00	100	755.30	202.11
	RENTS	48,215.00	3.4	25.58	6.89

Store Areas

Type of Store	Existing Footage	Proposed in Report
Food	4,200 sq. ft.	3,000-3,500 sq. ft.
Drug	2,160 sq. ft.	2,500 sq. ft.
Variety	3,600 sq. ft.	6,000 sq. ft.
Stationery and Magazine	500 sq. ft.	
Beauty Shop	670 sq. ft.	
Barber Shop	670 sq. ft.	
General Merchandise and Valet	1,350 sq. ft.	
TOTAL OF STORES	13,150 sq. ft.	11,500 to 12,000 sq. ft.
Office Space of Greenbelt Co-operative	2,600 sq. ft.	
Movie	590 seats	500-600 seats
Gas Station		

GREENBELT STORE INCOMES			
Date	1941	1943	1946
Population	3,000	7,000	7,000-plus
Gross Income from Sales	$449,867.91	$1,001,668.94	$1,414,741.00
Rents	19,078.13	35,320.85	48,215.00
Maintenance Cost	5,232.56	6,731.00	9,554.00
Taxes	4,000.00	6,492.00	7,605.00
Net Gain	9,845.57	22,097.85	31,056.00
% Rent/Income	4.2%	3.5%	3.4%
PER FAMILY STORE INCOME			
Sales	$508.35	$531.34	$755.30
Rents	21.55	18.74	25.58
Maintenance	5.91	3.57	5.07
Taxes	4.52	3.44	4.03
Net Gain	11.12	11.73	16.48
STORE INCOME PER CAPITA			
Sales	$158.90	$143.10	$202.11
Rents	6.74	5.10	6.89
Maintenance	1.85	.96	1.36
Taxes	1.41	.93	1.08
Net Gain	3.48	3.15	4.45

The gross income from sales for 1949 was about $2,200,000. It is apparent that outside business is being attracted, partly by the new supermarket, partly by better parking and shopping conditions, and partly by outside interest in the cooperative method.

1941 and, when the town grew to 7,000 population, 3.4 to 3.5 per cent. The rentals in dollars were higher than the estimate in the 3,000 person town ($19,000 as compared with $13,950), and were very close to the estimate in the larger town ($35,000 instead of $32,000).

MAINTENANCE COSTS were difficult to figure. The PHA (or its predecessors of varied other initials) as representative of the landlord, the U.S.A., kept accounts of the whole first development as a single unit. The maintenance costs for the stores as well as for the community schools, including heating, etc., were not allocated to residential, commercial, or educational buildings in the accounts. Instead they were taken as a whole, and then distributed as part of the expenses of the houses. The Community Manager has unscrambled these accounts for me with the greatest possible accuracy. His estimates, on which we have based our maintenance figures are, I believe, close enough to serve our purposes. They double or more than double our estimated figures.

NET INCOME in our estimate was intended to cover the return to the community. We had hoped that the store buildings would ultimately be owned by the town, and that the returns from them could be used to decrease rentals, or in a sense be a dividend to the people. In such a procedure there would be no real need to differentiate between taxes or rent to the community.

What we refer to in the estimated incomes as *per capita* net income from all stores is the proportion per person of the difference between rental and maintenance. In the figures of what actually happened the net-gain equals rents minus maintenance and taxes. This actually did not go directly to the community, but it served to decrease the cost per unit of housing expenses. So I have called it net gain per family or *per capita*. This net income or gain *per capita* was estimated as $4.00 for 3,000 population and $4.35 for 7,000. In 1941 it was approximately $3.48, and in 1943 it was $3.15 when the population was 7,000. In 1946 it was $4.45.

Government

The fact that the federal government has been the owner of Greenbelt and the landlord of practically all its citizens might give the impression that it is a 'freak' town. On the contrary, the citizens take at least as active a part in determining civic policies as in most small American municipalities. Their local government, the Town (now the City) Council is democratically elected. Administration is under a City Manager directly responsible to it and the Mayor. The only difference between it and other Maryland municipalities with managers is that all voters have been tenants of the single owner of all taxable property, the U.S.A.

Although there has been no serious difficulty so far, there have been indications from time to time of some sense of irresponsibility on the part of the local governing body. This is because the Federal Government foots the bill for all new installations and services through its payments in lieu of taxes. On the other hand the Council, on the advice of the Town Manager, determines the budget and expenditures. In spite of this I think that, as a whole, in budgeting and operation great care has been taken to give as complete service as economically possible. The good record has been due in large part to the technical efficiency and the dedication to public service of the town managers.

Greenbelt has been integrated into the pattern of Prince George's County and Maryland State governmental procedure in a manner similar to to other municipalities. Such was the intention of the Resettlement Administration as stated in its early memorandum of objectives:

'A municipal government to be set up, in character with such governments now existing or possible in that region; co-ordination to be established, in relation to the local and state governments, so that there may be provided those public services of educational and other character which the community will require; and finally, to accomplish these purposes in such a way that the community may be a taxpaying participant in the region, that extravagant outlays from the individual family income will not be a necessity, and that the rents will be suitable to families of modest income.'

So as to assist the Resettlement Administration in carrying out this statement of objective, and particularly the latter part of it, I made the study of operation-maintenance costs for the purpose of:—

1. Setting up minimum desirable standards of housing and community equipment.

2. Estimating the costs of operating and maintaining the facilities and services required.
3. Measuring these costs of operation-maintenance against the ability to pay of families at various income levels.

In regard to its scope and limitations the report said:[34]

'For the purpose of this study a median family income of $1,250, an average family of four (consisting of two adults, one child of 10, one child of eight), and occupancy at one person per room were assumed.

'The study deals only with operation-maintenance costs of government and housing. These costs are basic and must be met by the inhabitants. Additional amounts to be paid as amortization and as interest on capital invested are matters of policy to be determined by the administration. The study differs from statements of operating costs in existing communities in that it does not include the factors of payment on capital outlays or debt service.

'The study is organized in such a way as to show the relative effect of change of policy or of cost of any single factor such as education, type of house, grouping of houses, manner of disposing of waste, income group to be housed, portion of income that can be afforded for rent, distance and cost of transportation, etc.

'Certain matters that are self-evident from the studies are:

1. Education is the largest single factor in operation-maintenance cost. However, it is most subject to probable economies or reduction, and appears to be the pivotal point on which Suburban Resettlement communities will reach closer to or away from low income groups. The actual cost per pupil will vary in each project with:
   (a) The standard of education in each state on which state assistance is based.
   (b) Extent to which the program of education in each community exceeds the minimum standard.
   (c) Extent of state aid.

'The transportation factor will be a most important item of cost in the family budget in Suburban Resettlement communities. A base figure of 10 cents per trip has been figured in these studies,

which brings the total family expenditure for transportation at the $1,250 income level to double the customary amount. This cost should be considered an integral part of the rent, and no rents are comparable unless weighted with transportation costs.

'Unless radical savings can be made in the costs of education or transportation, the $1,250 income group can pay a rental equal only to the cost of operation-maintenance in towns of 4,000 population and over. For families below this level operation-maintenance costs exceed the ability to pay except at the expense of minimum requirements for food, clothing, etc.'

It was apparent at an early stage of the investigation that the size of the population greatly affected the costs of both housing and governmental operation. So we made a comparison of cost of operation-maintenance of well-organized municipalities of various sizes run by town managers in a business-like way. We restricted our studies to communities of 3,000 to 7,000 population, as this was to be the size limits of these New Towns, at least in the first stage of construction. Most statistical data on this subject was based on generalities. There were too many variations to form scientific or factual conclusions. Costs of government in existing towns were too often affected by:

1. Debt.
2. Antiquated laws and customs.
3. Obsolete machinery and poor organization.
4. Low standards or limited services.
5. Motivations other than service, such as politics.

We proposed to, and in fact did, set up statistics relating to municipalities with as high as possible a standard of service, having:

No debt.

Town management form of government.

New equipment, and no old restrictions.

The budget of government cost was laid out as far as possible on the basis of what was to be done by each department or division, what employees and materials would be required, and how much the annual cost of these would be. In a few instances where we had had parallel experience (in parks at Radburn, for instance) I based probable cost on comparison with these. But in most cases we set up the work to be done just as one might in budgeting for a factory or, and this came closer to my own experience, for the operation-management of a housing development. This required judgment as to what services should be given and how carried out. I fortunately had the advice of one of our most expert small town government authorities, Major John O. Walker, who was afterward in charge of operating the Greenbelt Towns. We both hoped for a broadening of the local government expenditure in that department than was or is customary in small towns. Public health services have improved in the last decade in America but mainly at the expense of federal or state agencies.

The cost of the function of government that we found most difficult to predict was the most expensive of all, that is, education. The quality and therefore the expenditure for schooling differ greatly in various parts of the country. Greenbelt, Maryland, pays much less per child than do the other two Greenbelt Towns, which are in northern states with higher standards. The administrative and fiscal set-up for public education differs in various parts of the country. The functions of state, county, school district and local authority vary as do the portion of the costs paid by each of these, and the method of collecting and distributing monies for that purpose. For the time being in the comparative cost of government of the three towns, I have separated the costs of education from the other municipal expenditures, so that I may have an opportunity to analyze separately these later costs and services.

The estimated local government and community services' costs exclusive of education showed a continuous decrease in unit cost as the size of population increased from 3,000 to 7,000 persons(from $27.57 to $17.22). The actual figures, although they differed in detail, as was to be expected, show

the tendencies we predicted. The cost of governing Greenbelt (exclusive of education), with a population of 2,831, was $23.61 per person in 1941. With a population of 7,000, in 1943, the cost had dropped to $14.57 per person.

The proportion of decline in operation-maintenance costs between the larger and smaller-sized town is somewhat less when taken on the basis of family rather than individual unit. This was because the size of family, which in 1941, was 3.2, due to the large percentage of small apartment units, had grown in 1943 to 3.7, whereas in our theoretical set-up we presumed an average family of four persons. These differences have only very slight effect on the relation; so the total cost per family of serving the larger and smaller communities with protection, public works, recreation, and the other typical governmental services, which we had estimated at $110.34 for the town of 3,000 population (with 750 families), and $68.84 for the 7,000 persons (or 1,750 families), was in Greenbelt in 1941 (with 885 families), $75.35, and in 1943 (with 1,885 families), $54.08. In short the trend downward followed much the direction we had indicated.

How long would that tendency continue as a town increases in size? We know that beyond a certain expansion, unit cost of operating municipalities increases. But where and why? Over-expansion, increased complication, greater amount of expenditure for 'administration' in place of 'doing,' changing degree of participation by the public— all of these and other factors have their influence. To take just one example. Small American towns such as the three Greenbelt Towns have volunteer firemen. When a municipality reaches a size where paid firemen replace the volunteers, the unit cost of administration goes up.

Astoundingly little factual investigation of the effect of size of governmental units on cost of operation has been made. Further research of this type is urgently required in determining policy and a plan for New Towns. This should serve as an important factor in deciding what is the desirable size.

The comparative cost of local government and community activities for communities of approximately 3,000 and 7,000 as estimated in 1935 and as realized at Greenbelt are summarized on Tables I and II. On Table III are shown the approximate breakdown of similar costs including Greendale and Greenhills. As cost accounting methods have been slightly different in the various towns, there may be some slight variations in the breakdown.

The cost accounting has special difficulties because of the unusual relation of the Federal Government to the Greenbelt Towns. It is, at the same time, the main taxpayer and the landlord of properties used by all levels of government and landlord of nearly all the residential property.

This is a particularly difficult time to describe the relation of the various levels of government at Greenbelt. The disposal of the town required by national legistlation (1949) is about to be negotiated. The Federal Government will, in all probability, shortly retire not only from ownership of the town, but also from the administration of certain functions normally carried on by the municipal or other levels of government. In fact during the past year or two certain of these have been handed over to the municipality in preparation for the retirement of the Public Housing Administration (which I will refer to hereafter as the PHA).

Another change that has taken place during the past year is the designation of Greenbelt, by the Maryland legislature, as a City instead of a Town. Apparently this does not give the municipality additional powers. Now that Greenbelt is about to be entirely on its own, the change was made so that it would be in a position of equal importance

TABLE I

PER PERSON

ESTIMATED AND ACTUAL COST

LOCAL GOVERNMENT AND COMMUNITY ACTIVITIES

	CSS est.	Green-belt	CSS est	Green-belt
Date	1935	1941	1935	1943
Units	750	885	1,750	1,885
Population	3,000	2,831	7,000	7,000
Administration	$2.66	$3.45	$1.43	$1 78
Recreation and Community Activities	7.00	5.06	4.50	2.94
Parks	1.33	2.00	1.04	.71
Public Works and Services	6.27	7.29	3.91	5.05
Repair Shop (Equipment)		.71		.31
Protection—Fire, Police	4.43	3.47	2.11	2.71
Health	3.33	1.20	2.25	.60
Cemetery		.01		.002
Civilian Defense				.09
Insurance	.17	.42	.09	.24
Contingency	2.38		1.89	.14
TOTAL	$27.57	$23.61	$17.22	$14.57
Education	22.50	17.05	22.50	14.76
GRAND TOTAL	$50.07	$40.66	$39.72	$29.33

TABLE II

PER FAMILY

ESTIMATED AND ACTUAL COST

LOCAL GOVERNMENT AND COMMUNITY ACTIVITIES

	CSS est.	Green-belt	CSS est	Green-belt
Date	1935	1941	1935	1943
Units	750	885	1,750	1,885
Population	3,000	2,831	7,000	7,000
Administration	$10.66	$10.95	$5.71	$6.61
Recreation and Community Activities	28.00	16.19	18.00	10.91
Parks	5.35	6 39	4.14	2.63
Public Works and Services	25.07	23.32	15.64	18.74
Repair Shop (Equipment)		2.27		1.16
Protection —Fire, Police	17.73	10.99	8.44	10.05
Health	13.32	3.84	9.00	2.23
Cemetery		.05		.006
Civilian Defense				.33
Insurance	.67	1.35	.37	.88
Contingency	9.54		7.54	.53
TOTAL	$110.34	$75.35	$68.84	$54.08
Education	90.00	54.56	90.00	54.87
GRAND TOTAL	$200.34	$129.91	$158.84	$108.95
Omitting Contingency, TOTALS	$100.80	$75.35	$61.30	$53.55

TABLE III

LOCAL GOVERNMENT AND COMMUNITY ACTIVITIES
COMPARATIVE COSTS PER PERSON IN THE
GREENBELT TOWNS

	CSS est.	Green-belt	Green-dale	Green-hills
Date	1935	1941-1942	1943	1940-1944 av.
Units	750	885	572	676
Population	3,000	2,831	2,610	2,500
Person per family	4.0	3.2	4.5	3.7
I. ADMINISTRATION	$2.66	$3.45	$4.09	$1.15
II. RECREATION AND COMMUNITY ACTIVITIES	7.00	5.06	2.54	6.89
III. PARKS	1.33	2.00	.96	2.83
IV. PUBLIC WORKS AND SERVICES	6.27	7.29	11.78	10.49
V. REPAIR SHOP (EQUIPMENT)		.71	.99	2.98
VI. PROTECTION, FIRE, POLICE	4.43	3.47	4.60	5.12
VII. HEALTH	3.33	1.20	.50	.20
VIII. INSURANCE	.17	.42		
IX. CONTINGENCY	2.38	.01		
TOTAL	$27.57	$23.61	$25.46	$29.66
X. EDUCATION	22.50	17.05	35.95	33.37
GRAND TOTAL	$50.07	$40.66	$61.41	$63.03

NOTE: The exact comparison of the actual cost of operation and maintenance of various services performed by local government with the figures in the estimate of 1935 is difficult because certain of the functions are distributed differently in Greendale, Greenhills and Greenbelt, not only from each other but from that presumed in the original set-up. In some cases, instead of the local government's taking financial responsibility, in part expenses have been covered by the federal government through PHA, FHA, etc., or through school boards, etc. One example of this is in regard to supplying water. In the estimate it was presumed that this would be a local function. In the case of Greenbelt this has been distributed by PHA as a service of housing management. Again, certain of the community activities, such as adult education or library have come under various agents of different levels of government.

with nearby small cities. From now on, the Town Manager will be titled City Manager, and the Council the City Council, and the people of Greenbelt will have the satisfaction of being citizens of a city.

As I am going to deal with the past in my summary description of governmental relations and functions, I may use past titles and speak of relations that have of late changed.

There have been two types of managers at Greenbelt, as well as the other Greenbelt Towns: the Community Manager, representing the PHA, and the Town (now City) Manager in charge of the administration of local government.

Under the Maryland State Legislation, by which Greenbelt was incorporated as a chartered town in Prince George's County in 1937, the charter created a town-manager form of government, acting under a municipal council of five members, elected for a term of two years. Until a few years ago the town council always elected as town manager the person who represented the Federal landlord as community manager under the Housing Agency.

There was a certain economy in the administration of the town in having these two functions carried out by one official. However, they have now been separated, for political or other reasons, in all three towns. In Greenbelt, after the change took place in 1948, the incumbent of the two offices was re-elected Town Manager. The present City Manager, Charles T. McDonald, has had a varied experience in connection with the operation of all three towns.

The PHA management collects rents and makes payment in lieu of taxes. As the Federal government is not permitted constitutionally to pay taxes to a lower level of government, it has made equivalent payments in lieu of taxes—or in many cases it has directly paid the costs of new installations and services.

EDUCATION. The PHA, in addition to payments made to the municipality, finances education by payments in lieu of taxes to Prince George's County. It is somewhat difficult to figure the exact cost of education, as these payments to the county are used in part for certain other county purposes. But the greater portion goes to the Board of Eudcation. The fact is that the school buildings were built by various federal agencies, and have been either operated in whole or part by PHA, or have been loaned to the Board of Education of Prince George's County. Of these relations I have already spoken.

The cost of education at Greenbelt has been not only lower than that which we estimated in 1935 at $90, but also much less than Greendale and Greenhills, due, as I have said, to the lower educational standards of Maryland.

The town has supplemented the education given by the County by directly financing adult education, the library, and the two kindergartens. Child care has been either a co-operative undertaking or a war-time federal expense. The county expenditures have also been supplemented by PHA in the form of janitorial and other services.

PROTECTION. The proposal to combine fire and police protection made in the studies for the Resettlement Administration has been followed successfully in all three towns. At Greenbelt the number of men permanently employed and the costs of operation have been very much as predicted. The Public Safety Department takes care of both fire and police protection. There is a staff of five full-time professional policemen who have also trained as firemen at a University of Maryland night course. When Greenbelt had a population of 2,831, there were four policemen. By 1943, there were five policemen for a population of about 7,000. In 1948, the staff consisted of a Director of Public Safety, an Assistant Director, three officers, and two part-time clerks, plus the help of two part-time relief officers for special occasions.

Police work consists of traffic control, and the inspection and registry of bicycles (at a charge of 25 cents, and children seem to enjoy having a license plate). Police perform other services, such as keeping the development's main switchboard open after regular working hours and on Saturdays, Sundays and holidays. They take messages for the doctors, and keep a list of those willing to be blood donors in emergencies.

FIRE PROTECTION. The staff of professional police-firemen is assisted in fire prevention by volunteers who receive 50 to 75 cents an hour for their participation in the fire-fighting and training program. During the war, under the Civil Defense

Act the force consisted mainly of old men and high-school boys, but since the war there are 16 well-trained young men, many of them veterans. In emergencies they can be supplemented by 8 or 10 of the project employees — heating men, plumbers and electricians. These men have been trained in fire fighting, but the Department tries to call on them as little as possible. Actually there have been few fires in the dwellings, and the main concern of the department has been brush fires. This, combined with the prompt response of the volunteers to fire calls, has kept fire losses very low.

PUBLIC WORKS AND SERVICES. A number of services have been distributed or operated by the PHA and not the municipality—at least up to a short time ago. These include water, sewers (both sanitary and storm), and electricity. Water as well as electricity is purchased in bulk from an outside public utility corporation. Water is furnished by the Metropolitan (Washington) Sanitary Commission. It is delivered to a standpipe, of 2 million gallons capacity. The distribution system has been owned and operated by the PHA. Water was sold to the Town of Greenbelt for hydrants and other purposes, and to the Consumers Services, Inc. The water costs to the municipality have been far less than we etsimated, because it has paid only for what it used and has not had to operate and maintain the plant.

GARBAGE AND TRASH DISPOSAL. Although PHA owns the incinerator plant, it has been leased by the municipality, which operates large trucks for collection and disposal. This service is included in the payments in lieu of taxes, by PHA. These complicated relations may be simplified when the government sells the town.

THE SEWAGE SYSTEM remained in the possession of the Federal Government, but it is operated by the municipality. The disposal plant is large enough for 3,000 houses. The trunk sewers run through parks as well as streets. The cost of sewage disposal remained very much the same for the 7,000 population town as for the 3,000, as we had predicted. Costs were less as no assistant operator was needed.

PUBLIC WORKS. The 1935 Report proposed that all of the functions listed as Public Works and Services should be managed as one department with an efficient engineer at its head. Fewer skilled assistants could then have been put in charge of the various functions. In reality public works are all under one head, but municipal functions and housing functions are not under the same engineer. The volume of work was found to be too great for a single person to discharge both responsibilities.

HEALTH was one of the items for which our 1935 budget estimate was much higher than the ultimate costs in any of the three towns. Major John Walker and I both strongly believed in a municipal preventive program. We were apparently a little ahead of the time, and as the need of a program such as we suggested became a public policy the functions or costs of public health, in whole or part, were taken over by government at higher levels. We had proposed:

  (a) medical inspection of school children
  (b) immunization against small-pox
      and diphtheria
  (c) school hygiene
  (d) first aid in cases of emergency nature.

Thus, services in all cases were to be preliminary to reference to a physician when medical care was required.

The planned set-up also contemplated a first-aid station with a full-time nurse and doctor in attendance, preferably located in the school. We also said:

'It will probably be advantageous to place the nurse under the jurisdiction of the County Health Service, thereby permitting the Community to participate in the benefits of such service (laboratory facilities, sanitary officer, etc.). The cost of hospitalization is not included and is assumed to be contained in State or County levies. It is not proposed to erect a hospital in any of the towns as part of first construction.'

Strange as it may seem, the Town Council of Greenbelt did actually vote in 1940 to build a hospital, in spite of the fact that there were a dozen hospitals within as many miles of Greenbelt. Although the Town and Community Manager opposed it as financially unsound, in 1941, none the less, $16,607.60 was spent on changing some dwellings into a small hospital building. By 1943 the hospital had been abandoned, and the Greenbelt Health Association used the space.

GROUP HEALTH. The Greenbelt Health Association was active in the earlier years of Greenbelt's history. It provided a means of paying medical bills in advance. For a payment of $1.00 to $2.25 a month, depending on family size, members were allowed unlimited office visits and charged only 50 cents for the first home visit in each week of illness. Moreover, members obtained complete obstetrical care (exclusive of hospitalization) for the exceptionally low rate of $25.

In 1939, 130 families out of a total of 885 belonged to the association. In 1943, 375 families out of a total of 1,885 had joined. Greatly increased demand for public health service was to be expected under war conditions. The low number of families taking advantage of Group Health during the war years may have been partly due to the lack of sufficient doctors. Originally there had been three physicians, but during the war there was only one.

The Health Association, with its present staff of three full-time doctors and two nurses, seems to be overworked in spite of its reduced membership. The two other doctors and a dentist have busy private practices at Greenbelt.

PUBLIC HEALTH WORK has been confined to: (a) examination of school children, (b) operation of various adult clinics, and (c) immunization of young folks against contagious disease. The staff has consisted of one part-time health officer and one public health nurse.

The cost of public health service in 1941 was $3,399.00 for a population of 2,831. This included $500 for supplies. Space used was supplied free by the FHA. In 1943, for 7,000 people, the total cost was $4,214.00, including $3,260.00 for salaries, and $953.87 for supplies and services. By 1947 it had risen to $5,168, that is, $2.74 per family or about $0.75 for each person.

This is to be compared with our own 1935 Report's estimate, for the 7,000 population Town, of $15,000. However, there are additional health facilities made available by county and other governmental agencies. The latest of these is the Mental Hygiene Clinic of Prince George's County, which is housed in the University of Maryland, and the cost of which is in part paid for by the Federal Government. The services of the clinic are free.

RECREATION AND COMMUNITY ACTIVITIES have been discussed elsewhere. In carrying out the program there are varied parts, played by the PHA, in operation of the Community-School Building as well as the housing of the Child Care Center, of the Board of Education of Prince George's County in adult education, etc., and the private co-operation activities such as the nursery school.

This all naturally lessens the expenses that might otherwise have to be met by the municipality. The Recreation Department, which functions under the Town (now City) Manager, operated in 1941 (population 3,000), at a cost of $14,330 as compared with the 1935 estimate of $21,000. For the 7,000 person community the estimate was $31,500, the actual expenditures were in 1943 $20,564, in 1945, $37,108 and in 1947, $40,079. (The decreased buying power of the dollar in war and postwar years should be noted.)

The Recreation Department supervises the playgrounds, athletic fields, tennis courts, ice-skating rink, swimming pool, teen-age youth center, and all organised sports. During the summer months the program is very extensive, from baby playground programs to semi-professional baseball series. During the winter the recreational staff organizes and directs adult gym classes and teaches the elementary physical education classes in the two public schools.

The music program, which now consists of two elementary glee clubs and a children's string orchestra, is under the superision of the Recreation Department. There are several annual special community programs such as a Fourth of July celebration and a Christmas program. These are planned and carried out by the Recreation Department.

THE SWIMMING POOL has been operated as a separate feature by the municipality. It has required 20 half-time workers for a period of three months of the year. It now more than pays for itself. Expenses are $7,000 to $9,000 a year; income, $8,000 to $10,000. The extra income is used for other recreational expense. Charges are: Adults $.35, or 10 tickets for $2.00; children $.20, or 10 tickets for $.75. The pool did not pay during the first year, although it was crowded. It was opened only to Greenbelt people and their friends. Members of the community were able to purchase a pass for $6.00 a year for the family, $2.50 a year for individuals. The present rate schedule produces more revenue than the above system, thereby resulting in a successful financial operation.

Cost Accounting

There is much to be learnt from the decade of experience in Greenbelt, Greendale, and Greenhills that can help in the further development of functional contemporary towns. One of the difficulties I have found in trying to uncover the experiences is that results are not always clear.

It has been much like laboriously excavating archeological ruins. Many of the experiments that might be of great assistance in planning or running future communities have not been sufficiently observed or recorded. Often this is merely a matter of bookkeeping, or the method of setting up figures. Here is just one example.

In the heating of the houses a number of different methods have been used. In the Resettlement Development each row of houses has one boiler. As these were coal-burning, to tend the boiler and collect ashes a man had to travel from one group to another. This always has seemed an unnecessarily complicated system. So, when the Defense Homes were built, group heating for a number of rows was tried: some for as many as 200 units, others for lesser numbers. Here was an opportunity to get information that could be of much future value, not only as to practical experience with the number of units served by a single boiler, but also the difference in efficiency of using coal or oil. But the accounting records were set up so that the comparison could not be made between cost and efficiency of heating in units of 6 or of 200. This is due in part to the fact that the heating of all the buildings of the earlier development are accounted for together, and then divided by the number of house units. As the Community-School and shopping center were included, and their costs distributed among the 885 houses, the information as to heating costs is vague to say the least, and is of no use for purposes of comparison. I note that the British Mission to study District Heating in American Housing had similar difficulty in securing what might have been valuable information on heating at Greenbelt.[35]

An Unfinished Story

The Greenbelt Towns are often referred to as *demonstrations*. Perhaps it would be better to say that they have been *indicators*. They have indicated that certain unusual policies and practices in the planning, organization and operation of communities are both attractive and highly practical. They have indicated very strongly that certain development methods and forms that have been followed in the past are obsolete, unnecessarily wasteful and ugly. One illustration is the contrast between the concentrated Greeenbelt shopping center and nearby roadside sprawl.

Perhaps the co-operative shopping center is the appropriate place to leave Greenbelt. For physically this marketplace, with the nearby related community buildings and recreation fields, is the heart of Greenbelt, and the dominant spirit of Greenbelt is that of doing things together—or co-operation.

This is an unfinished story because a town as vibrant with life as Greenbelt is constantly changing and its history can only be sketched in this limited space. I have tried, however, to indicate as adequately as possible how the three planning conceptions, the Garden City, the Radburn Idea, and the Neighborhood Unit, have actually worked.

This is written as one chapter of the history of Greenbelt is about to close and another to begin. Early in 1950 the Federal Government will end its guardianship of Greenbelt. The town will be sold, but on exactly what terms none of us know yet. However, the Congress has authorized the Public Housing Commissioner in the disposing of the Greenbelt Towns 'to give the first preference . . . to veteran groups organized on a non-profit basis (provided that any such group shall accept as a member . . . any tenant occupying a dwelling unit in such project . . .).'

It further permits the Commissioner to preserve the green belts by authorizing him to 'transfer . . . adequate open land surrounding or adjacent to each project to the appropriate non-federal governmental agency.'

We can only hope that these powers will be used in such a way that the spirit and form of Greenbelt will survive and that it will develop into a complete New Town.

Fig. 133—Double crescent roads encircle the community center for shopping, education, swimming and other recreation and community activities. This photo shows most of the Resettlement Development of 1937 as well as the lake in the distance. (Fairchild Aerial Surveys, Inc., New York)

GREENHILLS

Justin R. Hartzog and William A. Strong, Town Planners

Roland A. Wank and G. Frank Cordner, Architects

Fig. 134—Airview of Greenhills taken in 1949 toward the northeast. All houses shown were part of the original Federal government construction excepting a small number (121 lots) to the extreme right and on Gambier Circle at the top of the picture. These were finished in 1947.

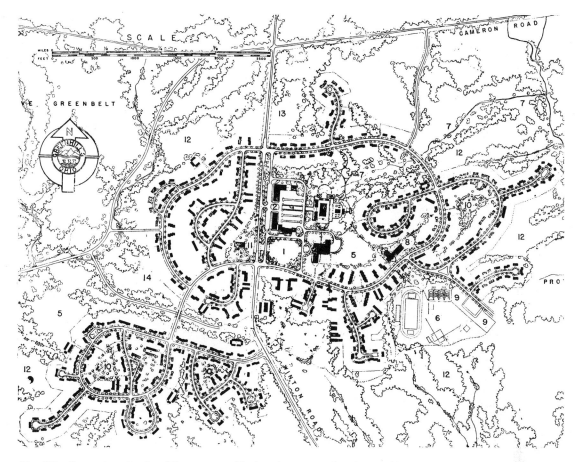

Fig. 135—Town plan showing (1) common; (2) shopping center (northern half not yet built); (3) community school; (4) swimming pool; (5) inner park; (6) playfield; (7) stream; (9) parking areas; (10) small children's play areas.

Fig. 136—Greenhills School, with the administration building in the background beyond the Common.

Greenhills is situated on an undulating, wooded site, five miles north of Cincinnati. The initial plan was for 676 dwelling units which were built in the first stage (Fig. 134). The form of the plan was suggested and limited by the rolling ground and many ravines. The latter have been preserved in the open space system as delightful and naturally wooded parks.

In Greenhills the Radburn Idea has been followed but not as completely as at Greenbelt. The turn-arounds of the dead end lanes are better than those at Greenbelt, Greendale or Radburn. Cars entering the lanes may easily return without backing or maneuvering. The arrangement of the elements in the Community Center is noteworthy (Fig. 137).

Of the 676 dwelling units there are 112 one-bedroom apartments, 40 two-bedroom apartments, 18 single-family detached four-bedroom dwellings, 6 single-family detached three-bedroom units; and, in row houses, 260 two-bedroom units, 208 three-bedroom units, and 32 four-bedroom units.

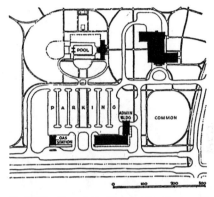

Fig. 137—Greenhills Community Center. Community school building and the administration building face the Common. The parking area lies between the shopping center and the swimming pool. The back of the pool shelter was designed to be used as an outdoor stage. The central part of the parking area was intended to be used as a farmer's market, but the farms in the area sell most of their products to the larger dealers in Cincinnati. The community building serves for gatherings of all kinds as well as for school. The auditorium-gymnasium is equipped for theatrical performances and the libraries and art studios are open in the evenings for adults. The large cafeteria in the basement is open day and night.

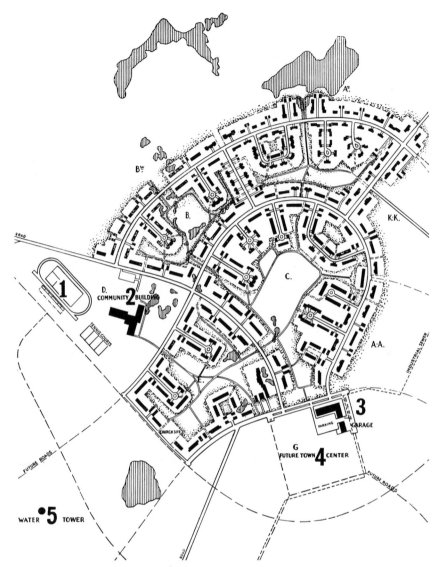

Fig. 138—Greenbrook, New Jersey. Initial project plan, showing the residential blocks with interior commons and walk systems and (1) athletic field; (2) community building; (3) shops and garage; (4) future town center; (5) water tower.

GREENBROOK

Henry Wright and Allan Kamstra,
Town Planners
Albert Mayer and Henry S. Churchill,
Architects

Greenbrook, the fourth of the Greenbelt Towns, was never carried out. Work on the project was begun in October, 1935, and ended in May, 1936, when legal controversies arose. Rather than risk holding up all four projects, the Resettlement Administration decided that the Greenbrook project, on which controversy centered, should be dropped.

Subsequent events have proved that the location of Greenbrook was well chosen. It was on the southwest edge of the rapidly growing New Jersey industrial belt, five miles west of New Brunswick, and adjacent to the main lines of communication between New York City and Philadelphia. Within 40 minutes of the site by motor there was employment for about 50,000 in industry, with an anticipated growth making 10,000 more jobs available in two to three years. There was also an abnormal shortage of low-rent housing in adjacent areas.

The site was to have been of between 3,800 and 4,200 acres, of which about 1,400 acres were for the ultimate built-up area. The initial project was for: 750 dwelling units, occupying 125 acres; a community center, commercial area and town common of about ten acres; with 25 acres in roads (Fig. 138). Of the dwellings, 3 per cent were to be detached houses, 20 per cent double houses; 70 per cent rows of 3 to 6 houses; and 7 per cent multi-family dwellings. Seventy per cent of the dwellings were to have had garages, 35 per cent to 40 per cent of that number as integral parts of the dwellings, and the balance in compounds located not over 200 feet from the farthest dwelling.

The final scheme for the ultimate town provided for 3,990 families at 4.9 families per net acre (exclusive of streets but including all interior open spaces, school areas and peripheral blocks, to the rear lot line). There was to have been an industrial area of 125 acres.

Fig. 139—The Community-School at Greendale. The school and community building contains thirty classrooms, an auditorium and gymnasium, recreation room and youth center, and the municipal library. It is surrounded by parks and is adjacent to the major playground.

GREENDALE

Jacob Crane and Elbert Peets,
Town Planners
Harry H. Bentley and Walter G. Thomas,
Architects

Greendale[36] is superby related to its natural site. The form of the land has indicated the location of roads paths, and buildings. Attractive features of nature have been preserved: for example, the stream that flows through the wooded park in the very center of the village.

Greendale was planned and built as a harmonious whole. It shows that regimentation and monotony are not necessarily the product of over-all design of the street pattern and buildings of a village. The buildings are harmonious in spite of the diversity of their form and placing. The care with which the planners related structures to site and to one another is the result of skilful practice and a real affection for the place they helped to create. The varied architectural beauty accentuates rather than overshadows its natural setting. A restful and gracious unity is the result.

SAFETY PLANNED AND ACHIEVED. Greendale is safe. There has not been a single automobile fatality, and not one serious accident during the ten years of its existence.

It is not by chance that Greendale has this remarkable record. Its streets are planned for through traffic or direct access. As a result, only the machines that are serving the houses on a lane or a street are likely to go there. Also, the pedestrian paths are in large part separated from highways.

BUILT FOR GOOD LIVING. Greendale is a spacious, comfortable, convenient place for living. The green breadth of Broad Street that leads to the Village Hall introduces the visitor to the roomy character of the village. The Central Park along Dale Creek at one side and the commercial buildings and theatre with their own service road, as well as the mall and tennis courts at the other, open broadly to the view. Around the houses are goodly private gardens—most of them beautifully kept, I observed. The houses were carefully located so that they are not cramped and crowded as most speculative housing is. This, in spite of the need of economizing on the length of utilities and roads, so that rent could be low.

PROTECTED BY ITS GREENBELT. Greendale is shielded from external dangers and encroachments as were medieval towns. But there is a great difference. The old communities were protected by gray fortifications: Greendale is secured by a belt of natural green.

A wide-open area is needed to prevent destruction from the spread of blight just as much as from forest fire.

That is what the greenbelt around Greendale does. It guarantees the integrity of the town.

It serves other purposes too. It brings country and semi-wilderness within walking distance of

Fig. 140—View of pedestrian walk and garden court.

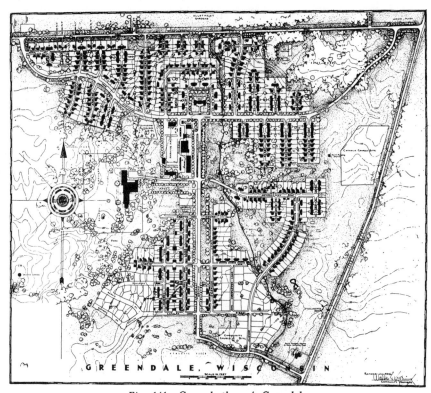

Fig. 141—General plan of Greendale.

homes. Farms and forests are familiar to kids from daily experiences, not merely from pictures in school books and movies. Picnics and hiking can be enjoyed by the family as a whole. The nature of changing seasons becomes a beautiful reality.

Town folks and farm folks know each other as neighbors, friends and associates. They come together in town meeting, churches, village and social affairs and at the co-operative, or the tavern. One more barrier that creates strangeness and misunderstanding among different groups of people is dissolved and broken down.

But the greatest advantage of the greenbelt is that it definitely limits the size and growth of the community. That is desirable, because only so can the neighborly character be sustained—and the common interest of all in their common affairs be kept alive.

GREENDALE A NEIGHBORLY COMMUNITY. The neighborhood community is now accepted as the basic unit of city building as well as planning. Small neighborhoods are essential for eye-to-eye democracy—and this is basic, not only for local contentment, but for national freedom and worldwide security.

It is just that kind of neighborly community life that makes Greendale such an important demonstration of the kind of towns we need all over America. All through the activities of Greendale one feels a spirit of fellowship—and as far as I could observe, it does not interfere with privacy or family life.

THE FUTURE. One of the fine qualities of Greendale is that it is small. But don't misunderstand me—I did not say Greendale was of a perfect size. In fact, I think it is apparent now that it has certain disadvantages because it is too small. A place that has a high standard of community and local-government services must spread the costs among an adequate group. Education and culture in Greendale require a large population to support them economically.

Greendale has plenty of space on which to grow. Less than 300 acres of the 3,140 acres (that originally were purchased by the Federal Government through the Resettlement Administration in 1936 as the site of Greendale) have been developed for houses and community facilities. So far, 525 acres of the greenbelt area have been dedicated to Milwaukee County for park and recreational purposes. It would be wise to deed permanently to the state or county the remaining greenbelt area surrounding the future expanded Greendale. Thus, the temptation to use portions of the protective belt for other than public or agricultural purposes might be done away with for all time. The smaller separation greens between the various neighborhood villages should be owned and operated by Greendale itself. They should be permanently dedicated to public use as one of the first steps toward the development of the future of the village of Greendale.

NO UTOPIA. Strangers who read my description in praise of Greendale may think that I am writing about Utopia. But those who live there know that Greendale is not a phantom, but a fact. It is a living, growing reality.

It has had more luck than most villages. First, the conception of a community planned in orderly fashion for the motor age and increased leisure time, with its character and integrity protected by its greenbelt, was a great step forward. Then the detailed planning and development a decade ago was a very able job—thanks to the ability of the planners, Jacob Crane and Elbert Peets—their skill and more than that, the love that they put into the work. Then, there has been exceptional leadership on the part of one of America's ablest town managers, Walter Kroening. Here again has been a case of devotion as well as unusual understanding and skill. But none of these things would matter if it were not for the fact that Greendale has gathered together a lot of folks that appreciated its physical qualities and have made it a living community.

9   BALDWIN HILLS VILLAGE

Reginald D. Johnson and Wilson, Merrill, and Alexander, Associated Architects

Clarence S. Stein, Consulting Architect

Fig. 142—View of garden and garage courts, looking toward the village green.

At Baldwin Hills Village in 1941 the Radburn Idea was given its most complete and most characteristic expression. There, in Los Angeles, with an average of over one automobile per family, was needed—perhaps more than anywhere else in the world—the combination of complete convenience in the use of the automobile and a peaceful escape from its dangers. And so at Baldwin Hills all the original elements of Radburn reappear—superblock, specialized means of circulation, complete separation of pedestrian and auto, park as community heart and backbone faced by all houses. They were freshly developed in a comprehensive, straightforward manner without compromise or indecision. Here, these basic elements have been clearly expressed and crystallized into more functional unity.

Economic Background

Baldwin Hills Village was another child of the long depression. During its final stage a forward-looking group of Los Angeles architects devoted three years to the development of plans for a new community, inspired by Radburn, but essentially local in character, to be built on a great empty ranch bordering Los Angeles. Too much of these three years was spent in securing approval, loans and mortgage insurance from cautious government officials in the Federal Housing Agency and the Reconstruction Finance Corporation. The bureaucrats, although they vaunted their progressive planning viewpoint, delayed and postponed all action that would result in any but 'safe' commonplace form or plan. Because of this procrastination there was time for the original conception of 1938 to be thoroughly studied and refined; about fifty plot plans were developed and the buildings were redrawn in detail some ten times. Yet it is remarkable how fresh and simple and straightforward the project was, when it was realized at last in 1941.

Pearl Harbor closely followed the arrival of the first of the 627 tenants. Rents, which had been set low, averaging $12.27 per room per month, were frozen. Financial plans, which had been figured tightly to keep rentals low, were disrupted as a result of unforeseen restrictions caused by wartime conditions. For instance, the proposed public omnibus that was to have carried tenants to the nearest transportation line was forbidden by the local authorities, and one had to be run by the Housing Company at a financial loss. Also no private direct telephone lines were permitted. So

BALDWIN HILLS VILLAGE

the company had the added unexpected expense of running a telephone central. In addition all operation and maintenance costs rose far above the estimated figures on which the fixed rentals were based.

In spite of this (due largely to the fact that it has continuously been 100 per cent occupied and not 90 per cent full as figured in the financial setup insisted on by FHA) Baldwin Hills Village has always paid its way; for eight years rentals have covered all operation and maintenance costs as well as debt services on mortgages and loans. In short, the only debts that were postponed were the interest and amortization of the equity, which had all been invested by the owner of the land, the architects and the builder. Now their investment has been returned with all back interest. This is the result of the sale of Baldwin Hills Village in 1949, to the New England Mutual Life Insurance Company of Boston, at a price sufficiently above its original cost to more than repay all equity and interest for eight years. And yet this wise company, I understand, knows that it has made a shrewd long-time investment.

The Site

The site consisted of some eighty acres of almost flat vacant land, with nothing on it higher than a blade of grass. It was part of an immense ranch that had changed hands only twice; first when the King of Spain deeded it to a conquistador; second when 'Lucky' Baldwin purchased it from his descendants over seventy years ago. It sloped slightly up to the low barren hills on which grow oil towers in place of foliage. The site is between Baldwin Hills and Beverly Hills, which create a 'draw' for cooling summer breezes from the nearby Pacific.

I had been shown this property by a broad-minded local builder, Joshua Marks, when I was looking for sites in 1935 for the group of communities of the Valley Stream type. I had recommended its use, in spite of the prevalent opinion that the peat in the soil of this valley made it undesirable for building. In the Baldwin Hills Village this difficulty was overcome by the use of floating foundations.

During the postwar boom the surrounding miles which had been empty were covered with speculators' disorderly housing. Baldwin Hills is now the population as well as the geographic center of the Los Angeles metropolitan area. It is within twenty minutes' auto ride of the business center, universities, airport, the beaches and other public recreation resorts, as well as the business centers of Los Angeles, Hollywood, and Beverly Hills.

The Objective

The purpose of Baldwin Hills Village was to demonstrate the practical possibilities of spacious homes and surroundings in an orderly community at low rentals, using the basic features of the Radburn Idea: superblock, homes facing central greens — twenty acres of green parks — pedestrian and auto completely separated.

The difficulties of carrying out these objectives in the Los Angeles area were twofold:

1. *The dominance of the automobile.* Nowhere else in the world are the problems of man's relation to his individual little railroad as acute. In Los Angeles there is an average of one automobile for every two-and-a-half persons—that is, more than one per family.

2. *The past control of housing by speculative subdividers and speculative builders* throughout Los Angeles. The old conventional type of street pattern and land subdivision best served their purposes of rapid sale. This gridiron pattern was adopted in spite of costly waste and its dangers to pedestrians.

The system of continuous through-streets had official recognition and legal backing. Municipal engineers had nailed down the typical pattern of streets in the official maps. They recognized no other arrangement. Change meant work — and making up one's mind — and possibly courting disapproval of superiors. In fact they looked upon new-fangled arrangements such as cul-de-sacs as dangerously revolutionary—or just the crazy idea of impractical architects.

Even where no streets had as yet been put on the city map the form of the circulation pattern was predetermined as though by command of the Almighty. The property that was to be Baldwin Hills Village was annexed to the city at the request of the architects so as to obtain city utilities, and

Fig. 143—Aerial view of Baldwin Hills Village showing the contrast between the development according to the Radburn Idea and the typical speculative development to the north and south. Baldwin Hills are at the south (bottom of the picture).

BALDWIN HILLS VILLAGE

at that time had no mapped streets. Nonetheless the plan to dispense with through highways between La Brea Avenue and Hauser Street—a distance of about three thousand feet, was disapproved repeatedly by City Engineer and City Planning Board. The intermediate streets to the north they insisted must be extended through the 1100-feet width of the project. It was the same struggle between the past and the future city pattern that we had fought at Sunnyside and Hillside.

It looked for some time as though the city engineer would be as obstinate as his professional brothers in the Boroughs of the Bronx and Queens. The City Planning Board was, however, finally induced to eliminate the streets that were to have dissected the residential area on the plea that these roads would be dead-ended by the hills beyond Coliseum Street and so might as well end at Rodeo Road.

In this eighty-acre superblock, therefore, we were free to work out a commonsense, logical and functional plan. However, the highway that separated this area from that which was zoned as business, they decreed must create an island to be surrounded by roads. We had hoped to design a market-place here with direct safe entrance from the residential park area of Baldwin Hills Village, in much the same way that I had indicated in the diagram illustrating the Neighborhood Shopping Center article.[37] The dismemberment of the superblock by cutting through Sycamore Avenue made this impossible. Natives of the Village, I understand, speak of this as a 'death trap.' Although I do not believe there have been any fatalities as yet, people are constantly dodging trucks and the bus which turns there. There have been a number of serious accidents, and recently the elderly guard of the theater building was injured for life.

The complete difference of the realtors' street pattern and the community pattern stands out in the air-view (Fig. 143). Below Baldwin Hills Village (to the north), built about the same time as the Village, a few meaningless curves are added to the typical gridiron. The through streets do not tie into any scheme of circulation—they go from nowhere to nowhere. The southern subdivision is more liberal of space than most of such wholesale developments. It was built only a few years ago,

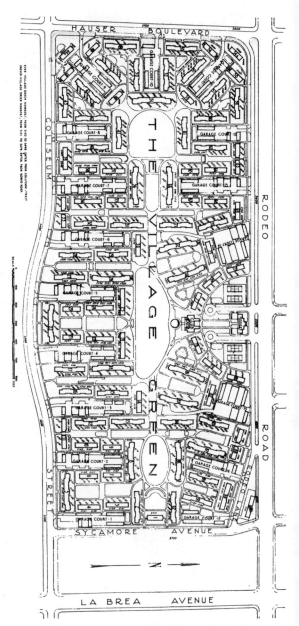

Fig. 144—Plan of Baldwin Hills Village. Only 15 per cent of the 80 acres of the site is covered by buildings, including the garages.

where we architects had hoped to locate an addition to Baldwin Hills Village that would have made it large enough to support a centrally located public school. It climbs the hill in a purposeless way. The outstanding feature of both these subdivisions is the undue importance and comparative spaciousness of streets. There is no concentration of green open spaces. Yet there are only 3.5 to 4 houses to the acre as against 7.8 dwelling units per acre in Baldwin Hills Village, with its spacious, verdant openness. The dissecting divisions of wide gray paved bands characterize, and dismember, these typical subdivisions to north and south.

The Village Plan

'Very pretty' says the Californian as he flies over, 'but is it practical? Where are the streets to take autos to the houses, and where do folks park and garage their machines?' There is no parking or storing of autos on public streets—in fact there are no streets within the 1100-feet by 2750-feet superblock. The highways that surround it are exclusively for movement—as they should be everywhere in all our cities. Rodeo Road, the one heavily used thoroughfare, is relieved of local traffic by the secondary roadway that parallels it on the Village property. This gives a safe approach to parking areas and auto courts. The two functions of through flow and access to groups are thereby separated and channeled, with entrances to Rodeo Road at only a limited number of points. On the periphery of the other surrounding highways there is off street parking space with indented curbs.

Not only are there no streets within the eighty acres of the Village, but even the dead-end of the Radburn type has been replaced. It has here been changed into a concentrated but adequate garage court. A new form has developed and come of age. Here is realistic modern functionalism replacing outworn traditionalism. Within the court is one garage for each home around it; also parking space for one car per family or its visitor. There remains adequate space for maneuvering, turning, backing into garages (Fig. 147 and 149). The automobile —arriving, departing, at rest, in storage—has all the room needed. Its local functions are not interfered with by through circulation.

Within each court are also the public group

laundries with washing machines and out-door, but enclosed, drying yards. These were given increased space to meet war-time conditions. Now that wash can be sent out again, the additional drying enclosure is once more being devoted to parking.

There are less than four dozen families served by a garage court. Their houses surround it. This is similar to the location of the courts in the second (Defense) development at Greenbelt. But here the likeness ends. The dangers of too direct access to the paved courts by pedestrians do not exist at Baldwin Hills. There are only a limited number of entrances. A child running out of the house will be stopped by a high wire fence or planting. The view of cars is hidden, or at least lessened by the vines that overgrow the fences, as well as by the intervening planting (Fig. 146). This also serves to decrease the annoyances of auto sounds and smells.

PATIOS offer additional reposeful retreat on the garage court side of the houses. The patio is the indigenous private outdoor livingroom, dating back in California to the Spanish conquest. Although small, these six-foot redwood walled garden spaces, directly accessible to diningroom or kitchen, serve for sun-bathing, children's play and outdoor dining and lounging, as well as limited gardening during the lengthy mild sunny season. All ground floor dwellings and even some upper apartments have patios. Other second-floor tenants were compensated for lack of private grounds by private balconies. The new owner is so impressed by the advantages of these private enclosed courts that he is now building additional patios for those upstairs families that now have none. These will surround the entrance doors giving access to the second-floor apartments. Thus every one of the 627 families will have its own outdoor privacy (Fig. 146).

Another improvement planned by the insurance company is the building of additional garages. There are now 100 per cent garages, 100 per cent parking in courts, and about 100 per cent parking space in indented curbs—and yet more is needed! Where but in Southern California could this happen?

The orderly concentration of automobiles and servicing on one side of the houses leaves the other side free for pedestrians, play, and peaceful loafing. Here is another, a different, urban world; a world

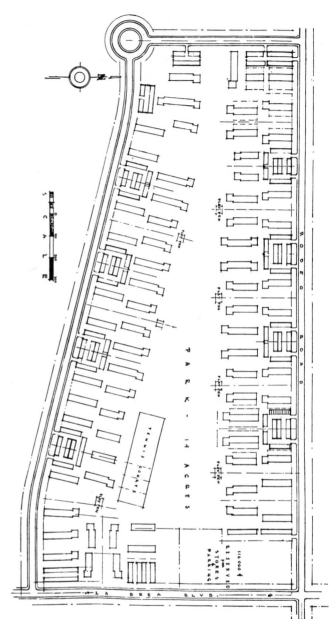

Fig. 145—First site planning study.

of quiet tranquility within the framework of per-
petual, congested movement. It is toward this calm
and restful verdant space that all livingrooms and
main bedrooms face.

About one-quarter of the area of Baldwin Hills
Village is devoted to green commons consisting of
inner parks and garden courts. The central park,
first planned as a single unbroken area, was afterward broken into three main bodies of different
shapes and sizes. The narrow connecting links
give scale and increased interest to the larger open
areas. The central green, although its maximum
width is only 250 feet, has a surprising sense of am-
pleness. This is due partly to the limited two-story
height of the long horizontal buildings. The central
greens serve for strolling, children's unorganized
play or romping, or even for informal ball games
by their elders. But above all their main function
is visual—or perhaps I should say spiritual. The
calm, long, orderly lines of the row houses and contrasting sweep of the brown hills behind—low hills
though they are, they seem to tower above the
domestic human scale of the homes—give the
feeling of spreading spaciousness. A tenant said to
me 'When I can't sleep nights I walk down the
length of the three central greens. I can hardly
believe I am in the heart of a great industrial me-
tropolis. The quiet sense of security and peace is only
broken by an occasional song of a night-singing
mockingbird.'

Although the Management leaves the great
central parks freely open for recreational use, they
look empty much of the time. Many of the youngsters seem to find the smaller proportions of the
garden courts, which form bays off the central
greens, more congenial. They are nearer home,
and the little ones love to use shrubs as hiding
places. Other causes for the sense of vacancy or
only partial use of the parks may be the omission
of benches which the planners proposed, and also
the insufficient shade of young trees. At the moment
the parks serve, above all, to form a visual foreground and spacious center of the architectural
composition (Figs. 151 and 164).

THE GARDEN COURTS are 100 feet or more wide.
Contrasted with the long horizontals of the row
houses less than twenty feet high, they have an
appearance of generous spaciousness. The homes

*Fig. 146—The enclosure of patios facing the garage
court. The serpentine brick wall has been added so that
the second-floor tenants might have privacy in their
patios. The ivy-covered wood walls surround the original
patios for the occupants of the first floor.*

Fig. 147—A garage court entered from Coliseum Street.

Fig. 148—View toward Baldwin Hills from garden court with entrance from Coliseum Street.

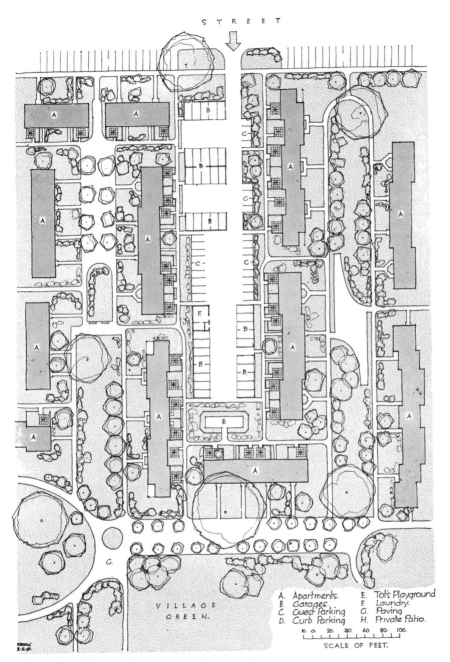

STREET

A. Apartments.   E. Tot's Playground
B. Garages.   F. Laundry.
C. Guest Parking   G. Paving
D. Curb Parking   H. Private Patio.

VILLAGE GREEN.

10. 0.   20.   40.   60.   80.   100.

SCALE OF FEET.

Fig. 149—Details of a garage court and two garden courts.

have a certain privacy as the public paths are twenty feet away and the intermediate space is planted with ivy or other ground cover. But there is no fence or hedge to make this space into a private yard, where one may plant one's own flowers or enclose one's baby. (That type of retreat is left to the patio on the other side of the houses.) These vine-covered foregrounds, along with the broad central lawns and the parks, are all part of the general landscape picture. They are very attractive, very orderly, very harmonious, with pleasing variety, like the buildings that surround the courts.

Baldwin Hills is so satisfying to the eye, and to the soul, of the visitor, that I hesitate to suggest ways in which it might possibly be improved. But let us look at it from the point of view of the people who live in the houses. They are all enthusiastic about the patios because of the privacy they give them. A good many of them, I imagine, want more of this. So I propose that when we take the next step in the evolution of the Radburn Idea we might increase in depth the individual space in front of each house, at the expense of the central part of the green courts, and then hedge them in, just as at Radburn or at Greenbelt. Look at the pictures of these two places (Fig. 37 and Fig. 123) and see what pleasure the people get out of having their own little outdoor kingdoms. The actual ownership of the land is not, I believe, the thing that matters. The man with the beautiful flower garden at Greenbelt has as much love for it and pride in it as any one in the subdivisions to the north or south of Baldwin Hills Village. He has much use of it and pleasure out of it, and as much sense of it being his own.

The maintenance of these private yards by the tenants would be a great advantage to the management. It could mean a decided saving in landscape upkeep—which is an important item in an open green community. Greendale, where a large portion of the open spaces are in enclosed yards, as compared with the other Greenbelt Towns, showed the economic advantage of increased tenant maintenance. The costs chargeable to management for gardening were far lower. Greendale's experience seems also to answer the question of whether a tenant will care for his garden as would an owner. This they emphatically—and proudly—do.

I do not believe the hedging in of varied gardens need spoil the orderly urban sense of openness in the courts—the big harmonious picture. It would make the Village what we at first proposed to call it: *Thousand Gardens.*

Do not let this thought for the future lead you to think that my enthusiasm about Baldwin Hills Village is diminishing. I will leave it to a more disinterested as well as a better critic to evaluate its design. Lewis Mumford said of Baldwin Hills Village: 'Here every part of the design speaks the same robust vernacular: simple, direct, intelligible. I know of no other recent community that lends itself so fully to strict scrutiny, simply because every aspect of its physical development has been thought through.

'The site plan represents a further development of the Radburn Idea, made possible by the use of the row house, with the removal of the garage to the service road. One of the most important facts about this plan is its clarity and readability; the buildings all form a comprehensible whole, which can be taken in at a glance; the stranger is not puzzled or led astray by any mere jugglery of the structures for the sake of achieving specious aesthetic effects or pinchpenny economies. Such order is a vital attribute of a modern urban environment.'[38]

Form, Mass and Pattern

The general design of Baldwin Hills Village differs in various ways from the other developments; Sunnyside, Radburn, Chatham Village and the Greenbelt Towns.

Baldwin Hills has an organized unity of overall pattern; a more formal grouping that suggests the balanced treatment of the squares of eighteenth-century London or of the *Places* built by Stanislas in Nancy. This is in large part the result of its being conceived and built as a single related operation with adequate time for thorough study, simplification and integration of the varous parts. Sunnyside and Radburn or the other hand show the effect of a continuous process of development from year to year, in which the original conception persisted as guide, but the detailed grouping and relations of parts altered on the basis of experience and changing requirements. There was no complete

Fig. 150—View from the Baldwins Hills to the south, showing part of the western section of the village. This photo was taken in 1956. Note how the trees have grown since the early photos were taken.

Fig. 151—A ballgame on the village green.

Fig. 152—Plan and site of a garden court and garage courts.

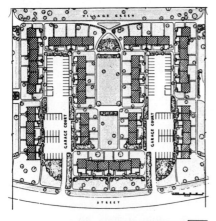

Fig. 153—Summertime in a garden court.

design of Sunnyside or Radburn at any time. They grew. The fundamental Sunnyside and Radburn Ideas were strong enough to unite them.

Chatham Village and Greenbelt's first development have much of the homogeneous architectural quality of Baldwin Hills, but in quite different ways. Greenbelt has more of the thorough, conscientiously studied simplicity of external treatment—perhaps slightly less polished—Chatham Village is more romantic. The hilly topography and the existing trees in both cases guided the architects in the location of buildings and dictated the picturesque variety of grouping. The almost flat site of Baldwin Hills on the other hand required that the over-all pattern be set entirely by the planners.

The architects in all three designs had the advantage of using row or terraced houses as the minimum unit. These are long enough and sufficiently varied in length to permit freedom of composition and adequate scale as part of the design of a large development. The typical American small free-standing dwelling is too spotty to count as a related part of a general picture. Radburn illustrates this in spite of continued architectural controls to preserve architectural unity. Most of the early free-standing houses were somewhat awkwardly cramped until the foliage had time to unite them by dominating them. It is true that the planners of Greendale composed some of their individual cottages so that they make interesting street pictures by contrasting one roof shape with the repetition of another form and by facing the structures on a gradually winding street. But even this type of design would be monotonous if it were not relieved by the long horizontals of the row houses.

Chatham Village and Baldwin Hills both illustrate excellent but dissimilar methods of composing long rows. The differences are the results of topography, climate, soil, external materials, and the local habits as well as taste, both of the architects and of the place and time. At Chatham Village the sloping land and its ultimate terracing suggested a more picturesque architecture and a more broken roof line. The desert-like soil of Los Angeles lacked the natural verdant background and foreground of the great old trees in the rich ground of Penn's ancient manor. The trees at Baldwin Hills, even after eight years, are mostly too small to be dominant. There are charming landscaped courts, some with spaced olive trees shading the gravel-covered spaces for walking and children's play. But it will be years before trees in the central parks or courts are large enough to form an important, rather than a minor, natural decorative element of the big composition. Local custom and economy in building material dictated brick walls, cast stone doorways, slate roofs, in Pittsburgh, contrasted with the painted stucco over wood frame predominant in Baldwin Hills. Climate—and particularly snow—required steeper sloping roofs at Chatham Village.

The shape of the land, the weather, local taste and habits, regional architectural customs — all played a part in forming the external design of Baldwin Hills Village. But the architect planners had unusual freedom of opportunity to fix form, mass and pattern. They set the borders of the project (the Baldwin Estate owned the surrounding land) and even determined the location and form of Coliseum Street. At their request the county moved the boundary of the city so that all the development might be within the Los Angeles municipality. There were no bisecting streets to prevent the free development of the 80-acre superblock, and each road and path was located where, in the architects' opinion, it would best serve firstly for convenience, secondly for good living, and thirdly for the beauty of the community.

The resulting design of Baldwin Hills Village is dominated by long restful horizontal lines and planes; long green courts paralleled by long low buildings. This horizontality is accentuated by the unbroken line of the delicate cornice and the deep shadow cast by its overhang, which is sometimes three feet wide. The horizontality is emphasized by the thin parallel line of porch and entrance roofs and the flat surface of balcony fronts (Fig. 165).

The forms of the buildings are all simple. There is no extraneous ornament or moldings. Adequate and rhythmic pattern is secured by means of the organization and grouping of the simple, straightforward essentials: windows, doors, balconies. There are contrasts in mass of different lengths of buildings consisting of two to six houses, and of heights of one and two stories. Additional variety comes from the different direction in which the structures run, resulting in varied play of light, shade and shadow. Add to this the contrasts of pastel coloring — bluish green, suede grey, dark tobacco brown, grey blue—and holding these together large masses of white, slightly greyed, reminiscent of the house rows of Denmark and Sweden. There is added diversity in the individual landscape treatment of different courts (Figs. 159 and 161).

In spite of the harmonious unity of its horizontal treatment Baldwin Hills is never monotonous. It has a simple, decided rhythm. The big composition, that follows the dominating line of the flat ground, is relieved by the contrast of the long curves of the brown hills that form a background.

There is no waste motion, no pretence about the design. It is straightforward and entirely serviceable (which word is used to replace that overworked term: functional). The individual house plans are integral parts of the community plan. They all open out to its expansive beauty; living-rooms and principal bedrooms face towards the greens, while kitchens, though convenient to the service side, open to the patios. In these houses and the surrounding open spaces it is easy to live the kind of life people in Southern California seek in the present time. This, it seems to me, makes the buildings contemporary architecture far more than could any veneer of stylized 'modern.'

The House Units

The individual houses are so integrated into the whole scheme that I have already told much about them in speaking of the Village plan. They are extraordinarily commodious for rental houses—far more so than is required by the building code or by the FHA which, in insuring the loans on most builders' housing, fixes minimum standards of space and quality; and of course minimum standards really become maximum attainment. The Baldwin Hills houses are far more spacious and better built and equipped than houses 'normally' approved.

The size and openness of the rooms can best be read in the plans (Figs. 156 and 157). Note that they are all unusually well supplied with storage space; every bedroom has either two closets or a long closet with double doors. There is additional storage room under stairs, in the rear of garages,

Fig. 154—The center green.

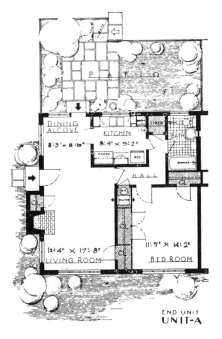

Fig. 155—Plan of Unit A.

BALDWIN HILLS VILLAGE

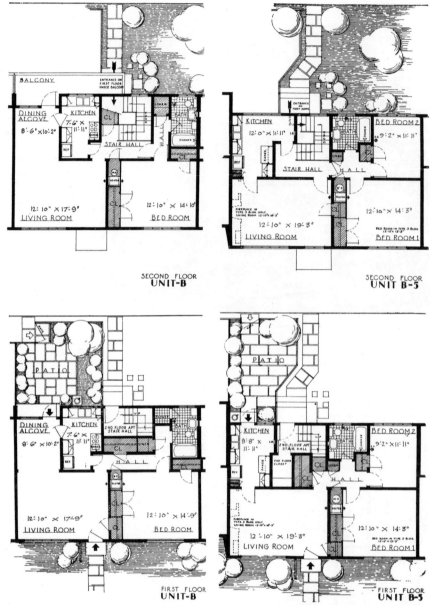

Fig. 156—Unit B is a two-family house. The entrance to the upper apartment is on the garden court, though family and many guests use the patio entrance. Unit B-5 has two bedrooms in each apartment. Note the large ground floor closet for the upper apartment at foot of stairs. Unit A (see Fig. 155) is of one story and used either at the end of a two-story row or as one of three attached bungalows. Gas-fired heater and water heater are centrally located in small closet. Bathrooms have electric heater. There are 55 one-story units.

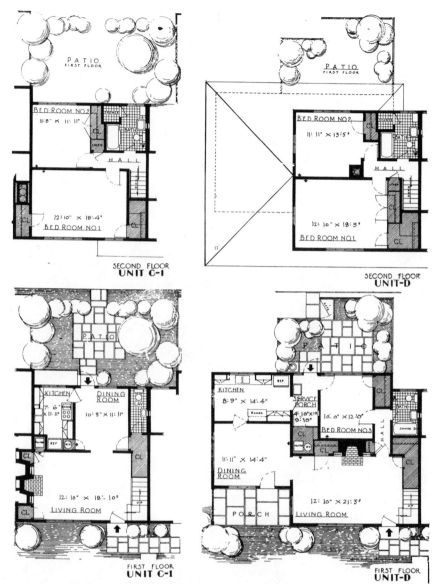

Fig. 157—Unit C-1 is a single-family two-story house. There are entrance doors on either side; thus circulation through living rooms is minimized. The ground-floor lavatory and bathrooms, with walls of ceramic tiles, have shower stalls as well as bath tubs. Unit D is the largest house. The ground-floor bedroom, with patio entrance, may be used for guests or servant. The dining room, with entrance from the porch, may be used as study, and the kitchen is large enough for children to dine. Doors of second-floor bedrooms are placed to allow varied arrangements of furniture and long closets. Dwellings of all kinds number 627. Of these, 55 are one-story bungalows, 216 are two-story houses, and 356 are flats in two-story units. There are dining-rooms in 356, dining alcoves in 143, and in 128 the family eat in the livingroom; there are 40 dwellings with 3 bedrooms, 312 with two, and 275 with one.

Fig. 158—A single-family house (Unit A) at the end of a row of two-family houses.

Fig. 159—Entrance side of row houses.

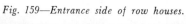

and elsewhere. There are wood-burning fireplaces in one-third of the homes. The bathrooms have tiled floors and wainscots and about two-thirds of them have additional separate shower stalls tiled to the ceilings. In the larger houses there are supplementary bathrooms or toilets on the ground floor. The floors are oak. Those on the lower stories are 3/16-inches parquet in mastic above full-floating slag foundations, with a membrane below the parquet.

There are three types of house: one-story bungalows—as the Californian calls them—fifty-five of them in groups of three or at the ends of rows of taller buildings; two-story houses—216 of them; and the flats, with one family above the other.

About half of these units have two bedrooms each and forty have three sleeping rooms. There are diningrooms in over half the units and dining alcoves in over a quarter, which means that only 128 families in houses or flats have to eat in a livingroom or, if they prefer, in the open on balcony or patio, or even in the convenient kitchen. Just a word about the kitchens. It is difficult to get visitors from abroad to go anywhere else—even out to see the green—when they discover the stainless steel drainboards, large divided sinks, and much cupboard space.

The flats, along with all the other units, are always full. They have many advantages over the typical two-family house. Each upstairs unit has its own entrance and private hall, distinctly separated from the tenant below. This entrance faces the garage court, which is the point at which almost everyone arrives. The ground-floor tenant can come in from either front. The upper-floor families all have large balconies—and in the future they are each promised their own patios.

In spite of all these advantages, I have a preference for single-family houses. This comes from our experience at Sunnyside, Radburn and elsewhere, where there was much dissatisfaction on the part of people on the lower floor who claimed to be disturbed by the movement or voices of people above. I do not know why tenants of apartment houses complain so much less about such annoyances; perhaps because they accept apartments at first as a temporary way of life, and then get accustomed to their annoyances and accept

Fig. 160—The entrance to an upper story apartment before the addition of the serpentine brick wall shown in Fig. 146.

them as part and parcel of urban living.

In trying to think of the exceptional ways in which Baldwin Hills might be improved the next time that type of development is projected, I would propose fewer — many fewer — families on the second floor. Two-story houses, similar to those at Chatham Village, might provide more suitable accommodation. An even better solution for Southern California might be to use a larger number of bungalows, which are customary and popular there.

GARAGES—which were built in rows for about ten cars—have end walls of shiplap, but no separation between stalls. They have floors of asphalt concrete, continuing the paving of driveways and motorcourts. In the back of each stall is a storage closet for the use of each tenant. As a whole these economically built garages have stood up very well. There was only one main criticism: that there were no doors in the beginning. The omission of these was one of the exceptional and unwise economies in a job that was unusually liberal in expenditures. As a result the experience of Greenbelt was repeated; the garages became one of the favorite play and hiding places for children—and both cars and children were in danger. But now at Baldwin Hills overhead doors have been installed in the greater part of the garages—with an additional rent charge.

The Architects

It is impossible to divide credit for Baldwin Hills Village among its architects. Lewis Wilson and his associates did a splendid job in connection with the conception and development of plans. Reginald D. Johnson, in his simple, delicate, but dignified designs, surpassed even the great mansions for which he is justly famous.

An indication that the architects approve of their own work is that most of them have lived in the village. The Alexanders brought up their children there, and he has his office in the shopping center. The Johnsons and Lewis Wilson have both for a time given up their large dwellings for the simpler life of the Village.

The Village as a Community

The general plan and the air view may suggest that the central axis is over-emphasized and out of harmony with the unpretentious urban quality of the rest. This apparent formal monumentality is more evident in the drawing or as viewed from the air than in reality. The individual on the ground sees only a small picture at a time, and he is not likely to observe the main axis, excepting in the relation of the two community buildings at either end of the charming formal garden court (Fig. 152).

The community group consists of the Administration Building and the Community Club. The former serves for contact between tenant and landlord. It is the center for information and complaints and for receiving packages. It was the telephone center for the Village, with extensions to houses from its large switchboard, during the war when direct wires could not be secured. The office also supplies maids on an hourly basis.

The Club House is used for various community activities. It consists of a great room some ninety feet long, that can be divided into three sections; also an adjoining kitchen, space for a darkroom, and a small lending library. There are weekly dances. Until just recently, when a church was built nearby, non-sectarian services were held there every Sunday morning. On weekdays it is used for parties, gatherings, committee meetings and general loafing. On its large terrace, shaded by awnings, badminton and other games are played.

A Child Center was originally designed to occupy what is now the Club House. But the little ones, to make room for their elders, have been located in two remodeled houses close by, containing room for thirty children. It has a spacious, well-equipped play space. Just outside, there is a large, wire-fenced enclosed play space with sandboxes, swings and other apparatus next to the nursery school (Fig. 149).

For little children who do not go to the Child Center there are a dozen or more small fenced and equipped play areas. These are generally placed just outside the ends of the enclosed motor courts, within sight, or at least hearing of mothers in their kitchens.

Convenient tennis courts are at either side of the Administration Building. Not far from the Village are public golf courses. There is also a 30-

acre public playground; but this is at the other side of two busy streets, La Brea Avenue and Rodeo Road.

A well-equipped playground for boys and girls of all ages, in easy safe walking distance, preferably within the superblock, is needed. This could be added now, possibly in the Western Central Park. It would be of great value even though it would have to be a little restricted in area. The next time it should be planned as an essential part of the development. Surrounding houses should be mainly those for families with children; though there should be some for old folks, as they like to be within sight of the activities of the younger members of a community.

The idea of devoting certain portions of the development to families with boisterous children— or any children for that matter—has been tried out at Baldwin Hills Village. Those without youngsters claim to have more peace and quiet as a result. This age zoning was the idea of the management; the architects did not plan for it. It would be wise to study carefully its success and the pros and cons of this kind of segregation, so that houses may be planned and grouped to meet special requirements —if this is found advisable.

A swimming pool is another addition that would probably have been very welcome at Baldwin Hills. The fact is, if I remember rightly, a swimming pool was suggested at one time, to be placed directly in front of the Community House. Los Angeles with its long warm season would be an ideal place for this. That a swimming pool makes a popular center for a community is vouched for by the experience of Radburn, Greenbelt and Greenhills. And they show that it can be run so as to pay its way. An adequate swimming pool might be difficult to add now—but the next time there should be one.

A wading pool was installed in front of the Village's Community House. For some reason it was decided that babies would not be safe in the pool. Now it is a flower garden (Fig. 154). I wonder if the pool was thought too small to make it worth while to have a guardian or some mother in charge when it is used. Experience elsewhere, at Hillside for instance, where a second one was later installed, is that these pools are extremely popular and need not be dangerous.

The Cost of Spacious Housing

Catherine Bauer wrote a splendid description and criticism of Baldwin Hills Village (for *Pencil Points,* September, 1944) which she speaks of as 'the most seriously progressive experiment in home building by private enterprise since Radburn, New Jersey, . . . probably the most spacious urban rental housing ever built in the United States . . .

'If Baldwin Hills Village is in many ways the most attractive, livable rental community in the country, how much does this extra degree of amenity cost? Some of it comes from good modern planning techniques, of course, and costs nothing but sense and sensibility on the part of the planner and entrepreneur. And cheap land facilitated great openness. But a lot of the attractiveness of the Village derives from standards of space, facilities, and equipment measurably higher than those in other large-scale housing, public or private.'

She then analyses and compares the costs of Baldwin Hills and the costs of subsidized public housing developments in the same city, Los Angeles, and built at about the same time. I am repeating here the analysis of Cost of Dwelling Unit, which I know has been carefully checked, as Catherine Bauer's facts and figures always are. Here is a condensation of some of her conclusions.

'All housing costs are subject to varied conditions dependent on time and place. And in the early 1940's other fluctuating conditions entered the picture which make any rigid comparison difficult if not impossible. Nevertheless the Los Angeles City Housing Authority, an efficient agency which employs good architects and has achieved about the highest local level of public housing quality in the country, did build a number of projects at about the same time as Baldwin Village. It may be worthwhile to set down a few figures on some of these projects next to the figures for the Village (see Table).

'The over-all cost per dwelling unit for Baldwin Village is $4911, and the average for the five public projects is $4385—11 per cent lower, or a difference of $526 per family. This is not a fair comparison, however, due to the high cost of central sites and slum clearance for three of the public projects . . . For a closer comparison it seems desirable to eliminate the land factor and also,

Project	Baldwin Hills Village	Pico Gardens	Aliso Village	Rose Hill Courts	Hacienda Village	Channel Heights	
Sponsorship	Private FHA Insured	Los Angeles City Housing Authority; mostly for war workers, but all 'permanent,' all but Channel Heights built under U.S. Housing Act.					Average Cost for Public Projects
No. Units	627	260	802	100	184	600	
Construction	Stucco, wood frame (ex. 9% masonry)	Stucco, wood frame	Some masonry; some stucco, wood frame	Stucco, wood frame	Wood, stucco wood frame	Wood, stucco, wood frame	
Families per gross acre	7	16	19	16	19	9	
Height	2 story some 1	2 story	2 and 3 story	1 and 2 story	1 story	1 and 2 story	
Rooms per unit	4.3 (FHA count)	5.2 (FPHA)	4.3 (FPHA)	4.4 (FPHA)	4.3 (FPHA)	4.2 (FPHA)	
Contract awarded	Feb. '41	Jan. '42	Feb. '42	Dec. '41	Nov. '41	May '42	
Completed[1]	Oct. '42	Aug. '42	Mar. '43	June '42	July '42	July '43	
COSTS: Land	$314	$1311[2]	$1022[2]	$796[2]	$279	$103	
Site impvmt.[3]	637	407	437	357	412	1163[4]	
Dwelling construction[5]	3730	2977	3441	2912	2704	2825	
Garages	138	none	none	none	none	none	
Community buildings	926	107	132	165	138	236	
TOTAL PHYSICAL COST PER UNIT	$4911	$4802	$5032	$4230	$3533	$4327	$4385
TOTAL EXCLUDING LAND	$4597	$3491	$4010	$3434	$3254	—	$3547[7]

COSTS PER DWELLING UNIT

NOTES: Figures include: Contractor's, architect's, engineer's fees; supervision. Excluded are carrying charges, pre-occupancy, administrative, or financial expenses. 1, occupancy often earlier. 2, including slum clearance. 3, including utilities and landscaping. 4, extremely rough site. 5, including equipment. 6, including administration, club and laundry buildings, but not dwellings now used for nursery school, etc. 7, excluding Channel Heights.

Fig. 161—Approach to a garden court from Coliseum Street.

Fig. 162—Looking across West Green.

because its peculiar site resulted in abnormal land development costs, to exclude Channel Heights entirely. Excluding land the cost per unit of Baldwin Village is $4597, and the average for the four public projects is $3547 . . . 23 per cent lower, or a difference of $1050 per family.

'No resounding generalizations should be drawn from these figures . . . But perhaps it would be reasonable to claim some evidence that, excluding the land and location factor, permanent community housing of "decent, safe, and sanitary" but minimum standards costs 20 to 25 per cent less than community housing of luxury standards in Los Angeles in the early 1940's. What does one get for this extra $1000?

'Landscaping and outdoor recreational and service areas much more highly developed than in public projects, and covering about twice as much open space per family;

'Garages; lawn sprinkler system; laundries with enclosed drying yards; enclosed playgrounds; athletic facilities;

'Private patios and balconies;

'Much larger rooms, particularly living-dining areas; luxurious storage space;

'Better heating and hot water systems, plumbing and electric installations;

'Oak floors, tile baths, stainless steel drainboards, Venetian blinds, etc.;

'Many fireplaces, some extra bathrooms.

'This is a lot . . . there is evidence that even 10 per cent more leeway in the costs and standards of "minimum" modern housing might bring a social return much greater than 10 per cent in more space, more amenity, more convenience.

'Perhaps the most significant single item is the cost of site improvements, landscaping, and utilities. The cost per unit for Baldwin Hills Village is $637, for the public projects (excluding Channel Heights) $403 . . . only $234 difference, although the Village has only half the density of population, and open space far more highly developed for varied use and beauty than do the public projects.'[39]

New Towns: 1766 and 1941

The closest historical parallel to Baldwin Hills Village is the New Town of Edinburgh, built in 1766 from the design of James Craig. Both layouts were reversals of the past planning practices of their city. The formal, balanced Georgian development of Edinburgh contrasted as sharply with the picturesque medieval congestion that herringboned from the High Street ridge as does the open orderliness of the Village, united around its expansive greens, differ from the repetitive monotony of the road-sliced subdivisions of Los Angeles.

Both developments were on open areas, unrestricted by existing streets and buildings — the planners worked out both patterns freely on clear, and approximately flat, land. The similarity in the size of the Edinburgh and the Los Angeles New Towns is remarkable—both are one thousand feet wide (Figs. 163 and 164).

The people for whom the developments were built were in each case united by social and family customs and taste, as well as by economic standards. The Scots were the prosperous burghers, in large part merchants, impressed with their own importance, who desired more spacious living, and greater opportunity for display and entertainment than was possible in the cramped quarters of the old town.

To Baldwin Hills Village came the typical mid-income Californians; lovers of informal life in the sunshine and open spaces, they sought freedom from care and worry for their children's safety, in spite of lack of servants to guard them.

In both cases land was in single united ownership; there was a definite clear conception of purpose, and the means of attaining the objective was fresh and new for its city; there was concentrated leadership; a unified design of which the whole development and each detailed unit all formed parts of a comprehensive picture, including the pattern of circulation and of open spaces. The street facades, from the massing and grouping of the building down to the last detail of windows, doors, projections, coloring and planting—all contributed to the unity of the single compositions.

The houses in both places were built according to standardized plans, and individualized by the variety of the family life and taste in interior decoration. They were constructed as a single or continuous operation. In all this the two developments closely paralleled each other.

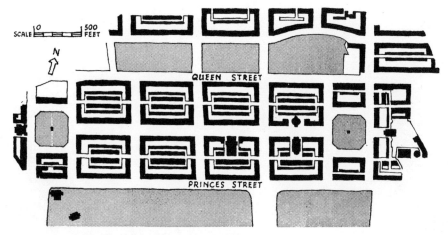

Fig. 163—Plan of first section of the New Town, Edinburgh. George Street in the center links the two squares.

Fig. 164—Plan of Baldwin Hills Village to the scale of the plan of New Town, Edinburgh.

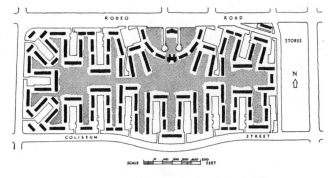

Fig. 165—Typical row of houses.

Fig. 166—Entrance side of row houses.

But here the similarity ends — and the much greater dissimilarity that grew out of time, place, climate, the way of life, and the status of technology differentiate the two.

Of the social and cultural life of Edinburgh in 1766 for which the New Town was created and which served as its stage, E. J. MacCrae says:[40]

'The keynote of society was elegance, whether in dress, the dance, social recreation or buildings and furniture. The tempo of life was the easy speed of horse-drawn vehicles. This was reflected in the dignified orderliness of society and the literature of the Golden Age. Naturally, the adjustments of life to the new were revolutionary in their social implications. In the characteristic words of Lord Cockburn, "It was the rise of the New Town that obliterated our old peculiarities with the greatest rapidity and effect. It not only changed our scenes and habits of life but, by the mere inundation of modern population, broke up and, as was then thought, vulgarized our prescriptive gentilities".'

Cold winds and mists, predominating most of the year in Edinburgh, gave emphasis to indoor life. The sunny temperate clime of Los Angeles invites outdoor living. This dictates closer contact between the inside and outside of the houses. As a result, clothing, homes and living are freer and more informal.

Let us now see how the two physical plans crystallized the differences of period, place and people.

The dominant framework of the New Town of 1766 is rigid straight avenues; that of Baldwin Hills is flowing parks. Edinburgh's George Street, a broad and imposing corridor connecting two formal squares, was intended primarily to be viewed from moving vehicles or by the man on horseback. Straight broad avenues facilitated movement of horse and coach, and offered a stage for display of this symbol of social or commercial standing. From the moving vehicle it is the perspective that counts; one wants orderly regularity, repetition, the horizontality of uniform roof and cornice lines, in short, regimentation. Finally, and at not too great a distance, the perspective of the corridor should terminate in points of interest, and so George Street leads to the tall dome of St. George's Church at one end beyond the green of Charlotte Square; at the other it approaches the graceful Excise House facing St. Andrew's Square.

The more leisurely, less tense rhythm of walking or loafing in the parks of Baldwin Hills calls for a greater variety and for a less rigid setting. Flowing paths; variety of width of open greens, of direction and length of building masses, of color and of planting; even the calm repose of long horizontal lines which unifies and gives repose to this variety is softened by the trees and the background of rolling hills.

There is one architecturally composed front to the Edinburgh houses, that on the avenues approached by the master's vehicle. The backs of the houses, for servants only, are of haphazard and unorganized design. At Baldwin Hills all sides are equally important. They are all approached by the tenants or their friends. So all facades were studied with similar care.

Edinburgh's New Town was built in the Grand Manner, which was best expressed by the Renaissance regal palace. This degree of external importance could only be attained by uniting groups of houses in a single external design. The style chosen was the graceful refined baroque, similar to that used by John Wood in Bath, and in the Squares of the Bedford Estate in London.

Life now in every way is more informal—and so is dress. As a result, so is architectural expression: patios and balconies for sunbathing; open green spaces close to the doors. Baldwin Hills is quite as orderly but the architectural composition is based on simple, more utilitarian motives such as windows, doors and balconies. Its stucco or brick exteriors, although by no means plebeian, are certainly less formal as well as less reminiscent than the typical Edinburgh stone facades.

Both developments were for communities of one class. But in Georgian Edinburgh that class was given distinction and supported in its luxury by many servants. Therefore it was possible to devote spacious halls and salons solely to entertainment and conspicuous display. These and the great stairways rising through many floors could be cared for by the many servants who inhabited the basements and attics.

This almost servantless age must be more economical of space and of labor. This means no nonessential space or projections to collect dust, fewer stairs, the same rooms for entertainment, generally informal, as for family use. The mother-cook in the kitchen must be where she can easily see and hear the children without devoting herself to their constant care. The lack of servants calls for few stories and closeness to the ground, and so does the informal Los Angeles life in the open. It is the unity of indoors and out that characterizes the California home life of today—the easy imperceptible flow from one to the other. And this is why the Radburn type of plan with its center of safe verdant openness fits so well the requirements of present-day Los Angeles.

Parks also form part of the New Town of Edinburgh. To the north and south are large open spaces that were landscaped as parks after the buildings were erected. The gardens to the north are enclosed for the use of the surrounding dwellings—but both are separated from the houses by busy streets—and so children must be guarded.

After almost two hundred years much of the monumental grandeur and beauty of George Street and its terminating squares, as well as Queen Street, still remain. But the invasions of commerce have destroyed the design of the Princes Street facades, and attacked the symmetry of the other street fronts. The plan was too static to bridge the change of two centuries. I wonder if the Baldwin Hills Village arrangement is flexible enough to weather the more rapid changes of the times in which we live. The fact that the buildings are cut off from the flow of traffic, and so are not likely to invite other than residential use, gives hope. The open spaciousness between buildings toward the greens offers opportunities for progressive and harmonious changes such as enclosed gardens,

organized or unequipped play spaces of varied kinds, and even a fairly large playground or a swimming pool. The greatest weakness is a certain incompleteness as a neighborhood. There should be a closer coordination between the residential superblock, its shopping center and its community facilities. This lack of adequate unity that requires an even larger, more comprehensive neighborhood plan and control is particularly apparent in the relation to the elementary school. If Baldwin Hills Village had been about twice its size it could have had a school located near its center. The architects had hoped that the land that climbed the hill south of Coliseum Street would be reserved for an addition that would have given the Village some 1250 families, and that the school and its playground might have been located on or near the center axis. But it was not to be. And so the children of the Village must risk their lives daily in crossing Rodeo Road, a busy highway.

If Baldwin Hills Village has not answered all of the physical problems of modern community development, it has found a saner and more progressive solution to certain basic difficulties in making city planning realistic and contemporary— of really making it work. We must recognize that to break all the chains that bind us to obsolete forms and procedures of past city building is a complicated task. We apparently must progress step by step. At Baldwin Hills Village the problem of co-ordinating full, direct, convenient service by automobile with spacious, peaceful, harmonious living came closer to solution than ever before. In its plan today's problems were frankly faced and answered both logically and beautifully. And so another step has been taken Toward New Towns for America.

INDICATIONS OF THE FORM OF THE FUTURE

This book has been called *Toward New Towns for America* because I have told the story of new communities at Sunnyside, Radburn, Chatham Village, Phipps Gardens, Hillside, Greenbelt, and Baldwin Hills Village primarily to see what could be found to help us in successfully conceiving, planning, constructing and operating New Towns. Although the developments described are not New Towns, they are steps toward creating New Towns. Each is limited but rich in suggestions. Note that I do not call them solutions. That is too final a word: at least they point the way. They contain many new ideas and are living experiences, not blue prints. I have reviewed them to see what might be regarded as warnings against errors, or might form the basis of future work.

Each of the developments has its own distinct individuality. Built in a period of twenty years of unprecedented technical progress, they are in different metropolitan areas, spread from the eastern to the western coast. The schemes differ in size and contain many types of residential buildings: apartments, row and free-standing houses. They have been constructed and operated by private corporations, foundations, or the Federal government for diverse income groups, and the dwellings have been for sale or rent.

In spite of these differences they are unified by common objectives, by the spirit in which these were pursued as well as by the three basic conceptions, the Garden City, the Radburn Idea, and the Neighborhood Unit, that served as guides in planning. Each heralds progress, some in one of the fields of organization, promotion, design, construction, or operation—some in another, but all are experiments leading toward New Towns.

Contemporary Towns

What do I mean by New Towns? Not merely that they are newly created. Many towns have been and are being built that are immediately obsolete and out-dated. They may have been fitted to an age long past; but they have nothing whatsoever to do with the life people now want to live, or would if they thought it were attainable.

New Towns are contemporary. This does not necessarily mean that they should have any particular type of 'New Look,' a different architectural style or veneer. By contemporary I mean towns that are planned, built, and operated to serve present day needs and conditions. During the past half-century or more we have rushed through history as never before. As a result our requirements for living, here and now, are utterly different from those met by the cities in which most of us live. This is apparent if we consider only a few of the main requirements of the period which New Towns are to serve:

1. *Increasing Leisure Time* means a shorter working day, and more hours for recreation. It allows evenings on playgrounds, in swimming pools, and loafing on the green, or for community affairs, lectures, clubs, and workshops. Free Saturdays as well as Sundays offer opportunities for hiking on a green belt, for long excursions, for keeping house and garden spic and span.

2. *Increasing Equality of Opportunity* to enjoy the goods of the world is available to an ever-larger proportion of American workers, together with some form of insurance schemes for unemployment, health, and old age. Sanitary and mechanical facilities are becoming standard equipment in the homes of those with moderate incomes and—thanks to public housing—even in those of the poor. Bathrooms, central heating, mechanical refrigerators, and even television are becoming universal. Community facilities, such as schools, cinema, outdoor and indoor recreation, libraries, are fundamentally the same for employer and employee, and for all groups. The opportunity for a good life is con-

stantly broadening. What is needed is a better community setting and organization, and it is these which New Towns can provide.

3. *Mechanization.* The form and organization of our New Towns will to a large degree determine whether the machine shall serve, command or destroy our civilization.

4. *Disappearing Domestic Service.* In comparing Baldwin Hills Village and the 18th century New Town of Edinburgh (see pp. 212-216), I indicated how the lack of servants was leading to simplification of planning and an organization of house and community pattern that would lighten the mother's care of home and children. Nursery schools are only a first step toward organized or associated care of little ones to allow more freedom for parents. Central kitchens and laundries are a few of the indications of increasing simplification through mechanization or organization to replace the maids and cooks of yesteryear.

The Present Period of Growth and Change— technical, social, economic and political—is unprecedented. It is leading, through changing phases, to a different and, we hope, more stable economy. It demands new town forms and environment, a new stage and direction—and the possibility of revising the setting to keep in harmony with the changing show.

From Obsolete Cities to New Towns

To serve the evolving culture and civilization of which I have mentioned only a few principal characteristics, New Towns are essential. This is because the existing cities cannot fit the needs of this age without a complete rebuilding. It is not merely that the elements and the details of plan and mass urgently require new forms, but that the relation of these to each other, must be radically revised. For this, one must begin with a clean slate and a large one. Therefore it seems to me that the sane policy is first to direct our energy toward building new and complete communities from the ground up: that is to say on open land outside developed urban areas. This we should do until such time as we have adequately demonstrated, by contrast, how unworkable and wasteful are the obsolete patterns of the old cities, and how completely they demand replacement. It is futile to

attempt this in a small, piecemeal manner. Meanwhile, where attempts are made to redevelop our old cities it must be on an adequate scale to form New Towns or at least modern neighborhoods within the old cities, but to a pattern far different from the old. Each redevelopment project should be a further exploration of the new patterns that we have, at least in part, evolved through our trials and demonstrations, from Radburn to Baldwin Hills Village. Redevelopment will be useless unless each scheme is part of a coordinated process that will ultimately make the old cities into New Cities— modern cities.

Here are some of the basic evils and limitations of the old cities which New Towns and worthwhile redevelopment of existing urban areas must eliminate:

Dangers to Health and Life: The strained nerves, tension, physical disabilities, declining birthrate, breakdown, and madness, resulting from 'normal' urban life. Death at every street crossing perpetually haunting parents. Sunless, insanitary, filthy, congested slums spreading blight throughout the towns. The constant threat of catastrophic breakdown of water, food, fuel, machines, movement, all dependent on long tenuous supply lines, is ever present and horribly intensified by the menace of atomic war.

Congestion: Life and movement is imprisoned by gridiron streets forming an archaic pattern within which houses, factories, shops, and offices are crammed. Sunlight and breezes are blocked; privacy and effective working conditions are lacking. Buses and subways are packed tight with human indignity; 100 m.p.h. machines crawl snail-like as traffic is congealed.

Loneliness: Man is submerged in the colossal human swarm, his individuality overwhelmed, his personality negated, his essential dignity is lost in crowds without a sense of community.

Lack of Nature: In the canyons of the city, nature is obliterated by the hard masonry. Man is lost in the stony urban desert, with increasing distances between him and his natural abode of fields and woods, free-flowing breezes, and the sight of sky, sea, mountains, and wilderness.

Waste of Time, Money, Energy: In the city people are always going somewhere instead of doing things. The everlasting journeys to work and to play consume the hours and wealth that should go into productive, worthwhile, enjoyable occupations. The growing costliness of great cities absorbs an ever-larger share of the incomes of individuals and municipalities.

Ugliness: Monotony is produced by the endless repetition of similar rectangular blocks and the decaying wreckage of past disorder. Vision is limited by confining ugly walls. There is monotonous regimentation, smoke, and dirt.

The grave faults of the obsolete urban environment inevitably lead one to seek physical patterns more in harmony with present-day culture. The developments described in the preceding chapters have been proving grounds, and partial demonstrations of the evolving form of the future, in which:

Safety will take the place of danger when pedestrian and automobile traffic are entirely separated by the use of properly designed superblocks and specialized means of circulation throughout our cities.

Spaciousness will banish congestion when an orderly relationship is established amongst circulation, buildings, and open spaces, including open greenbelts and expansive block centers.

Nature will dominate, and all cities will be green cities, with parks in the heart of each block and encircling belts of agriculture, natural playgrounds and wilderness. Man's desire for a good life and his love of nature will determine the form of the town.

The Neighborhood, which will have a limited area and a central meeting place, will provide a setting for neighborly friendship and co-operative participation in common activities.

Beauty will be derived from the composition of building groups, their color and texture, and their relation to each other and to nature.

Economy of money, time, and energy will permit creative and recreative leisure activity and will come from:
1. Efficient planning for use, in place of speculative sale.
2. Large scale building and operation.
3. More efficient government and community organization, made possible by a well designed town of limited size.
4. The related location of homes, community facilities and work places to facilitate safe convenient walking and bicycling.
5. The decrease in the journey to work and other unproductive travel. (Over 10 per cent of America's consumption expenditure is for transportation, much of which would be unnecessary if industry and business were located within convenient distance of workers' homes.) [41]

In the distribution of industry in relation to living quarters we have made little progress. Solutions are to be found not only in terms of individual Garden Cities but also in regional constellations of varied types of New Towns set in a broad background of agricultural land and regional parks.

A Different Technique

New Towns mean new plans and different physical arrangements, with green belts and inner block parks, neighborhoods and superblocks, community centers, and the separation of roads and walks. These modern urban forms are bound to replace the obsolete, socially repellent, barren real-estate gamblers' checkerboard. But communities fitted to the life of today—and fit to live in now—will neither come into being nor have any lasting existence merely because the plan is modern. Creating New Towns implies more than designing new forms. A new technique is required, and this will involve a different procedure all the way from raw land to the neighborhood built and lived in.

The New Town technique must differ from the customary process of city growth in every element: its promotion and organization for development, its design, its construction, its marketing and its operation. It even requires another kind of legislative background and different ownership or control—at least control of land if not of building. These differences grow out of a fundamental contrast in objectives. The purposes of New Towns are basically opposed to the influences responsible for the growth of our old cities.

THE OBJECTIVE of New Towns is fundamentally social rather than commercial. Bluntly, the distinction is that between building for people or building for profit. Whereas the customary motive is primarily that of trade in real estate in whatever form and manner is most profitable, New Towns will be created for use as communities, vital and contemporary, to encourage and foster present-day good living.

THE PROMOTER creating New Towns or communities must differ in his methods and procedure from the speculator. Quick profit requires rapid sale, whether it be in the subdivider's lots or the promoter-builder's houses. This is a game made for irresponsible traders. For long-time investment quite a different type of promotion is essential. This demands large-scale finance for a long period. It is the field for limited dividend corporations, for companies with large capital to invest such as insurance companies and foundations. It is likely to be increasingly carried out by co-operatives and unions. It is more and more bound to be an activity of government, either as principal or as assistant, of co-operative or private group endeavor.

This type of promotion brings no quick profits as does the speculators'. But as in the cases of Hillside and Chatham Village, where the homes were on a rental basis, it has already proved a very sound investment. They both paid their way, amortized their capital costs and paid regular dividends. Because they are for lasting investment they were built soundly and spaciously planned, as communities, so that they would remain full of satisfied tenants—and they do. Under an economy illustrated by the valleys as well as hills pictured in the graph at the beginning of this volume, it seems the only way to make housing and New Town building a safe and sound investment (Fig. 1).

The New Town promoter naturally tends to be progressive: his purpose is to serve the public, to demonstrate a finer and more fitting background for community and family life. He and his architect and builder, and the other technicians, because they are in search of new and better ways of planning, constructing, and operating, do work that is both imaginative and scientific. They are pioneering. Not so the speculative builder. He takes the minimum risk and plays safe: that is the easiest way to get a loan. As a result his plans, exteriors, even the relation of his houses to each other and to their surroundings, are dull and conservative. They are just as near as possible like something

that has already been done. He repeats even his own past blunders. And so his products are, as likely as not, conventional and nearly always obsolescent before they are occupied.

BUILDING, both in its character and in its quality, is largely determined by its objective. The New Town investor counts costs on a long-term basis. The yearly expenses of operation and maintenance are more important to him than the original capital investment. So he constructs soundly. At Hillside the buildings were fireproof throughout, instead of the less expensive semi-fireproof the law permitted —and yet the annual cost, that is, the carrying charges on the investment, was decreased as the loan charges on the safer construction were less and for a longer term. At Chatham Village wood was eliminated as far as possible from exteriors because brick required less care.

Keeping all buildings full during depressions, as well as in periods of housing scarcity, is essential to moderate rental housing. No vacancies, no bad debts, over the period of years in which the original investment is paid off, more than balance higher original costs for sound construction, spacious greens and gardens, as Hillside, Chatham Village and Phipps so well testify. At Baldwin Hills Village the large rooms, the many closets, the well-equipped kitchens and bathrooms not only spell good living but sound investment. In short, in New Town building the time factor is the prime consideration in counting costs.

This is not so in speculative building. The only time that interests the speculative builder is the short period between securing his mortgage and unloading his product. The speculator is more likely to put his money in gadgets, in advertisements, selling force and ballyhoo than in sound lasting qualities or in livability or neighborhood features. There are exceptional speculative builders such as the builders of Levittown, but most of them give no more in size and quality than the scant requirements for FHA insurance.

City Planning New and Old

To build a substantial setting for neighborhood and family life, rather than to control and regulate, requires a completely different kind of planning. That is why I intend to call it community development or *New Town Planning* to differentiate it from the procedure that is generally called city planning in America. There is actually an antithesis between the two procedures. The prime objective of one is to assist in the marketing and protection of property, of the other to create communities. The latter deals with the realities of living rather than with trading. The two are at cross-purposes: preserve and protect in contrast with devise and produce.

New Town planning is an integral part of a co-ordinated procedure for building communities that will be both contemporary and dynamic. Note:

CO-ORDINATED, not disorganized
BUILDING, not delineating
COMMUNITIES, not lots or streets
CONTEMPORARY, not obsolete
DYNAMIC, not static.

New Town planning is not a separate function; it is an integral part of a procedure that creates a complete, solid, living community. It is an essential link in the chain of related and interdependent processes that actually turn open country land into complete, vibrant towns—good places to live in.

City planning is too often an afterthought; in other words it is no more than city patching. It is not the work of a creator, but of a surgeon called in too late to operate on a decaying carcass. Such city patching deals with *means* rather than ends. It creates superhighways, supercomplicated intersections or other gargantuan minutiae while neglecting the causes and sources of congestion. Thus it often fans the flame instead of extinguishing the fire. It is so fully concerned with mechanical or engineering feats that it loses sight of the ultimate goal of planned development—better living.

The New Town planner requires a broad understanding of aims and objectives, and of all the related functions with which he must work to realize them. As his technical work is part of a larger process of creating a community background, that is to say of building, and not mapping or drawing, he must work as part of a team. That was one of the great and and inspiring features of the work of the City Housing Corporation under the leadership of Alexander M. Bing in building Sunnyside and Radburn—the teamwork of a group with such varied knowledge and ability as had Herbert

Emmerich, Louis Brownlow, Henry Wright, John O. Walker, Frederick L. Ackerman, Charles S. Ascher, Ralph Eberlin, Marjorie Cautley and myself.

The old type of city planning is merely one of a disorganized series of unrelated activities that produce chaotic cities, including land speculation, lot subdivision, skeleton highway plans, individual house plans, regulations, spotty location of public buildings, and ultimately rebuilding unrelated structures one after the other, when zoning inevitably surrenders to the greed of individual lot owners.

In all this the city planner plays but a minor role. It is not his detailed factual surveys, his traffic counts, his calculations of population growth, his clever graphs, his many colored diagrams of use and heights, nor his superbly presented reports that determine the ultimate form and substance of our cities. Look at the ugly, dangerous, irrational, chaotic messes we call cities: certainly these are not the result of a purposeful plan for good living or even for efficient industry and trade. The essential reality of these cities has not been conceived, devised, pre-determined.

This present kind of city planning does not deal with substantial realities; but with phantom cities, outlines of cities. It delineates bodiless skeletons instead of creating habitable, solid cities. Its subject is primarily a framework for saleable lots, not a community. It is concerned with separate and limited units: lots, individual houses, a single road, not community building. Because city planning outlines and regulates, and does not relate these units in a composed group or neighborhood, it must generalize. This requires stereotyped, conservative, easily classified, standardized objects; these are more easily marketed and regulated.

The present city form is not molded by the planner. It is the random consequence of the separate and unrelated decisions of subdivider, municipal engineer, zoning board, speculative builder, aided and abetted by the FHA and the lending institutions.

Finally, the shape and appearance of things, and the relation of the parts that make the chaotic accidents called cities, are the summation of the haphazard, independent whims of a multitude of individuals. They ultimately determine the pattern for living by filling in the cubby-holes marketed by the subdivider; and for the individual there seems to be no alternative.

To fill in the form, the body, the reality of the town, city planning proceeds not by positive action but by negations. It restricts and regulates, and limits use, height and bulk by zoning laws.

These regulations are usually commonplace generalizations. They result in monotonous similarity of use, height, coverage and outline of neighboring buildings. Predetermined related variety of mass, height, and a common pooling of open spaces is found in our cities only in such exceptional large-scale unified developments as Rockefeller Center. This kind of purposeful organized design that produces architectural and civic beauty as well as better lighting and ventilation is never attainable by the old highway-framework-subdivision process of city planning, even with the addition of the best-intentioned and most expert zoning. Nor can the special community facilities be grouped in a serviceable or attractive manner by this type of wishful negation.

The kind of city planning of which I have just spoken was not helpful in creating the communities described in these articles. It was foreign to their objectives: they would have been hampered, not aided, by its use. Experiments such as the Radburn Idea never could have been realized within the framework both legal and physical, that has circumscribed the city planners' thinking and activities. At Radburn we were able to work on a clear slate because we got there before the zoners and the subdividers and the municipal highway engineers. Their immovable framework would have held up progress there and, afterwards, at Chatham Village, the Greenbelt Towns and Baldwin Hills Village.

The full realization of the economic as well as the living advantages of the Radburn Plan cannot be attained by the ordinary piecemeal process of city planning for lot subdivision. It must be built in—houses, roads, walks, parks, gardens—and a definitely determined reality must be created that will fit a desired way of living long enough to pay off its capital, maintenance and operational costs. It must furthermore be arranged to allow the

changes required to keep it in harmony with this changing world.

To attain the economies that the Radburn type of planning officers, the gambling chance of increased monetary values of a lot must be given up. If the less costly types of specialized means of communication, such as the cul-de-sac at Radburn or garage court at Baldwin Hills Village, are to be used, there is little opportunity of finding a better paying future use for an individual piece of property, for example, for a commercial purpose. Therefore zoning would be only reiteration. The future use is more purposefully and lastingly set by group buildings than by regulations open to constant change.

The green inner core of the superblock is the cheapest as well as the most satisfactory way of securing nearby verdant openness. But the unusual location of the inner block commons requires an unusual form of community organization or of legal framework to maintain and organize it.

In creating New Towns, planning and building go hand in hand. They must be united as two inseparable parts of one process. Just as architecture is concerned with the solid realities of structures, so New Town planners must deal in terms of three-dimensional actuality. As city architect or civic designer he must mold form and mass as well as predetermine city plan or outline. A beautiful and livable urban environment requires a comprehensive design embracing the site, the form, the mass and the detail of every building and the relation of each building to the whole site and neighboring structures — in short all the visual surroundings.

Civic design is foreign to the methods of the old city planning. It cannot be clamped within the confines of lots or of the conventional gridiron. It requires the unified design of a portion of the city at least large enough to form a complete visual picture. This picture the New Town planner must paint on a broad canvas, a canvas large enough to comprise all that the human eye can envisage at a time. The developments which are illustrated in this book have done this in different ways. In every case the landscape and the structures have been blended into a unified composition, with great foregrounds of lawns and related verdure, and the mass and color of buildings composing pleasantly together and with this background. In Baldwin Hills Village the long horizontal lines of the houses contrast with the rounded slopes of the surrounding hills (Figs. 142-148); in Chatham Village the houses climb up the hills (Figs. 57, 61) and in Greenbelt the simple rows are arranged one above the other on the rising ground. In each one of them the great mass of spacious green around which they are set unifies and dominates the composition. At Radburn the broad lawns and spreading trees are the center of visual beauty just as they are the center of the community (See Figs. 17, 31, 38, 40). It is this spaciousness that is the keynote of the wholesome, good living of these places. And the comprehensive views of grouped buildings are dependent on the openness of the central greens, around which each one is composed in a different way. Even the greens of Sunnyside, in spite of the more restricted gridiron frame, give a natural charm and beauty to the simple rows of brick buildings (Fig. 12).

The contrast between the massing of open spaces at Baldwin Hills Village and the spotty, disorderly distribution in the typical lot unit development, with half the number of homes per acre, is apparent in the airview (Fig. 142). The spacious green inner park within the superblock, protected and insulated from auto traffic, has been applied only to limited neighborhood communities, as at Radburn, Greenbelt, and Baldwin Hills Village. It is still to be applied to a *city as a whole* (although Mayer and Whittlesey propose to do just that in the plan they are making for the New Capital City of East Punjab in India).

But it seems to me that the few examples in this book should indicate why and how the principles of New Towns should and can be applied to the planning and replanning of whole cities. So let me repeat, with somewhat greater emphasis on the City as a work of art, some of the reasons for the Radburn type of planning.

GOING PLACES and ENJOYING THE USE OF PLACES are quite distinct and different functions. What serves one is antagonistic to the other. Therefore a circulatory plan and a plan for a maximum practical and aesthetic use of the building and spaces of a city must be kept separate.

The same forms or means cannot serve the two at one time or at one place. Although they complement each other, they require different locations and forms, diametrically contrary in use. To coordinate these two is a basic problem of contemporary planned city development. That is the purpose of the Radburn type of plan.

CIVIC DESIGN for inspiring delight, and CITY TRAFFIC PLANNING for safe, easy, quick flow of modern traffic must be harmonized if a modern city is to be completely practical for circulation and use, and at the same time, full of beauty. Although these are by nature antagonistic, they must be integrated into a practical beauty. They will cripple or destroy each other unless they are functionally and spaciously separated and at the same time mutually serve each other.

Let us examine and compare the requirements of City Traffic Planning and Civic Design.

A CITY TRAFFIC PLAN requires for speed, safety and maximum steady flow:

1. Straight roads or long sweeps with clear visibility at crossings and of approaching traffic.
2. As few crossings as possible.
3. No access to or from buildings on primary roads.
4. Minimum visual distraction—the auto driver's attention should be kept on the road.

The objective of such planning is to allow vehicles to move from one place to another as safely, quickly, directly and easily as possible.

CIVIC DESIGN, on the other hand, deals with the presentation of a city's buildings and open spaces so that they give the greatest pleasure and enjoyment. That each individual building should have beauty of form, mass and color is not sufficient.

The display of a building as part of civic design has much in common with display of the treasures in a well-designed museum. Buildings, like art objects, must be placed so that they will be observed, examined, appreciated and enjoyed. This is impossible in a formal monumental museum and equally so in a gridiron-patterned city.

The automobile has made obsolete the classical monumental type of city plan, dominated by highway axes leading from one important structure to

INDICATIONS OF THE FORM OF THE FUTURE

another. Terminal vistas are not for the auto driver; he has not time to enjoy them while keeping on the move; and even if he did, his attention should not be distracted. In Edinburgh's Georgian 'New Town' the man on horseback, or in a horse-drawn carriage, had an opportunity to observe and enjoy the street composition while approaching its terminal of church, monuments or government building. This met the requirements of the Eighteenth Century. But it is meaningless in a Twentieth-Century city. Vistas of dominant buildings there should be for leisurely enjoyment. Therefore they should face parks or public places from which vehicular traffic is excluded.

Even less appropriate to the needs of a contemporary New Town than the Worlds' Fair kind of city plan is the typical gridiron plan, in which all buildings are filed away in cubby-holes at either side of a highway, so that one passes them by no matter how significant they may be. The architectural masterpieces might as well not exist for any citizen or visitor of a gridiron-planned city. He passes good and bad alike, with merely a hasty glance to right or left. His mind and eye are on the traffic and the distant perspective. He is going somewhere—he has neither the time nor the desire for visual enjoyment. Before him, if he is in an automobile, he sees and observes only flashing green and red lights, traffic police and congested highway. If he is on foot his attention is concentrated on the danger of street crossings, while he battles with the crowds. A striking group of buildings or a monument terminating a busy highway would be wasted on either pedestrian or driver. But in the typical gridiron city neither walker nor motorist approaches a building or an architectural group of structures in an attractive setting. If he did see them the composition, no matter how attractive, would be lost on him. His attention is elsewhere. He is not in the spirit for beauty, grandeur, inspiration.

The setting in which interesting buildings or groups of buildings are to be viewed must be separated from the massed flow of machines or people. It is not enough for one to give them a passing glance and be momentarily attracted, one must remain long enough for the beauty to become part of one's consciousness. This is not possible in the midst of rushing activity. Peaceful surroundings, away from the movement and uproar of the streets, is the proper setting for civic design. Here buildings can be enjoyed in relation to open places or in natural surroundings, across water or gardens. One should be able to remain long and comfortably to discover varied beauties, as the light changes. One should approach the great monument or group reverently, slowly, by foot. And there should be several approaches, so that one can see it at various angles, in different compositions of landscape and architecture.

Dynamic Cities

A new town must remain contemporary for a very long period. Only thus can we afford it. It must last long enough to allow its original cost to be amortized. That on the face of it may seem impossible, for the main characteristic of the present time is change—change in our way of living, in our thinking, even our objectives; and above all in our technical facilities and ability to make changes.

New Towns must not only be the flowering of today's life and civilization, but they must have in them the seed of the future—or at least the facility of growing and changing to fit it. They must be dynamic. Therefore our New Towns, if they are not quickly to become our Old Towns, must be flexible. We must plan so as to limit the difficulties we now face in the redevelopment of our old cities, which require extravagant destruction and the rebuilding of vast areas.

To make this possible we need:

1. A community of completely integrated neighborhoods.
2. A minimum original investment in buildings or equipment which are costly to alter or replace.
3. Plentiful open space in which the community form and pattern can be set and developed.

The cause of blight in the old sections of cities is due largely to the fact that they were built not as the living-working place of an interrelated, interdependent community, but as a conglomeration of crowded, unrelated units or cells. These are so packed together that there is no room for the individual house or workplace to stretch, expand or change. There is no space in which the community form or pattern can be modified or reorganized without complete destruction.

If revision to meet gradual and continuous change is not to be wastefully extravagant, we need the smallest possible investment in big buildings with complicated mechanical equipment and therefore high first costs. It is practically impossible to amortize such investment in either skyscraper office or residential buildings before they are functionally obsolete, or before the congestion they foster blocks city transit and transportation and makes their servicing and use unbearably slow and costly.

Large sections of New York are now being rebuilt with massed, regimented apartment houses, both by the Municipal Housing Authority and by large insurance companies. This tendency is being followed in various other cities in America and even in Europe. Here the basic living requirement of easy access to adequate natural green surroundings is neglected. If the life of these buildings were figured less on the basis of structural and more on that of social obsolescence in a changing world, I think the policy would be different.

Spacious planning with large areas left open for future change is the surest method of preparing for flexible growth. That is one of the principal advantages of Green Cities, with great open space surrounding them as greenbelts and in the centers of superblocks. There is room for change and for the growth of present requirements without complete destruction and rebuilding.

Many elements of the existing communities tend to grow and to demand more space, without having adequate room for expansion. The present trend to build one-story schools is an example. The increased acreage needs of play spaces for all ages is another. Additional community requirements, such as Health Centers, Nursery Schools, Youth Centers, are continually being recognized. As these new functions develop and need buildings, there should be room to place them in proper relation to other elements of the Neighborhood or District Center. Flexibility calls for, above all else, space—more space than is needed to compass the original requirements.

Parking space for motor cars is the type of unforeseen change that requires flexible spaciousness.

We now know that we must have immense parking space—far more than for building—if we are not to tie up all movement by filling our highways with parked cars. Yet old habits persist and many housing developments are still built with scant room for parking one car per family and no space for garaging.

These changes we have already seen. Others are sure to follow—for instance in transportation. If individual air traffic by helicopter or other means should replace or at least surpass the use of the automobile some day, nearby open areas either surrounding a town or neighborhood as green belts or in the middle of a superblock can be used advantageously to keep these towns contemporary.

The Basis of New Town Planning

THE UNIT OF DESIGN in New Towns is no longer each separate lot, street or building; it is a whole community; a co-ordinated entity. This means that the framework of the community and every detail down to the last house and the view from the windows must be conceived, planned and built as a related part of a great setting for convenient, wholesome, and beautiful contemporary living and working. In this way every house gains from its relation to the buildings around it. Beauty as well as convenience is produced by the rational relationship of the individual parts.

The planning of every house and every room in that house is part of the process which gives the superblock its ultimate shape and character. Thus, the size and specific requirements of inner green and private yard, of cul-de-sac or auto court, help mold the superblock in relation to good living in home, community and town.

As he designs, the New Town planner envisages the future home life of the individual and the family, and their life as part of the community. He sees it not only in terms of house and garden but in the grouping of houses in relation to each other so as to take the utmost advantage of sun and wind for every residence, and to open up pleasant, spacious and varied views from every house and, as far as possible, in every direction. He will in part be guided by the form and nature of the land, and how its trees and streams and rocks can best be used or preserved for the common use and enjoyment of the people who are going to form the community, and whose life, from birth to old age, will be molded by the place.

New Town planning deals with the fundamental realities of living in a contemporary community, and, since we cannot foresee tomorrow's needs, it must take the future into account and allow for flexibility. The town plan must be molded to the life people wish to lead, and to fit the special needs of this twentieth century with all its differences— mechanical and other—from the past. The form of the home and its surroundings and the whole city must fulfil the requirements and aspirations of those who are to live in them. What these needs and aspirations are the planner cannot learn from most books—certainly not from technical works that deal with merely spiritless forms. He generally cannot determine them by surveys of existing conditions and of past performance. That is more often the way to find out what not to do, because so much of the present-day form, structure, equipment and practice is outdated and obsolete, and unrelated to the needs of the day.

The planner cannot discover the needs of people merely by asking them what kinds of home and town or community they want to live in. They do not know beyond their experience. However, with their assistance—not their guidance—he must discover their requirements. He must explore patiently, realistically, imaginatively. He should live in the places he helps to create, as Raymond Unwin did at Hampstead Garden Suburb and Henry Wright did at Sunnyside and Radburn. If he does not become an active part of the community he should know the people and managers and storekeepers. He should visit them often and come to see the life there both through their eyes and his own. That is what I have tried to do, so that I might progress from one experience and experiment to the next, on the basis of the realities of living communities.

The guiding motive for the New Town planner in molding the whole and its part is this: he is creating a stage, a theater for the good life. Yes, the planner's work is in many ways surprisingly like that of the skilled scenic designer. Lee Simonson, who was trained as a painter, at first designed his sets as pictures that would surprise and delight the audience and draw their first applause. But, he has told me, he soon found that did not serve the need throughout the play: the actors did not seem to fit into the place. So he carefully studied the text. In his mind's eye he followed each character as he would enter, move, stand and relate himself to other actors. He saw the life of the play, and as he followed this *it* set the stage; it determined the location of every door and piece of furniture. The shape of stage-set and the background became inevitable. The rest was easy.

That is just what the good planner does. He creates a setting in which people—the kind of people that will live there—will fit, where they will live a varied life, a convenient life, a beautiful life; where they will grow and change, and their surroundings can also change with them. The planner's subject, then, is man. It is his fellows and their reaction to their environment which he must study and understand.

I do not mean to suggest that taste and imagination and a feeling for good and great design in form and color are not essential requirements of community planner and architect. But they are not enough. New Town planning as well as architecture is an art, a great art, but it differs fundamentally from painting. The resulting work is not merely a form or pattern that the artist evolves out of his inner consciousness and projects on the canvas. Community planning starts not with aesthetic conception but with exploration, discovery, unveiling. It facilitates growth and leaves a record of human ideals and purposes that may last beyond its time.

THE SPIRIT in which the communities illustrated in this book were conceived, planned, developed, and in which most of them were operated, was that of exploration. From the days of Sunnyside to those of Baldwin Hills Village we have been in search of new or revised solutions of the setting for communities as well as for family and individual living. We have sought ways of bringing peaceful life in spacious green surroundings to ordinary people in this mechanical age. We have tried to simplify the complexity of needs and desire as contrasted with means, and thus to make changes, from the obsolete methods of the dead past, economically feasible.

Investigation and research has been an important

guide in our progress. In this the economic study always paralleled the social or architectural, as illustrated by my studies for the Resettlement Administration and Henry Wright's analysis of building operations at Sunnyside.

It has been my experience that one can never accept a planning or architectural solution as final. Every problem seems to require fresh analysis, a new approach, a different angle. As soon as an idea has become formalized into a rule of procedure, and as soon as designers give up the adventurous search, the solution used in the past seems to dry up and lose its quality and clarity.

Perhaps this tendency for ideas, that have bloomed, flowered and been accepted, to wither and petrify when given administrative sanction, has led me to be suspicious of all accepted formulas, even when I have sown the seed from which they grew. When an idea becomes conventional it is time to think it through again. Never-ending exploration and the charting of new ways is the life-force of the architect and the New Town planner, whose shield of battle should bear the simple device —a question mark.

APPENDIX

The Appendix includes some of the Reports which formed a series prepared for the Resettlement Administration in 1935 while the Greenbelt Towns were being planned. The Reports are described on pages 121-2 and are referred to throughout the article on Greenbelt. They dealt with:

Appraisal of plans

Studies of the relative improvement costs of various schemes of house grouping

> *Appraisal of group plans: relative cost of improvements of various schemes of house grouping*
>
> *Outline of specification used for estimating purposes*
>
> *Details of schemes*

Studies of relative cost of construction and improvements of various schemes of house grouping

> *Brief outline specification for houses (omitted here)*
>
> *Relative cost of construction of various schemes of house grouping*

Studies of operation-maintenance costs in Suburban Resettlement Communities

Operation-maintenance costs of local government and community activity

> *Operation-maintenance costs of houses*
>
> *Shopping centers*
>
> *Analysis of family budgets*
>
> *Rents, amortization charges and interest*

Parts of some of the above appear in the text and therefore are not repeated in the appendix: These include; *Shopping centers*, pp. 162-3, 164-6; *Analysis of family budgets*, p. 163; *Studies of operation-maintenance costs of local government and community activity in Suburban Resettlement communities*, pp. 168-9, 174.

The purpose of the studies was to indicate a broad and practical method of approach to the inter-related problems of social, economic and physical planning. It was felt that they were needed because the conception and design of a complete town to be built quickly were new subjects to most of the technicians involved. Previously they had been dealing with unrelated parts of a process: the architects with individual buildings, the city planners with the mapping of streets, zoning and restrictions. The effective relationship of buildings to each other and to the community had hardly been considered.

Many of the controlling factors have changed since the Reports were made. To give examples; the value of the dollar has decreased and specifications have in some ways changed as have size and character of equipment. Again, experience has since taught me that plans should be more spacious in many ways.

Therefore, the diagrams and tables are included to illustrate a method of approach rather than to be copied or slavishly followed. Both Gordon Stephenson and I felt the method is of importance and that the material is of value if it suggests a comprehensive and practical approach to the planning of community development.

The last two tables, page 243, give the comparative costs of the *lane* in relative values and not in dollars and cents. In general terms both apply to present day conditions despite the fact that the cost of all operations has greatly increased in the last fifteen years and, as a consequence, money values are different.

Some of the Reports made for the Resettlement Administration

and contained in Memoranda to John S. Lansill

APPRAISAL OF PLANS

The considerations in appraising plans, in order of importance, are:—

1. Standard of living offered.
2. Operation-maintenance cost.
3. Capital cost.

Method of Appraising Standard of Living Offered

As a measuring stick, set up plans of adequate minimum space and equipment requirements for various functions connected with living in house. These will consist of kitchen, bathroom, stairs, dining and living space, bedroom for one or two persons, space for heating and storage.

Consider relation of units, i.e. rooms to each other for purposes of spacious family living, individual privacy, light, ventilation, sanitation, cleanliness (convenience in cleaning and protection from vermin).

These should be considered for varied sizes of families and varied types of families to be served on the basis of:—

1. Their habits of living.
2. Better habits that they might find desirable, or at least acceptable.
3. Their economic ability to pay for the operation-maintenance and furnishings of the required space and equipment.

Method of Appraising Operation-Maintenance Cost

Make tentative house plans and grouping of houses that will fulfil standard of living requirements at minimum cost. All increase in space, equipment, and structural standards beyond these must be justified in terms of cost.

In considering cost, operation-maintenance cost should be considered first.

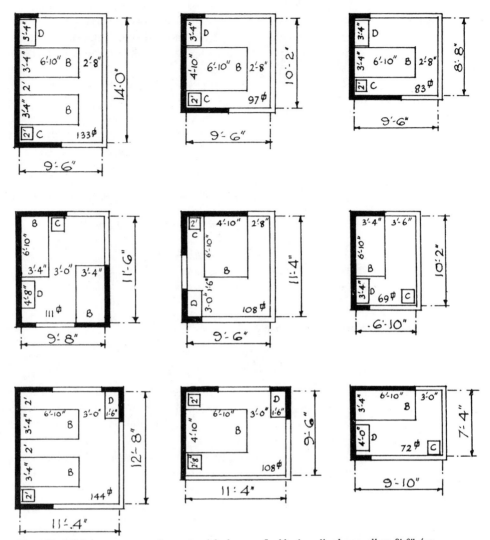

Fig. 167—Minimum space requirements of bedrooms. In blank walls shown allow 3'-0" for entrance door, 2'-6" for closet door, and space for windows. Add 6" to size of room where radiators and visers occur.

Operation-maintenance measuring stick must be cost of each factor of operation-maintenance of a given size and type of house grouped in a specified manner and of a specified type of construction.

In considering each proposed plan, measure the effect of change from standard of heating, painting, repairs, etc. as a result of:—

1. Change in size.
2. Increase or decrease of exterior wall.
3. Change in specifications.

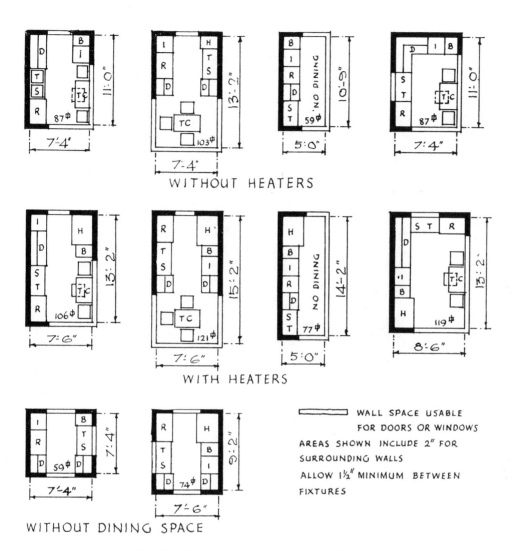

WALL SPACE USABLE FOR DOORS OR WINDOWS

AREAS SHOWN INCLUDE 2" FOR SURROUNDING WALLS

ALLOW 1½" MINIMUM BETWEEN FIXTURES

Fig. 168—Minimum space requirements of kitchens.

D	Dresser	2′ 0″ × 4′ 0″	L	H	Heater	2′ 6″ × 3′ 6″ W
B	Brooms	1′ 10″ × 1′ 4″ W		T	Tub	1′ 10″ × 3′ 6″
I	Refrigerator	2′ 0″ × 2′ 0″		S	Sink	
R {	Range	2′ 0″ × 3′ 0″		TC {	Table	2′ 0″ × 3′ 0″
	Range	1′ 0″ × 1′ 10″			Chairs	1′ 6″ × 1′ 6″

4. Changes in equipment such as refrigeration, heating, etc.

5. Relation to other buildings (grouping as affecting utility and road costs as well as house costs).

6. Relation to ground (site planning).

APPENDIX

METHOD OF APPRAISING CAPITAL COST

Capital cost should be measured by comparison of breakdown of all costs of each proposed plan as compared with the tentative plans. This must consist not only of the cost of all material, labor, and equipment required for the house itself, but also of the utilities, roads, walks, and gardens required to serve the house when arranged in proposed typical grouping.

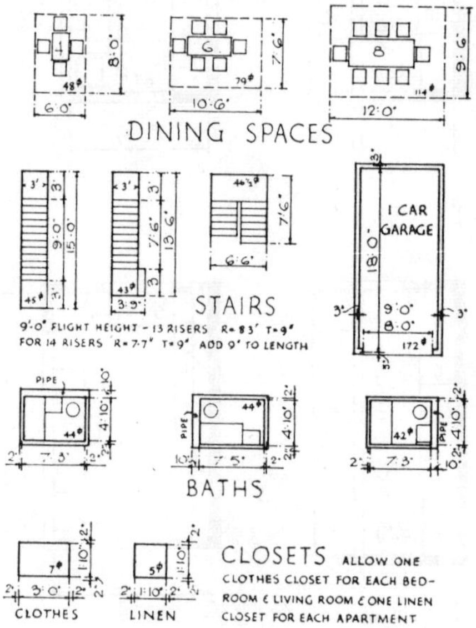

Additional capital cost beyond that required for adequate standard can only be justified by the fact that it will decrease operation-maintenance costs. Even if capital cost is not charged to tenant, it must be kept to a minimum so as to:—

1. Take care of as many families and persons as possible within the appropriation.

2. Set standards of planning and building that will be sufficiently economical to serve as a guide to others in building in the near future.

CLARENCE S. STEIN.
November 23rd, 1935

Fig. 169—Minimum space requirements.

Memorandum to Mr. John S. Lansill

From Clarence S. Stein

Subject: *Studies of the relative improvement costs of various schemes of house grouping.*

The purpose of these studies is to measure the comparative efficiency of various methods of grouping houses as affecting street, yard, and park improvement costs. The same type of house has been used throughout. We have compared: houses facing on main roads and on lanes with and without vehicular roads; similar lanes of different lengths; houses in groups of different lengths with and without garages attached, as well as free-standing houses; houses with long and with narrow side towards the road.

The attached table showing cost per family, indicates that improvement costs may vary as much as approximately 54 per cent in Schemes 4 and 11. This would make a difference of approximately $457,000 for a development of 1,000 houses. These figures naturally do not take into consideration the possible differences of contour and soil conditions. They are based on approximate costs in the New York region at the present time under normal building conditions. They indicate, however, the relative—if not actual—difference in costs. Bearing this in mind, a few of the conclusions that may be drawn from these studies are:

1. The cost of improvements per house is greatest when houses are built facing on main roads. (Houses on main traffic ways are also probably the least desirable for good living). Schemes 10 and 11 show similar arrangement of houses, the one on a lane and the other on a main road. The estimates of these two indicate that conditions of soil and contour being equal, the latter will cost about 38 per cent more than the former.

2. Improvement costs of houses on lanes are increasingly cheaper per house as the length of lane increases. (See comparison of Schemes 2 and 3). It is apparent that a super-block of 1,000-ft. in width offers economic advantages over a block of half this width unless there are site conditions that over-balance the saving from decreased length of main highway and main lines of utilities per house.

3. The cheapest arrangement as affecting improvement costs, is that of row houses on lanes without vehicular roads in the lanes, but with garages grouped at entrance to lanes. (See Schemes 1 and 4). This arrangement has great advantages from the point of view of good living. It offers increased safety and quiet on the service side of the houses and at the same time, it permits complete privacy on the garden side. On the other hand, some Planners may prefer to sacrifice these advantages for the convenience of direct access to each house by automobile and greater ease in the delivery of bulky goods and fuel, and easier fire protection.

The lanes without roads show a cost advantage of about 18 per cent over those with roads (see Schemes 1 and 2). However, the length of lanes without

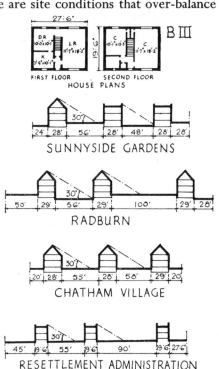

Fig. 170—Cross sections of lanes. House type B-III.

vehicular roads must be limited to facilitate delivery of heavy and bulky goods and of fuel. The proportionate difference of cost is greatly decreased when lanes with roads are increased to the greater length that their arrangement makes practical and acceptable (See Scheme 3). But, the economic advantage of the lane without roads will be increased on hilly sites where road construction is difficult and expensive.

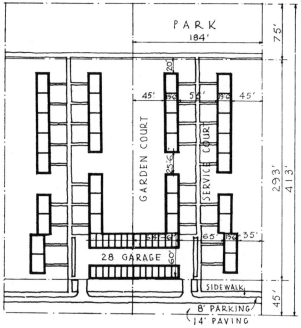

Fig. 171—House group. Scheme 1.

This study has been made with the assistance of Ralph Eberlin and of Albert Lueders.

CLARENCE S. STEIN.

November 19th, 1935.

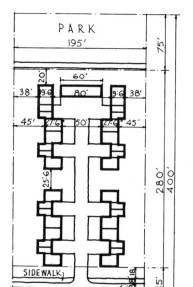

Fig. 172—House group. Scheme 2.

APPRAISAL OF GROUP PLANS
Relative cost of improvement of various schemes of

House Grouping

The diagrams are made for the purpose of measuring the comparative cost efficiency of various methods of grouping houses as affecting street, yard, and park improvements. The diagrams are not intended to be used as site plans. Site plans must be modelled to fit actual conditions of ground and the varied needs of those to be housed.

Costs will vary in accordance with wage rates, material costs, and organization of job operation in different locations. The costs here given were all arrived at on the basis of similar unit costs. They indicate the relative costs at the present time in the New York region. They are based on the theoretical use of approximately flat land and do not allow for grading. Actual costs will be modified by varied conditions of the contours and soil.

House Type B-III (See Fig. 170) has been used in all the diagrams. This type of house permits entrance to both kitchen and living room from a single vestibule at one side of the house. As a result, public passages at the garden side of the houses may be eliminated as in Schemes 1, 6, 8, 9. However, where there is a vehicular road on the service lane, a public path on the garden side is needed for the purpose of separating pedestrian and vehicular traffic. This principle of the 'Radburn Plan' has been adhered to excepting in Scheme 2.

The distance between houses, both on the service and garden side of houses is adequate, and if anything, liberal for moderate cost houses. Fig. 170 shows sections through lanes in Sunnyside, Radburn and Chatham Village for purposes of comparison with those used in these studies.

Parks are indicated in the diagrams as 150-ft. wide with houses set back 20-ft. from park line, making a total of 190-ft. between houses. This is the approximate average distance at Radburn. The amount of park land per family varies in accordance with the width of lanes and number of houses on each lane. Costs are given inclusive and exclusive of parks.

Where there is no lane and houses face on the main street, the park is indicated as only 50-ft. wide.

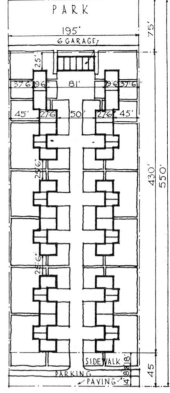

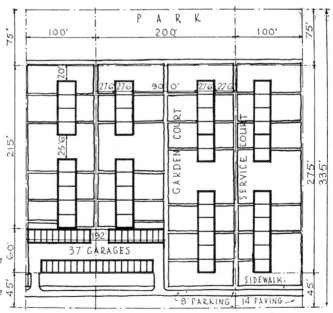

Fig. 173—(top right) House group. Scheme 3.

Fig. 174—(bottom) House group. Scheme 4.

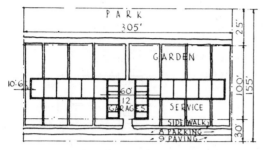

Fig. 175—House group. Scheme 5.

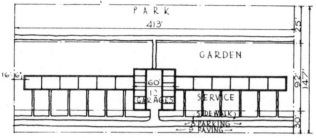

Fig. 176—House group. Scheme 6.

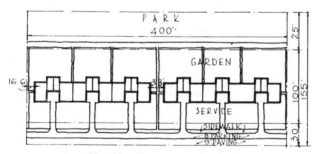

Fig. 177—House group. Scheme 7.

The depth of lanes is restricted in the case of those without vehicular roads directly to houses (Schemes 1, 4, 8, and 9) by limitations in delivery of fuel and in moving. A maximum distance of 225-ft. from road to house entrance has been used. This is not much greater than in large apartment groups such as Phipps and Hillside where furniture is carried from 180-ft. to 200-ft. It is presumed that there will be very little moving because of low rental charges for desirable houses. If coal is used rather than oil or gas for heating, it can be delivered in small quantities in hand carts with rubber wheels from municipal or co-operative centers.

In the case of lanes having direct road access to houses, the depth of the lane is limited by the distance from main road for delivery of fire protection and by the need of preventing congestion. Schemes 3 and 10 have approximately the same length as some of the longer lanes in Radburn. In Scheme 2, the lane was made shorter for the purpose of comparing with Scheme 1 which has the same number of houses, and with Scheme 3 which has similar arrangement of houses, but a longer lane.

CLARENCE S. STEIN.

November 19th, 1935.

APPRAISAL OF GROUP PLANS

Relative Cost of Various Schemes of House Grouping

In all studies one type of house has been used: a single-family, two-story, five-room house, 19-ft. 6-in. x 27-ft. 6-in.

Costs have been divided as follows:—

(*a*) MAIN STREET

Includes the following elements normally installed there even though some of the utilities may be actually located in areas other than in the main street and also some of the utilities that may be installed by the public utility corporation at its expense:—

Sidewalk—
 both sides of street.
Curb— ,, ,, ,, ,,
Grass area—unpaved areas between curb and property line.
Main sanitary sewer.
Main storm sewer.
Main water main.
Main gas main.
Main electric and telephone pole line.
Paving—between curbs.

In computing the cost of installing these elements, consideration is given to the fact that some of these utilities serve both sides of the main street and therefore one-half of the actual quantities are charged to one side of the street.

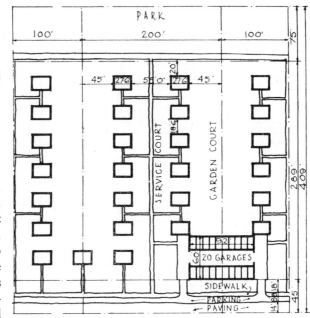

Fig. 178—House group. Scheme 8.

(*b*) GARAGE AND SERVICE ROADS
 Includes where they apply:—
 Garage driveways from curb. Garage driveways from service road.
 Parking areas within service road and lane paving.
 Curb at parking area within service road and lane paving.
 Service road and lane paving from curb.

(*c*) PUBLIC SERVICES EXCLUSIVE OF (*a*) AND (*b*)
 Includes where they apply:—
 Common footways.
 Park footways.
 Park lighting.

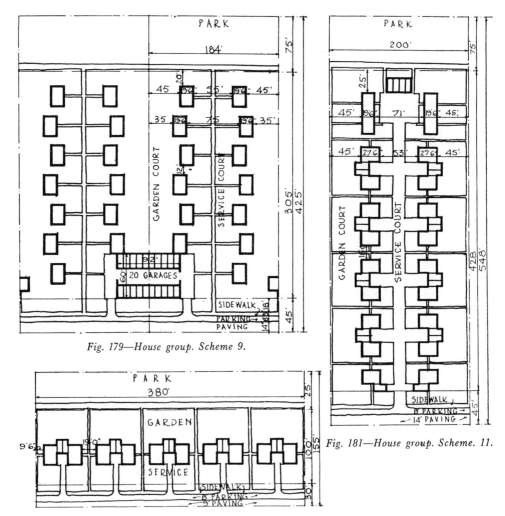

Fig. 179—House group. Scheme 9.

Fig. 181—House group. Scheme. 11.

Fig. 180—House group. Scheme 10.

Storm drain which serves for drainage of the park area and receives roof
drainage service lines.

Lane sanitary sewer—where an independent sewer line is installed in
the service lane to receive the house services.

Lane electric and telephone pole line—where an independent pole line
is installed in the service lane to receive the house services.

Lane water main—where an independent water main is installed in the
service lane to receive the house services.

Lane gas main—where an independent gas main is installed in the service
lane to receive the house services.

(*d*) House Services

Includes where they apply:—

Walks to buildings.

House sanitary sewer connections where these connections are made direct to an independent sewer.

Gas service where gas main is run through the length of the buildings and finally connects with one connection to the main gas main.

House gas service connections which are made direct to an independent gas main are considered as being installed free by the Gas Company.

Water service connections, where these connections are made direct to an independent water main.

House sanitary sewers where a common sewer is run through the length of the buildings and finally connects with one sewer connection to the main sewer.

Water service connections where a common water main is run through the length of the buildings and finally connects with one water connection to the main water main.

Roof drainage house connections from the roof leaders to the storm drain in (*c*).

(*e*) House Yards Exclusive of Walks

Areas to be landscaped in yards, i.e. finished with top soil, seeding and planting or other surfacing.

(*f*) Park Landscaping

Areas to be landscaped in park, i.e. finished with top soil, seeding, planting, or other surfacing.

OUTLINE SPECIFICATION
USED FOR ESTIMATING PURPOSES

The Specification is based on the premise that operation-maintenance is the first cost consideration. Increase in capita cost, beyond that needed for adequate service, is justified on by decrease in operation-maintenance cost.

1. Paving of main street service roads and garage driveways—concrete, 6-in. thick, with wire mesh reinforcing, broom finish.

2. Curbs—concrete, 6-in. thick at top, 8-in. at bottom, 18-in. deep with steel nosings.

3. All walks—concrete, 4-in. thick, monolithic finish: street sidewalks 5-ft. wide: house walks 3-ft. wide: common footways 4-ft. 6-in., and footway along perimeter of park 7-ft. wide.

4. Park light—ornamental standard fed by park cable.

5. Sanitary sewers in service roads where they apply—8-in. diameter vitrified tile pipe and house service connections to these independent sewers 6-in. diameter vitrified tile pipe. These house service connections twinned for two houses wherever possible. Where houses are planned in a row without attached garages, house sewer lines run in cast iron pipes along the length of the groups and then finally twinned together in one main tile pipe service connection to the sewer in the main street.

6. Water mains in service roads where they apply—6-in. diameter pipe with one hydrant and house service connections twinned for two houses wherever possible with a service line. Where houses are planned in a row without attached garages, house service lines run along the length of the groups and then finally twinned together in one main connection to the water main in the main street.

7. Gas mains in service roads where they apply—4-in. diameter pipe and house service connections are twinned for two houses wherever possible. Where houses are planned in a row without attached garages, house service lines run through the length of the groups and then finally twinned together in one main connection to the gas main in the main street.

8. Storm and sanitary sewers—based on a separate system. These, together with water and gas in main highways, of course vary in size depending on their location within the town. Therefore an average unit price was used for the estimates for storm and sanitary sewers, water, and gas mains. A hydrant was allowed for approximately every 400-ft.

9. Landscaping includes top soil, seeding, and planting.

Comparison of Various Schemes of House Groups

B-III Single Family, Two Story, Five Room House, 19-ft. 6-in. x 27-ft. 6in.

SCHEME	1	2	3	4	5	6	7	8	9	10	11
Number of Houses	16	16	26	21	12	12	12	13½	13½	22	10
Number of Garages	14	16	26	18½	12	12	12	10	10	22	10
Gross Area of Plot	75,992 sq. ft. 1.75 acres	78,000 sq. ft. 1.79 acres	107,250 sq. ft. 2.46 acres	79,000 sq. ft. 1.81 acres	47,275 sq. ft. 1.09 acres	60,711 sq. ft. 1.39 acres	62,000 sq. ft. 1.42 acres	81,800 sq. ft. 1.88 acres	78,200 sq. ft. 1.79 acres	109,600 sq. ft. 2.51 acres	58,900 sq. ft. 1.352 acres
Area of Park	13,800 sq. ft.	14,625 sq. ft.	14,625 sq. ft.	15,000 sq. ft.	7,625 sq. ft.	10,325 sq. ft.	10,000 sq. ft.	15,000 sq. ft.	13,800 sq. ft.	15,000 sq. ft.	9,500 sq. ft.
Area of Houses	8,356 sq. ft.	8,450 sq. ft.	13,943 sq. ft.	10,904 sq. ft.	6,160 sq. ft.	6,241 sq. ft.	6,325 sq. ft.	7,240 sq. ft.	7,240 sq. ft.	11,763 sq. ft.	5,362.5 sq. ft.
Area of Garages	2,322 sq. ft.	2,592 sq. ft.	4,212 sq. ft.	2,997 sq. ft.	1,944 sq. ft.	1,944 sq. ft.	1,944 sq. ft.	1,620 sq. ft.	1,620 sq. ft.	3,564 sq. ft.	1,620 sq. ft.
Paved Areas	Sq. ft.	Sq. ft.	Sq. ft.	Sq. ft.	Sq. ft.	Sq. ft.	Sq. ft.	Sq. ft.	Sq. ft.	Sq. ft.	Sq. ft.
(a) Main Road	4,048	4,290	4,290	—	—	7,021	6,800	—	4,048	4,400	6,460
(b) Service and Garage Driveways	3,032	10,702	14,886	—	—	1,646	5,046	—	2,614	14,630	4,205
(c) Walks	4,790	2,275	7,177	—	—	6,722	5,683	—	4,811	6,836	5,867
Number of Families per Acre	9	9	10.5	11.6	11	8.6	8.5	7.19	7.5	8.83	7.4
Gross Land Area per Family	4,749 sq. ft.	4,875 sq. ft.	4,125 sq. ft.	3,762 sq. ft.	3,940 sq. ft.	5,059 sq. ft.	5,167 sq. ft.	6,059 sq. ft.	5,793 sq. ft.	4,982 sq. ft.	5,890 sq. ft.
Park Area per Family	863 sq. ft.	914 sq. ft.	562 sq. ft.	714 sq. ft.	635 sq. ft.	860 sq. ft.	833 sq. ft.	1,111 sq. ft.	1,022 sq. ft.	682 sq. ft.	950 sq. ft.
Front Footage of One-half Main Street per Family	11.5 ft.	12.19 ft.	7.5 ft.	9.5 ft.	25.41 ft.	34.42 ft.	33.3 ft.	14.8 ft.	13.6 ft.	9.09 ft.	38 ft.

Relative Improvement Costs of Various Schemes of House Groups
B-III Single Family, Two Story, Five Room House, 19-ft. 6-in. x 27-ft. 6-in.

TOTAL COSTS

SCHEME	1	2	3	4	5	6	7	8	9	10	11
(a) Main Street	$2,233	$2,328	$2,321	$2,419	$3,172	$4,274	$4,007	$2,417	$2,232	$2,397	$3,829
(b) Garage and Service Roads	667	2,400	3,275	653	362	362	1,110	575	575	3,219	925
(c) Public Services exclusive of (a) and (b)	1,183	2,093	3,300	1,319	865	975	1,038	2,278	2,334	3,314	837
(d) House Services	1,660	823	1,732	1,952	1,106	1,106	1,185	1,229	1,345	1,986	1,568
(e) House Yards exclusive of Walks	1,533	1,351	1,902	1,366	761	1,068	1,067	1,763	1,691	2,037	1,068
(f) Park Landscaping	500	530	530	544	218	297	287	544	500	544	273
GRAND TOTAL	$7,776	$9,525	$13,060	$8,253	$6,484	$8,144	$8,694	$8,806	$8,589	13,497	$8,500
Total Exclusive of Park Landscaping	$7,276	$8,995	$12,530	$7,709	$6,266	$7,847	$8,407	$8,262	$8,089	$12,953	$8,227

COST PER FAMILY

SCHEME	1	2	3	4	5	6	7	8	9	10	11
(a) Main Street	$139.56	$145.50	$89.26	$115.19	$264.33	$356.17	$333.91	$179.00	$165.33	$108.95	$382.90
(b) Garage and Service Roads	41.69	150.00	125.96	31.10	30.17	30.16	92.50	42.59	42.59	146.32	92.50
(c) Public Services exclusive of (a) and (b)	73.94	130.81	126.92	62.81	72.08	81.25	86.50	168.74	172.89	150.63	83.70
(d) House Services	103.75	51.44	66.62	93.00	92.17	92.17	98.75	91.04	99.63	90.27	156.80
(e) House Yards exclusive of Walks	95.81	84.44	73.22	65.00	63.42	89.00	88.91	130.59	125.16	92.59	106.80
(f) Park Landscaping	31.25	33.12	20.38	25.90	18.16	24.75	23.92	40.30	37.04	24.73	27.30
GRAND TOTAL	$486.00	$595.31	$502.36	$393.00	$540.33	$673.50	$724.42	$652.26	$642.64	$613.49	$850.00
Total Exclusive of Park Landscaping	$454.75	$562.19	$481.98	$367.10	$522.17	$653.91	$700.50	$611.96	$599.18	$588.76	$822.70

Comparative Costs of Various Schemes of House Groups

B-III Single Family, Two Story, Five Room House, 19-ft. 6-ins x 27½-ft. 6-in.

TOTAL COSTS											
SCHEME	1	2	3	4	5	6	7	8	9	10	11
(a) Main Street	5.68	5.92	5.90	6.15	8.07	10.87	10.20	6.15	5.68	6.10	9.74
(b) Garage and Service Roads	1.70	6.11	8.33	1.66	0.92	0.92	2.82	1.46	1.46	8.19	2.35
(c) Public Services exclusive of (a) and (b)	3.01	5.33	8.40	3.36	2.20	2.48	2.64	5.80	5.94	8.43	2.13
(d) House Services	4.22	2.09	4.41	4.97	2.81	2.81	3.01	3.13	3.42	5.05	3.99
(e) House Yards exclusive of Walks	3.90	3.44	4.84	3.48	1.94	2.72	2.72	4.49	4.30	5.18	2.72
(f) Park Landscaping	1.27	1.35	1.35	1.38	0.56	0.76	0.73	1.38	1.27	1.38	0.70
GRAND TOTAL	19.78	24.24	33.23	21.00	16.50	20.56	22.12	22.41	22.07	34.33	21.63
TOTAL Exclusive of Park Landscaping	18.51	22.89	31.58	19.62	15.94	19.80	21.39	21.03	20.81	32.95	20.93

COST PER FAMILY											
(a) Main Street	0.36	0.37	0.23	0.29	0.67	0.91	0.85	0.46	0.42	0.28	0.97
(b) Garage and Service Roads	0.11	0.38	0.32	0.08	0.08	0.08	0.23	0.11	0.11	0.37	0.24
(c) Public Services exclusive of (a) and (b)	0.19	0.33	0.32	0.16	0.18	0.21	0.22	0.43	0.44	0.38	0.21
(d) House Services	0.26	0.13	0.17	0.24	0.23	0.23	0.25	0.23	0.25	0.23	0.40
(e) House Yards exclusive of Walks	0.24	0.22	0.19	0.16	0.16	0.23	0.23	0.33	0.32	0.24	0.27
(f) Park Landscaping	0.08	0.08	0.05	0.07	0.05	0.06	0.06	0.10	0.09	0.06	0.07
GRAND TOTAL	1.24	1.51	1.28	1.00	1.37	1.72	1.84	1.66	1.63	1.56	2.16
TOTAL Exclusive of Park Landscaping	1.16	1.43	1.23	0.93	1.32	1.66	1.78	1.56	1.54	1.50	2.09

This table was not included in the original Report. It was set up later to show costs in comparative terms rather than in terms of actual prices. Scheme 4, the most economical, was taken as the base and the grand total cost per family was assigned the value of 1.00.

These detailed estimates of cost were made in 1935. They are now out of date. They are included only to show method of estimating.

Estimate of Scheme 1

16 houses and garage group of 14 garages.
Gross size of plot—184-ft. x 415-ft.—76,360 sq. ft.—1.75 acres.

(a) MAIN STREET

Main street sidewalk		780 at 18c	$ 140	
Curb		196 at 75c	147	
Main Street paving		4,048 at 22c	890	
Grass area		2,875 at 4c	115	
Main sanitary sewer	92-ft. at 2.70	½ M.H. at 70	283	
Main storm sewer	92-ft. at 3.00	½ M.H. at 70 and ¼ C.B. at 100	336	
Water main	92-ft. at 1.45	½ Hydrant at 70	168	
Gas Main	92-ft. at 1.25		115	
Pole Line	92-ft. at 42c		39	
				$2,233

(b) GARAGE AND SERVICE ROAD

Garage driveway (curb to P.L.)	402 at 22c	88	
Garage and service roads	2,630 at 22c	579	
			667

(c) PUBLIC SERVICE EXCLUSIVE OF (a) AND (b)

Common footway	1,411 at 18c	254	
Park footway	1,288 at 18c	232	
Park lighting—one standard		125	
Storm drain connecting roof and park drains	348-ft. at 1.50 ⎱ 1.P.L. at 50 ⎰	572	
			1,183

(d) HOUSE SERVICES

Walks to buildings	1,311 at 18c	236	
House sanitary sewer (through length of buildings)		568	
Gas service ,, ,, ,, ,,		254	
Water service ,, ,, ,, ,,		476	
Roof drainage house connections (twinned)	252-ft. at 50c	126	
			1,660

(e) LANDSCAPE—PARKS AND YARDS—grass area

Parks	12,509 at 4c	500	
Yards	38,330 at 4c	1,533	2,033

For 16 houses	$7,776
For 1 house	$486

Estimate of Scheme 2

16 houses—attached through garages.

Gross size of plot	195-ft. x 400-ft.—78,000 sq. ft.—1.79 acres.
Park	195-ft. x 75-ft.—14,625 sq. ft.
Main Street	195-ft. x 45-ft.— 8,775 sq. ft.

(a) MAIN STREET

Main street sidewalk	159-ft. x 5	795 at 18c	$ 143	
Curb		199 at 75c	149	
Main street paving	195-ft. x 22	4,290 at 22c	944	
Grass area—main highway		3,000 at 4c	120	
Main sanitary sewer	97.5-ft. at 2.70	½ M.H. at 70	298	
Main storm sewer	97.5-ft. at 3.00	½ M.H. at 70 ¼ C.B. at 100	352	
Water main	97.5-ft. at 1.45	¼ Hydrant at 70	159	
Gas main	97.5-ft. at 1.25		122	
Pole line	97.5-ft. at 42c		41	
				$2,328

(b) GARAGE AND SERVICE ROAD

Curb in lane parking			60 at 75c	45
Lane paving—curb to P.L.	18-ft. x 23-ft.	414 ⎱		
	splays	172		
18-ft. roadway	200-ft. x 18-ft.	3,600 ⎰ 6,886 at 22c	1,515	
Dead-end	60-ft. x 45-ft.	2,700		
Garage driveways	18-ft. x 32-ft. x 6	3,456 ⎱		
	18-ft. x 10-ft. x 2	360 ⎰ 3,816 at 22c	840	
				$2,400

(c) PUBLIC SERVICE EXCLUSIVE OF (a) AND (b)

Common footway	23-ft. x 5—115 at 18c	21
Park footway	195 x 7—1,365 at 18c	246
Park lighting		125
Storm drain connecting roof and park drainage	333-ft. at 1.50 }	
	i.P.I. at 50 }	550
Lane sanitary sewer—262-ft. (8-in.) at 1.50 1 M.H. at 70		463
Lane Pole Line—245-ft. at 42c		103
Lane water main—245-ft. (6-in.) at 1.35 1 Hydrant at 70		401
Lane gas main (4-in.)—245-ft. at 75c		184

$2,093

(d) HOUSE SERVICES

Roof drainage house connections (twinned) 30-ft. a 2—60 } 510 at 50c		255
45-ft. x 10—450 }		
House sewer connections (6-in.) (twinned) 40-ft. x 5—200 } 270 at 1.25		338
70 x 1—70 }		
Lane water connection (1-in.) (twinned) 270-ft. at 85c		230

$823

(e) LANDSCAPE—PARKS AND YARDS—grass area

Parks 13,255 at 4c		530
Yards 33,769 at 4c		1,351

$1,881

For 16 houses $9,525
For 1 house $595

Estimate of Scheme 3

26 houses.
Gross size of plot 195-ft. x 555-ft. 108,225 sq. ft.—2.48 acres.
Park 195-ft. x 75-ft. 14,625 sq. ft.
Main Street 195-ft. x 45-ft. 8,775 sq. ft.

(a) MAIN STREET As Scheme 2 except—

Grass area	2,816 sq. ft. at 4c	113

$2,321

(b) GARAGE AND SERVICE ROAD

Lane paving—curb to P.L.—As Scheme 2	586 }	
18-ft. roadway—350 x 18	6,300 } 9,126 at 22c	2,008
dead-end—56 x 40	2,240 }	
Garage driveways—18 x 32 x 10	5,760 at 22c	1,267

$3,275

(c) PUBLIC SERVICE EXCLUSIVE OF (a) AND (b)

Common footway	2,169 at 18c	390
Park footway	1,365 at 18c	246
Park lighting		125
Storm drain connecting roof and park drainage	488-ft. at 1.50 }	
	i.P.I. at 50 }	782
Lane sanitary sewer 415 at 1.50 1 M.H. at 70		692
Lane Pole Line 395 at 42c		166
Lane water main 395 at 1.35 1 Hydrant at 70		603
Lane gas main 395 at 75c		296

$3,300

(d) HOUSE SERVICES

Roof drainage house connections (twinned)	795 at 50c	398
House sewer connections (twinned)	391 at 1.25	489
House water connections (twinned)	391 at 85c	332
Walks to buildings	2,848 at 18c	513

$1,732

(e) LANDSCAPE—PARKS AND YARDS—grass area.

Park 13,255 sq. ft. at 4c		530
Yards 47,550 sq. ft. at 4c		1,902

$2,432

26 Houses $13,060
1 House $502

These detailed estimates of cost were made in 1935. They are now out of date. They are included only to show method of estimating.

Memorandum to Mr. John S. Lansill

From Clarence S. Stein

Subject: *Studies of relative cost of construction of various schemes of house grouping.*

This is a continuation of the study which I submitted to you on November 19, 1935. The first report dealt exclusively with the cost of street, yard, and park improvements. In the attached study, the relative construction costs of the lanes already analyzed are compared. The same type of house has again been used.

We do not know exactly the type of construction that will be used. We have taken as basis, for estimating purposes, the type of construction of small houses that is used commonly in the New York region, i.e. brick veneer on wood frame.

Costs will naturally vary not only in accordance with type of construction used, but in method of organizing work. The costs given are approximately those in northern New Jersey at the present time under normal building conditions. The figures are intended to indicate the relative—if not the actual—difference in costs of construction of house type B-III grouped in different ways.

The findings of this study and of the earlier one are summed up on the table ' Relative Costs of Construction and Improvements of Various Schemes of House Grouping,' below.

In the preparation of this study I have been assisted by C. S. Carlson, F. E. Vitolo, and Albert Lueders.

RELATIVE COST OF CONSTRUCTION

OF HOUSES IN VARIOUS GROUPS

(All estimates are based on the use of house type B-III, see page 233)

(Costs do not include professional fees—or design and drafting; builder's fees—or supervision; insurance: or any charges for the use of money during construction)

COST PER UNIT	SCHEME 1		
$3,512 per family	16 houses at $3, 432 each	$54,912	
	8½ end walls at $130 each	1,105	
	17 windows at $10 each (in end walls)	170	
			$56,187
$225 per garage	14 car garage		3,150
	TOTAL		$59,337

Cost per Unit	Scheme 3		
$3,502 per family	26 houses at $3,432 each	$89,232	
	12 end walls at $130 each	1,560	
	24 windows at $10 each (in end walls)	240	
			$91,032
$275 per garage	10 two-car garage units at $568	5,680	
	1 six-car garage unit at $1,450	1,450	
			$7,130
		TOTAL	$98,162

Cost per Unit	Scheme 4		
$3,432 per family	21 houses at $3, 432 each	$72,072	
	No end wall required because this portion is included		
	in the above price		$72,072
$225 per garage	18½ garages at $225 each	4,163	
			4,163
		TOTAL	$76,235

Cost per Unit	Scheme 10		
$3,588 per family	22 houses at $3,432 each	$75,504	
	22 end walls at $130 each	2,860	
	55 windows at $10 each (in end walls)	550	
			$78,914
$270 per garage	8 two-car garage units at $566	4,644	
	1 four-car garage unit at $1,000	1,000	
	2 one-car garage units at $300	600	
			6,244
		TOTAL	$85,158

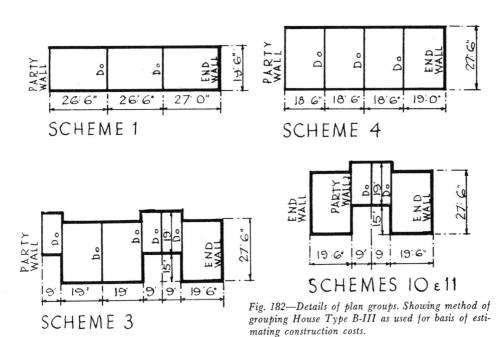

Fig. 182—Details of plan groups. Showing method of grouping House Type B-III as used for basis of estimating construction costs.

APPENDIX

RELATIVE COST OF CONSTRUCTION AND IMPROVEMENTS OF VARIOUS SCHEMES OF HOUSE GROUPING USING HOUSE TYPE B-III

(In regard to the cost of construction of houses, see page 246)
(In regard to the cost of improvements, see report of November 19, 1935—' Study of Relative Improvement Costs of House Grouping ')
(The cost of land is not included in this study)

TOTAL COSTS					
SCHEMES	I	3	4	10	11
Construction of Houses	$56,187	$91,032	$72,072	$77,914	$35,870
Construction of Garages	3,150	7,130	4,163	7,244	2,840
Construction Total	59,337	98,162	76,235	85,158	38,710
Improvements exclusive of Park Landscaping	7,276	12,530	7,709	12,953	8,227
Total	66,613	110,692	83,944	98,111	46,937
Park Landscaping	500	530	544	544	273
GRAND TOTAL	$67,113	$111,222	$84,488	$98,655	$47,210
COST PER FAMILY					
Construction of House	3,511.69	3,501.21	3,432.00	3,587.00	3,587.00
Construction of Garage	196.87	274.24	198.24	283.83	284.00
Construction Total	3,708.56	3,775.45	3,630.24	3,870.83	3,871.00
Improvements exclusive of Park Landscaping	454.75	481.98	367.10	588.76	822.70
Total	4,163.31	4,257.43	3,997.34	4,459.59	4,693.70
Park Landscaping	31.25	20.38	25.90	24.73	27.30
GRAND TOTAL	$4,194.56	$4,277.71	$4,023.24	$4,484.32	$4,721.00

BIBLIOGRAPHY

GENERAL REFERENCES

Bing, Alexander M., Henry Wright, and Clarence S. Stein, *Preliminary Study of a Proposed Garden Community in the New York City Region.* 1923. 43 pp. Typescript with illustrations.

Dahir, James, *The Neighborhood Unit Plan: Its Spread and Acceptance.* A Selected Bibliography with Interpretive Comments. New York, Russell Sage Foundation. 1947. 91 pp.

Feiss, Carl, 'New Towns in the United States.' In *Town and Country Planning,* Jan. 1955, vol. 23:129, pp. 37-41.

Stein, Clarence S., 'City Patterns, Past and Future.' In *New Pencil Points,* June 1942.

Wright, Henry, *Rehousing Urban America.* New York, Columbia University. 1935. 173 pp.

Wright, Henry, *Some Principles Relating to the Economics of Land Subdivision.* New York, American City Planning Institute, 1930. 20 pp.

1. SUNNYSIDE

Annual Reports to Stockholders of the City Housing Corporation. 1924-1929.

Ascher, Charles S., 'The Enforcement of Deed Restrictions.' In *City Planning,* Oct. 1932, vol. 8:4.

Bing, Aleanxder M., 'American Garden Colonies' (Sunnyside Gardens and Radburn). In *Housing and Building,* May-June 1930.

Bing, Alexander M., 'Sunnyside Gardens: A Successful Experiment in Good Housing at a Moderate Price.' In *Municipal Review,* June 1926.

Bing, Alexander M., 'A New Limited-Dividend Housing Company.' Reprinted from *Housing Betterment,* May 1924.

Bing, Alexander M., 'Minimum Costs for Low-Rental Apts.' In *The Journal of Land and Public Utility Economics,* May 1929.

City Housing Corporation, *Sunnyside Gardens, a Home Community.* New York, the Corporation. Undated.

City Housing Corporation, *Sunnyside and the Housing Problem.*

Friederick, Anton H., 'Case History of a Community of Mortgaged Home Owners.' In *Survey Graphic,* June 1933.

Ginzburg, Benjamin, and Alexander M. Bing, 'Sunnyside Back and Forth.' In *Survey Graphic,* Aug. 1936, vol. 25:8.

Larsen, C. Theodore, 'Play Areas for Apartment Houses.' In *The Architectural Record,* March 1931.

Lasker, Loula D., 'Sunnyside Up and Down.' In *Survey-Graphic,* July 1936.

Mumford, Lewis, *Green Memories.* New York, Harcourt Brace Co. 1947. pp. 30, 31.

Mumford, Lewis, 'Houses—Sunnyside Up.' In *The Nation,* Feb. 4, 1925.

Reports of the Commission of Housing and Regional Planning. Legislative Documents, 1923, No. 43; 1924, No. 78; 1925, No. 91; 1926, No. 40; 1926, No. 66.

Roosevelt, Mrs. Franklin D., 'The Vanishing "Vine and Fig Tree."' In *The Woman's Viewpoint,* October 1925.

Tough, Rosalind, Part I: 'Production Costs of Urban Land in Sunnyside, Long Island.' Part II: 'Building Costs and Total Costs at Sunnyside Gardens, Long Island.' In *Journal of Land and Public Utility Economics,* Feb. 1932, vol. 8:1; May 1932, vol. 8:2.

Wright, Henry, 'Housing. V. The Case for Group Housing. Sunnyside Garden Beginnings.' In *Architecture,* Aug. 1932, vol. 68:2. Afterwards part of the book *Rehousing Urban America.*

Wright, Henry, 'The Modern Apartment House.' In *The Architectural Record,* March 1929. Afterwards part of the book *Rehousing Urban America.*

Wright, Henry, 'An Account of Sunnyside Gardens in Relation to Problems and Development of Design and Site Planning and the Value of Same as an Experiment Directed towards an American Garden City.' 1926 Ms.

Wright, Henry, 'The Architect and Small House Costs.' In *The Architectural Record,* December

1932, pp. 389-394.

Wright, Henry, 'Study of Application of Sunnyside Planning Principles to a Larger City Area.' Ms.

Wright, Henry, and D. M. Kendall, 'Investigation of the Present Speculative Building Operations Now in Progress in Brooklyn and Long Island.' May 1924. Ms.

Wright, Henry, E. S. Palmer and J. G. Hutton, 'Sunnyside Gardens: General Report on Cost Accounting.' December 1925. Ms.

II. RADBURN

Ascher, Charles S., 'Government by Contract in Radburn, New Jersey.' In 'Private Covenants in Urban Redevelopment,' Part 3 of *Urban Redevelopment: Problems and Practices* (Woodbury, Coleman, ed.). Chicago, University of Chicago Press. 1953. pp. 278-309. See also pp. 233-234.

Augur, Tracy B., 'Radburn, the Challenge of a New Town.' In *Michigan Municipal Review*, Feb., Mar. 1931, vol. 4: 2-3.

Bing, Alexander M., 'Community Planning for the Motor Age: How the City Housing Corporation Separates Pedestrian and Motor Traffic in Its Unique Experiment at Radburn.' In *National Association of Real Estate Boards. Annals of Real Estate Practice*, 1929. Address before National Association of Real Estate Boards, June 27, 1929.

Brownlow, Louis, 'Radburn: a New Town Planned for the Motor Age.' In *International Housing and Town Planning Bulletin*, Feb. 1930, no. 21.

Brownlow, Louis, 'Some Problems in New Planning.' In *Proceedings of 21st National Conference on City Planning*, 1929. Refers to Radburn. Also reprinted as Bulletin no. 4, National Conference on City Planning.

Cautley, Marjorie Sewell, 'Planting at Radburn.' In *Landscape Architecture*, Oct. 1930, vol. 21 No. 1, pp. 23-29. By the landscape architect.

City Housing Corporation, *Radburn Garden Homes*. New York, the Corporation. 1929.

City Housing Corporation, *Regarding Radburn*. New York, the author. 1928.

City Housing Corporation, Leaflets descriptive of Radburn as an industrial town. New York, the author. 1928. Plans.

City Housing Corporation, Leaflets entitled: *A Town Planned for Modern Industry; The Way Out; Light on Labor.*

City Housing Corporation, *Radburn, Protective Restrictions and Community Administration.* New York, the Corporation. 1929.

City Housing Corporation, annual reports. 1928-1933.

Comey, Arthur C., and Max S. Wehrly, 'Radburn, Bergen County, N. J.' In U.S. National Resources Committee. Urbanism Committee. Supplementary report, *Planned Communities*. 1939; vol. 2.

'Evaluation of the Town of Radburn, New Jersey.' A study by students in the Department of Architecture, Columbia University; Ronnie Chelouche, Alfred Mercado, and Bert Whinston. Ms. with photographs by the authors.

Hudson, Robert B., *Radburn: a Plan of Living*. A study made for the American Association for Adult Education, under the supervision of John O. Walker. New York, the Association. C. 1934.

Olmsted, Frederick Law, *Forty-eight Years of Architecture*. Vol. 2: *Central Park*.

Radburn Management Corporation, *Radburn, Protective Restrictions and Community Administration*, n.d. 40 pp. 'Declaration of Restrictions No. 1: Certificate of Incorporation and By-laws of the Radburn Association.'

Rosenfeld, Isadore, *Memorandum Re First School District of Radburn*. March 20, 1929. Typewritten report made for the office of Henry Wright and C. S. Stein.

Smith, Geddes, 'A Town for the Motor Age.' *Survey Graphic* reprint for the City Housing Corporation. C. 1930.

Stein, Clarence S., *Radburn and the Radburn Idea* —Encyclopædia of Housing 1949-50. This contains some material used in the article above.

Stein, Clarence S., and Catherine Bauer, 'Store Buildings and Neighborhood Shopping Centers.' In *The Architectural Record*, Feb. 1934.

Urban Planning and Land Policies. Vol. II of *Supplementary Report of the Urbanism Committee to the National Resources Committee*. United States Government Printing Office. 1939. pp. 97-101.

Whitten, Robert, and Thomas Adams, *Neighbor-*

hoods of Small Homes. Cambridge, Harvard University Press. 1931. Harvard City Planning Studies, Vol. III.

Wright, Henry, 'The Autobiography of Another Idea.' Reprinted from *The Western Architect,* September 1930, by the Regional Planning Association of America. 8 pp.

Wright, Henry, 'Housing—Why, When, and How!' Part II. *Architecture.* August 1933. pp. 79-110.

Wright, Henry, 'The Radburn Plan.' In *National Real Estate Journal,* Sept. 30, 1929. pp. 74-76.

Wright, Henry, *Rehousing Urban America.* New York, Columbia University Press.

Wright, Henry, *Some Principles Relating to the Economics of Land Subdivision.* New York, American City Planning Institute. 1930. 20 pp.

III. CHATHAM VILLAGE

Bigger, Frederick, 'More Limited Dividend Housing: the Buhl Foundation Project in Pittsburgh.' In *Octagon,* Oct. 1931, vol. 3: 10.

'Buhl Foundation Housing Project in Pittsburgh, Pa.' In *Architectural Record,* Oct. 1931.

The Buhl Foundation, 'Chatham Village, a Modern Community of Garden Homes Combining Architectural Charm with Security and Cultured Living.' *The Foundation,* Jan. 1932.

The Buhl Foundation, 'Facts about Chatham Village. Pittsburgh, Pa.' *The Foundation,* Oct. 1943.

Comey, Arthur C., and Max S. Wehrly, 'Chatham Village, Pittsburgh, Pa.' In U.S. National Resources Committee. Urbanism committee. Supplementary report, *Planned Communities.* 1939, vol. 2, pt. 1.

Lewis, Dr. Charles (Director, The Buhl Foundation), 'The Large-Scale Planned Community as an Investment.' Speech given at 41st Annual Meeting of the American Life Convention, Chicago, Illinois. Oct. 1946.

Mather, Alan, 'The variation of roofs and imaginative planning on a hill-side site are distinctive of Chatham Village . . . Wright and Stein as Consultants on site plan,' in article: 'Henry Wright.' In *Pencil Points,* Jan. 1940, vol. 21:1.

Report of the Buhl Foundation. 1942.

Wright, Henry, 'Housing. V. The Case for Group Housing. Chatham Village.' In *Architecture,* Aug. 1933, vol. 68: 2.

IV. PHIPPS GARDEN APARTMENTS (1)

Rosenfeld, Isadore, 'Phipps Garden Apartments.' In *Architectural Forum,* Feb. 1932, vol. 56, pp. 111-124, 183-187; with photos, plans, tables.

V. HILLSIDE HOMES

'A Comparison of Two Ways of Housing 5,000 People.' In *The Architectural Forum,* February 1933.

Blackham, Louise P., *Community Service at Hillside Homes.* A four-year report, June 1935 to June 1939. Report to the Hillside Housing Corporation. Mimeographed. Hillside Homes, Bronx, N. Y. July 1939.

Blackham, Louise P., *Community Service at Hillside Homes.* A Review of Eight Years of Community Life at Hillside Homes, June 1935 to July 1943. Mimeographed. Hillside Homes, Bronx, N. Y. July 1943.

'Hillside Group Housing.' In *Architectural Record,* Oct. 1932, vol. 72: 4.

Saylor, Henry, 'The Hillside Housing Development: The Case History of an Idea from Its Birth in the Mind of Clarence S. Stein, Architect, to Its Material Realization in the Bronx, New York.' In *Architecture,* May 1935, vol. 71: 5.

Stein, Clarence S., 'Hillside Homes.' In *American Architect,* Feb., 1936, vol. 148. No. 2542.

VIII. GREENBELT TOWNS

Casseres, J. M. de, 'Amerikaansche reiservaringen op stedebouwkundig gebied.' In *Tijdschrift voor volkshuisvesting en stedebouw,* Feb. 1939, vol. 20:2, pp. 41-51; with photos, maps.

'Greenbelt Towns.' In *Architectural Record,* Sept. 1936, vol. 80:3, pp. 215-234; with photos, plans, sketch. Also reprinted.

'Greentowns All Sold by Federal Government.' In *American City,* March 1953, vol. 68:3, p. 113.

Mayer, Albert, 'Greenbelt Towns for the Machine Age. The government's plan to build four in this country directs notice to the successful ventures abroad.' In *New York Times* magazine, Feb. 2, 1936, pp. 8-9, 18; with photos, plans, sketches.

Mumford, Lewis, 'City and Region: . . . Greenbelt Towns.' In his *The Culture of Cities.* C. 1938. p. 452; with photos.

BIBLIOGRAPHY

Reiss, R. L., 'American Greenbelt Towns.' In *Town and Country Planning,* Jan. 1938, vol. 6:22, pp. 16-18; with plans.

Rigotti, Giorgio, 'I Borghi dalle "Siedlungen" alle "Greenbelt towns." ' In *Urbanistica,* Jan.-Feb. 1937, vol. 6:1, pp. 3-18; with photos, maps, plans.

'Site Plans of "Greenbelt" Towns, Layouts of the Resettlement Administration's New Suburban Communities Now Under Construction near Washington, Cincinnati and Milwaukee.' In *American City,* Aug. 1936, vol. 51:8, pp. 56-59; with plans.

Stein, Clarence S., Special reports made for the Resettlement Administration, Nov.-Dec. 1935. Studies of operation-maintenance costs in suburban resettlement communities; studies of the relative improvement costs of various schemes of house grouping; studies of relative cost of construction and improvements of various schemes of house grouping. See Appendix and body of book.

Stephenson, Flora C., 'Greenbelt Towns in the United States.' In *Town and Country Planning,* Winter 1942-43, vol. 10:40, pp. 121-123; with photos, plan. Also in *Planning and Reconstruction Year Book,* 1943, pp. 216-218; with plan only.

U.S. Congress, 81st, 1st Session, House, Suburban resettlement projects. Hearings . . . on H.R. 2440, a bill to authorize the Public Housing Commissioners to sell the suburban resettlement projects . . . 1949. (See also S351.)

U.S. Congress, 81st, 1st Session, House, An act to authorize the Public Housing Commissioner to sell the suburban resettlement projects known as Greenbelt, Maryland; Greendale, Wisconsin; and Greenhills, Ohio . . . 1949. (Public law 65.)

U.S. Congress, 81st, 1st Session, House, Disposition of greentown projects. 1949. (Report no. 402.)

U.S. Congress, 81st, 1st Session, Sale of greentown suburban resettlement projects. Hearings . . . on S. 351 . . .; with tables. 1949.

GREENBELT, MARYLAND
Comey, Arthur C., and Max S. Wehrly, 'Demonstration Projects: Separate Communities: Greenbelt, Prince George's County, Md.' In their *Planned Communities,* Monograph 1, in U.S. National Resources Committee. Urbanism Committee. Supplementary report. 1939, pt. 1, vol. 2, pp. 75-76.

Fulmer, O. Kline, *Greenbelt.* Introduction by Lewis Mumford. Washington, American Council on Public Affairs. 1941. 46 pp.; photos on covers.

Greenbelt News Review (formerly *Greenbelt Cooperator*), an independent newspaper published every Thursday by Greenbelt Cooperative Publishing Assn., Inc., and delivered to every home in Greenbelt. Office, 9 Parkway, Greenbelt, Md.

GHVC News Letter, House Organ of the Greenbelt Veteran Housing Corporation, published monthly at Greenbelt, Maryland, and distributed to most residents.

Gutheim, Frederick, 'Greenbelt Revisited.' In *Magazine of Art,* Jan. 1947, vol. 40:1, pp. 16-20; with photos.

Larsen, Christian L., and Richard D. Andrews, *The Government of Greenbelt.* Bureau of Public Administration, University of Maryland. 1951. 78 pp. Tables.

Thorpe, Merle, 'Fever Chart of a Tugwell Town. In *Nation's Business,* Nov. 1938, vol. 26:11, p. 13.

Walker, Hale J., 'Some Major Technical Problems Encountered in the Planning of Greenbelt, Maryland.' In *Planner's Journal,* Mar.-Apr. 1938, vol. 4:2, pp. 34-37; with photo.

Warner, George A., *Greenbelt: The Cooperative Community.* An Experience in Democratic Living. New York, Exposition Press, Inc. 1954. 232 pp.

GREENBROOK, N. J.
Mayer, Albert, 'A Technique for Planning Complete Communities.' In *Architectural Forum,* Jan., Feb. 1937, vol. 66:1, 2, pp. 19-36, 126-146; with maps, plans, sketch, diagrams, chart, photos.

GREENDALE, WISCONSIN
American Legion Community Development Corporation, *Greendale, the Answer to the Veterans' Housing Problem, a Plan Offered by the American Legion Community Development Corporation.* Greendale, Wis., the Corporation. 1948. 6 pp., Photo, map, sketches.

Crane, Jacob, 'Greendale: the General Plan.' In *Planners' Journal,* July-Aug. 1937, vol. 3:4, pp. 89-90. Discussion by Charles B. Bennett and Richard B. Fernbach, Nov.-Dec. 1937, vol. 3:6, pp. 160-161.

Greendale, Wis., *This is Greendale.* Greendale, Wis. 1948. 44 pp. Photos, map, plan, sketches.

Kroening, W. E., *The Story of Greendale.* A Government demonstration in community planning and public housing. Greendale, Wis., the author.

Lansill, John S., and Jacob Crane, 'Metropolitan Land Reserves as Illustrated by Greendale, Wisconsin.' In *American City,* July 1937, vol. 52:7, pp. 55-58; with maps.

Peets, Elbert, 'Studies in Planning Texture for Housing in a Greenbelt Town.' In *Architectural Record,* Sept. 1949, vol. 106:3, pp. 130-137; with plans, sketches.

Peets, Elbert, 'Greendale: the Town Plan.' A paper presented at the Milwaukee meeting of the American City Planning Institute, October 24, 1936. The Institute. 1936. 3 pp. mimeo.

Stein, Clarence S., 'Greendale and the Future.' In *American City,* June 1948, vol. 63:6, pp. 106-109; with photos, plan. Partially reprinted in this book and under title 'Greendale Revisited' in *Layout for Living,* Jan. 1949, no. 21, pp. 4-7; with photos, plan.

'Veterans Seek Purchase of Greendale and the City of Milwaukee Co-operates.' In *American City,* Jan. 1949, vol. 64:1, pp. 73-74.

Wisconsin. Historical Records Survey. Division of Community Service Programs. Inventory of the local government archives of Wisconsin. Village series, no. 141, Greendale, sponsored by the University of Wisconsin and State Historical Society of Wisconsin. Madison, *The Survey,* July 1941. 101 pp. mimeo; maps, chart.

GREENHILLS, OHIO

Greenhills, Cincinnati, Ohio, in article 'Farm Security Administration.' In *Architectural Forum,* May 1938, vol. 68:5, pp. 414, 424; with photos, maps, plans.

Hartzog, Justin R., 'Planning of Suburban Resettlement Towns: Greenhills.' In *Planners' Journal,* Mar.-Apr. 1938, vol. 4:2, pp. 29-33; with photo.

A planned community in Ohio provides housing, shopping, school and recreation facilities, in article 'Defense Housing.' In *Architectural Forum,* Nov. 1940, vol. 73:5, pp. 466-467; with photos, plan.

BALDWIN HILLS VILLAGE

Bauer, Catherine, 'Description and Appraisal, Baldwin Hills Village.' In *Pencil Points,* Sept. 1944, vol. 25:9, pp. 46-60; with photos, one colored; plans, cross-sections, tables.

Mumford, Lewis, 'Baldwin Hills Village.' In *Pencil Points,* Sept. 1944, vol. 25:9, pp. 44-45; with photo, colored.

SUPPLEMENTARY BIBLIOGRAPHY FOR 1966 EDITION

The New Towns: The Answer to Megalopolis. Sir Frederic Osborn and Arnold Whittick, with an introduction by Lewis Mumford. Leonard Hall, London, 1965.

The definitive book on the background and growth of the New Town movement in Great Britain, and on the creation of each of the British New Towns, with plans and photographs. Sir Frederic Osborn has been a central participant in all phases of the movement and its effective work, including the first prototypes of Letchworth and Welwyn Garden City, early in the century.

Community Planning in the 1920's: The Contribution of the Regional Planning Association of America. Roy Lubove. University of Pittsburgh Press, 1963.

This covers much more ground than just New Towns; it includes them as part of a total social-economic-physical community-regional conspectus. It gives an excellent background of the development and thinking in this country, intimately introducing the theories and achievements and influence of such men as Lewis Mumford, Henry Wright, Benton MacKaye, and others. A brilliant memoir.

Kitimat: A New City. Reprint of 3 illustrated articles in the *Architectural Forum,* July, August, October 1954.

The planners of Kitimat (Stein, Mayer, Whittlesey) explain the background and rationale, as well as the technical-economic-social-sociological process of actually building this new town in British Columbia, Canada.

"New Towns." *Architectural Record,* August 1964.

"The Role of Regional Policy." *Architectural Record*, September 1964.

Two articles by Albert Mayer and Clarence Stein.

These deal with both the fundamentals and the current issues in this country such as Land Ownership and Development. The September article contains the proposal of the Regional City as basic pattern for future cities as well as for Metropolitan development.

Town and Country Planning. Monthly publication of the Town and Country Planning Association, 28 King Street, London WC2, England.

A stimulating journal devoting much of its space to the British New Towns. Each January issue contains tables showing progress in growth of population, housing, industry, shops, schools, etc. Important source of current information and opinion. The January 1956 number contains articles and critiques of British New Towns by eminent critics from 11 countries, including the United States, as well as much other provocative material.

The Planning of a New Town. Based on a study for a New Town of 100,000 at Hook, Hampshire. Published in 1961 by London County Council. Hubert Bennett, Architect to the Council.

Excellent comprehensive and intimate study for a New Town, from site selection through all the planning phases, to economic and engineering detail; well illustrated. Useful for both professionals and laymen.

The Culture of Cities. Lewis Mumford. Harcourt Brace and Co., 1938.

This is one of three complementary books in which Lewis Mumford has brilliantly interpreted the relationship of man to his environment and to his cultural background throughout the ages. The others of the series are *Technics and Civilization,* 1934, and *The Condition of Man,* 1944.

REFERENCES

1 Bing, Wright and Stein: Preliminary Study. For further details of this and other footnote references, see Bibliography, p. 249.

2 Reports of Commission of Housing and Regional Planning, 1920-1926.

3 Tough: Production Costs.

4 Tough: Production Costs.

5 Bing, Wright and Stein: Preliminary Study.

6 Mumford: Green Memories.

7 Bing: Sunnyside Gardens: A Successful Experiment.

8 Tough: Production Costs.

9 Smith: A Town for the Motor Age.

10 Olmsted: Forty-Eight Years of Architecture.

11 Traffic Quarterly. April 1948, p. 205.

12 Wright: The Autobiography of Another Idea.

13 Report of the Special Evaluation Committee of the First Citizens' Association of Radburn.

14 Ascher: The Extra Municipal Administration of Radburn.

15 Hudson: Radburn, A Plan of Living.

16 Stein and Bauer: Store Buildings and Neighborhood Shopping Centers.

17 Wright: Rehousing Urban America.

18 Wright, Henry: The Architect and Small House Costs in Architectural Record, December 1932, p. 391. See also Architectural Record, December 1931.

19 Lewis: The Large-Scaled Planned Community as an Investment.

20 Lewis: The Large-Scaled Planned Community as an Investment.

21 Memorandum to Mr. John S. Lansill, October 1935. See Appendix, pp. 228 ff.

22 Memorandum to Mr. Lansill, November 1935. See Appendix, pp. 228 ff. for these memoranda.

23 Memorandum to Mr. Lansill, December 1935. Studies of Operation-Maintenance Costs in Suburban Resettlement Communities.

24 Memorandum to Mr. Lansill, December 1935. Notes on Cost of Local Government and Community Activity.

25 Report to Mr. Lansill, December 1935. Shopping Centers.

26 The New Exploration, pp. 147 and 188.

27 Agricultural Research Center of the United States Department of Agriculture. Agricultural Research Administration, U.S. Department of Agriculture.

28 H.R. 2440, Public Law 65, 81st Congress, Chapter 127, 1st Session.

29 81st Congress, 1st Session, Senate Calendar No. 292, Report No. 312, Disposition of Greentown Projects. (Report to accompany H.R. 2440).

30 Written in 1949.

31 Founded by the late Edward A. Filene to further the Consumers movement.

32 Shopping Centers: principles of planning and possible income to be derived from rental of stores. A Report by Clarence S. Stein for the Resettlement Administration, 1935.

33 Store Buildings and Neighborhood Shopping Centers, by Clarence S. Stein and Catherine Bauer. The Architectural Record, February 1934.

34 Studies of Operation-Maintenance Costs in Suburban Resettlement Communities. A Report by Clarence S. Stein for the Resettlement Administration, 1935. See Appendix.

35 See p. 57, District Heating in American Housing, National Building Studies, Special Report No. 7, London 1949.

36 From an article, Greendale and the Future, written by Clarence S. Stein on the tenth anniversary of the town in 1948, and republished in the American City, June 1948.

37 Store Buildings and Neighborhood Shopping Centers. By Clarence S. Stein and Catherine Bauer. The Architectural Record, February 1934.

38 Pencil Points (now Progressive Architecture) September 1944.

39 Pencil Points (now Progressive Architecture September 1944. pp. 58-60.

40 A Civic Survey and Plan for Edinburgh. Prepared for the Town Council by Patrick Abercrombie and Derek Plumstead. Oliver and Boyd, Edinburgh, 1949.

41 "America's Needs and Resources," by J. Frederic Dewhurst and Associates. The Twentieth Century Fund, 1947.

PHOTOGRAPHIC CREDITS

Fig.

6 Brown Brothers, New York
7 Museum of Modern Art, New York
8, 12-14 Gottscho-Schleisner, New York
15 Gretchen Van Tassel, Washington, D. C.
22 New York Public Library
23 Charles F. Doherty, New York
24, 31-33, 35-48 Gretchen Van Tassel
49 Fairchild Aerial Surveys, Inc., New York
50 Heinrichs Studio, Paterson, New Jersey
51 Gretchen Van Tassel
52 Aerial Surveys of Pittsburgh, Inc.
54 Leonard Schugar
58, 60-63 S. J. Link
64 McLaughlin Aerial Surveys, New York
65 S. J. Link
66 S. J. Link, courtesy of *Architectural Forum*
67 Leonard Schugar
68, 70, 72, 74 Gottscho-Schleisner
80 Standard Aerial Surveys, Inc., Newark, New Jersey
83 Palmer Shannan, New York
84, 87, 88 Gottscho-Schleisner
89 B. Popiel
90-94, 96 Gottscho-Schleisner

Fig.

102 Gretchen Van Tassel
103 United States Coast and Geodetic Survey, courtesy
     of Richard B. Hall
106 Library of Congress
107, 108 Library of Congress photo by Fairchild Aerial
     Surveys, Inc., New York
109 Library of Congress photo by Gretchen Van Tassel
110-117 Gretchen Van Tassel
120 Rothstein
121 Gretchen Van Tassel
122 Public Housing Administration
123, 125-131 Gretchen Van Tassel
132 Library of Congress photo by Gretchen Van Tassel
133 Fairchild Aerial Surveys, Inc.
134 Kinstler
139 Walter Kroening
142 Lewis Wilson
143 Fairchild Aerial Surveys, Inc., Los Angeles
146, 147 Lewis Wilson
148 Margaret Lowe
150, 151, 153, 158 Lewis Wilson
154, 159-162, 165 Margaret Lowe
166 Julius Shulman

INDEX AND LIST OF ILLUSTRATIONS

Ackerman, Frederick L. 12, 14-15, 21, 37, 65, 221
Adams, John Wolcott 45
Alexander, Robert E. 8
Appraisal of plans 121-122, 229
Ascher, Charles S. 221
Ashelman, Samuel F., Jr. 8, 160
Augur, Tracy 14
Automobiles:
    as social menace 37-38, 41, 47, 51-52, 189-190, 193, 218-222
    traffic 11, 16, 41, 44, 47, 51, 66-67, 115, 128, 131, 136-137, 139, 148-150, 173, 185

BALDWIN HILLS VILLAGE 8, 17, 19, 115, 188-216
    aerial view *Fig. 143*
    and New Town, Edinburgh *Fig. 163*, pp. 212-218
    architects 208
    by Catherine Bauer 209
    center green *Figs. 151, 154*, pp. 189-190, 195, 198, 202, 215
    child center 208
    children on green *Fig. 151*
    club house 208
    community building 208
    costs per dwelling unit 209-210, 212
    economic background 189-190, 211-212
    garage court *Figs. 142, 147*, p. 193
    garages 193
    garden courts *Figs. 142, 153*
        approach *Figs. 148, 161*
    garden courts and garage courts *Fig. 142*, p. 202
        plans *Figs. 149, 152*
    house units *Fig. 158*, pp. 195, 201-202, 207, 215-216
        plans *Figs. 155, 156, 157*
    objective 190
    patios *Fig. 146*, p. 193, 198, 215
    plan of village *Figs. 144, 164*, pp. 192-193, 198, 201-202, 208, 212
    play space *Fig. 154*, pp. 208-209
    row houses *Fig. 165*, pp. 195, 198, 201
        entrance side *Figs. 159, 160, 166*
    site 190, 201-202
        first planning study *Fig. 145*
    view across west green *Fig. 162*, p. 199
    village as community 208
Bauer, Catherine 14, 65, 94, 115, 163, 209
Bentley, Harry H. 185
Bigger, Frederick 14, 120
Bing, Alexander 8, 13-14, 19, 21-22, 37, 66, 68, 72, 85, 221
Black Rock Development, Bridgeport 12

Blackham, Louise P. 8, 107
Blocks, four ways of developing *Fig. 4*
Brownlow, Louis 59, 61, 221
Bright, John 14
Budgets for family of four 163
Buhl, Henry, Jr. 74
Butler, Charles 114

Cambridge, Mass. 11
Carlson, C. S. 246
Cautley, Marjorie S. 31, 88, 221
Central Park, New York *Fig. 25*, pp. 11, 16, 44, 52, 64
Chandigard, E. Bengal, India 9, 223
Chase, Stuart 14, 19
CHATHAM VILLAGE 19, 74-85
    air view, 1932 *Fig. 64*
    air view, 1935 *Fig. 52*
    conclusions 85
    cross section of hillside block *Fig. 57*
    economics 74, 78, 80, 85
    final plan of first unit *Fig. 59*
    garages *Figs. 57, 59*, pp. 76, 78, 85
    general plan *Fig. 55*, p. 76
    greenbelt *Figs. 54, 59, 67*, pp. 76, 85
    house types and plans *Figs. 56, 58*, pp. 62, 63, 65
        houses in first unit, 1938 *Fig. 61*
        row houses at different levels *Figs. 57, 61, 66*, pp. 76, 78, 86
    inhabitants 80
    investment finance 74, 80
    preliminary study *Fig. 53*
    site and plan *Figs. 53, 55, 59*, pp. 74, 76
    topography 74, 76, 86
    superblocks 76
Churchill, Henry S. 121, 182
City Housing Corporation 21-22, 28, 34, 37, 39, 47, 59-61, 68-69, 72, 85, 87, 221
City planning 220-225
Coit, Elizabeth 8
Commission for Housing and Regional Planning 14, 19
Conclusions on New Towns 216-225
Construction chart of projects *Fig. 1*
Cooley, Charles Horton 14
Coolidge, John 11
Cordner, G. Frank 178
Costs of operation-maintenance 169-175, 229
Costs of production, relative 246-248
Craig, James, of Edinburgh 212
Crane, Jacob 185, 187

Decentralization 7, 13-14, 130, 218

Density 16, 90, 136, 193
Dewey, John 14
Douglas, Senator Paul H. 133

Eberlin, Ralph 8, 59, 221, 234
Edelman, Kate 8, 136
Edinburgh, New Town 212, 215
Eken, Andrew 100
Ellington, Douglas D. 119
Emergency Relief Appropriation Act 119
Emmerich, Herbert *Fig. 16,* pp. 8, 38-39, 59, 221
England, influence of 7, 11-12, 19, 22, 27, 37, 44, 76,
    149, 158
Estimated annual store expenditure 164
Estimated family expenditure 164
Estimated store income 166

Fairchild Aerial Surveys Inc. *Figs. 49, 107, 108, 133*
Fairlawn Borough 48, 59, 61, 72
Federal Government 12, 14-15, 72, 93, 95, 117, 119,
    133, 156, 158, 160, 163-176, 178, 187, 189
Federal Public Housing Authority 39, 93, 157, 189, 202,
    220-221
Forest Hills 16
Fresh Meadows, New York 17
Fulmer, O. Kline 136

Garden Community Project, plan *Fig. 2*
Geddes, Patrick 14-15
Gobbel, James 8
Goodhue, Bertram Grosvenor 13
GREENBELT, MD. 8, 13-14, 16-17, 51, 118-177
    aerial views *Figs. 103, 106, 107, 108, 133*
    as garden city 130
    basic planning ideas 122-123, 127, 176
    bungalow *Fig. 111*
    community actiivties *Figs. 107, 129,* pp. 127, 130,
        133, 150, 153, 155-158, 160, 171, 175-176
    cooperation and shopping center 150, 153, 155, 160,
        162
    costs 121, 127, 160-175
        accounting 175
        of construction and maintenance 121-122, 137, 139,
            168
        of government 121, 168-175
        of transport 131, 155, 169
    Defense Homes Development *Figs. 108, 113, 115, 117,
        119,* pp. 128, 131, 134, 136-137, 139, 142, 148-149,
        153, 155-156
    family life *Figs. 120, 121, 123,* p. 166
    garage court *Fig. 114,* pp. 137, 139, 142
    garages 137, 139
    gardens *Figs. 122, 123,* pp. 139, 149
    general plan *Figs. 55, 105,* pp. 119-123, 127-128,
        130-131, 136-137
    government 127, 150, 157, 160, 168, 176
    group care for children 155, 158, 160

health 170, 174
    inner block paths *Figs. 102, 128,* pp. 148, 155
    lake *Fig. 109,* p. 160
    laundry *Figs. 116, 117,* p. 149
    living units *Figs. 118, 119,* pp. 122, 128, 139, 142
    managers 136, 150, 157, 168, 172, 174-175
    movie theater *Fig. 125,* pp. 150, 162
    neighborhood unit 122-123, 150, 153, 155-156, 176
    origins and purposes 119-123, 127, 130-131, 137
    parking court *Fig. 115,* pp. 137, 139, 142, 150, 155
    permanent greenbelt 130-131, 133, 176
    plan of shopping center *Fig. 124*
    play space *Figs. 130, 131,* pp. 139, 142, 149-150, 160
    protection 173
    public ownership 119, 133, 171, 176
    public works and services 150, 155, 169-170, 173-174
    Radburn Idea, the 119, 122-123, 127, 136-137, 150,
        176
    regional map *Fig. 104*
    religion 128, 158
    Resettlement Administration *Figs. 106, 107, 114,
        116, 118,* pp. 119-120, 122, 128, 136-137, 139, 142,
        148, 153, 162-177, 187
    residents 128, 130-131, 136, 153, 163, 166-169
    road crossing *Fig. 113,* p. 139
    safety for children *Figs. 102, 113, 115,* pp. 139, 142,
        148, 155
    schools *Fig. 121,* pp. 139, 148, 150, 153, 155-158,
        169-173
    service yards *Fig. 116,* pp. 137, 142, 148
    shopping center *Figs. 124, 125, 126, 127, 128,* pp. 122,
        148-168
        store sales and rentals 153, 160, 164-168
    site 127-128, 130, 133
    spaces, open *Fig. 121,* pp. 120, 127-128, 130-131,
        133, 136, 139, 148-149
    street and parking pattern *Fig. 127,* pp. 136-137, 139,
        142, 155
    superblocks 136-137, 148-150, 153
    swimming pool *Figs. 126, 131,* pp. 150, 153, 160, 175
    typical row house *Fig. 110,* p. 139
    underpasses *Fig. 112,* pp. 139, 148
    walk system *Fig. 128,* pp. 139, 148, 153
Greenbelt parks 9, 11, 16, 22, 35, 37, 67-68, 72, 76, 86,
    117, 120, 127-128, 130-131, 133, 136, 186, 198, 218-219
GREENBROOK, NEW JERSEY 16, 121, 182-183
    history 182
    initial project plan *Fig. 138*
GREENDALE, WISC. 8, 51, 121, 171-173, 184-187
    community school *Fig. 139*
    general plan *Fig. 141*
    greenbelt 185-186
    site 185, 187
    pedestrian walk and garden court *Fig. 140*
GREENHILLS, OHIO 8, 51, 121, 171-173, 178-181
    air view *Fig. 134*
    community center *Fig. 137*

community school *Fig. 136*
situation 181
town plan *Fig. 135,* p. 181
Griswold and Kohankie, Landscape Architects 78
Group plans 234-248

Hampstead garden suburb 16, 44, 76
Hartzog, Justin R. 178
HILLSIDE HOMES 8, 93-107
air view *Fig. 80*
basement services *Fig. 77,* p. 94
building 96, 100
central axis *Fig. 90*
community rooms 100, 107
court on central axis *Fig. 84*
economics 95, 100-101, 107
garden apartments *Figs. 78, 79, 92,* pp. 94-96
idea, the 93
life in Hillside 100
model used *Fig. 83*
nursery school *Fig. 88,* p. 107
planning Hillside 94-95
playground *Figs. 89, 91,* pp. 95, 100
plot plans *Fig. 75*
preliminary layouts *Fig. 79*
section showing use of slope *Fig. 78*
site 93
preliminary site plans *Figs. 79, 81, 82, 85*
final site plan *Fig. 86*
typical apartments *Fig. 76,* p. 96
unit plans Figs. *75, 79,* pp. 94, 96
workshop *Fig. 87,* p. 107
Howard, Ebenezer 7, 14, 19, 37, 120-121, 130, 149
Hudson, Robert 65

Ingham and Boyd, Architects 74

Jefferson, Thomas 11
Johnson, Reginald D. 188
Jordon, Frank 8

Kamstra, Allan 182
Keppler of Amsterdam 31
Kinzer, Mary Jane 8
Knisley, Ray 8
Kohn, Robert D. 12, 14
Kroening, Walter 8, 187

Lanes, cross sections *Fig. 170*
plans *Figs. 171-181*
tables of comparisons 233-238
Lanham Act 158
Lansill, John S. 120-121, 139, 162, 229, 232
Lawrence, Mass. 11
Le Corbusier 9
Legislation 119, 133, 158, 172
Letchworth 44

Lewis, Dr. Charles F. 80, 85
Logan, C. A. 131
Longwood, Mass. 11
Lowell, Mass. 11
Lueders, Albert 234, 246

MacCrae, E. J., on Edinburgh 215
MacKaye, Benton 8, 13-15, 19, 127
MacLane, Senator 120
McCamy, Win 8
McDonald, Charles T. 8, 172
McLaughlin Aerial Surveys *Fig. 64*
McNamara, Katherine 8
Manchester, New Hampshire 11
Markelius, Sven 9
Marts & Nichols *Fig. 103*
Mayer, Albert 8, 182
Mayer & Whittlesey 9, 223
Merrill, Edwin 8
Metropolitan Life Insurance Co. 16, 21, 24, 85
Minimum space requirements *Fig. 169*
of bedrooms *Fig. 167*
of kitchens *Fig. 168*
Mitchell, Robert 12
Morgan, Margaret 95
Morris, Henry 158
Mumford, Lewis 8, 14, 19
Introduction by 11-19
on Sunnyside 27
on Baldwin Hills 198

National Agricultural Research Center 126, 130, 133
National Capital Park & Planning Commission 133
National Housing Agency 119
National Industrial Recovery Act 119
National Public Housing Agency 119
New Amsterdam, 1660 *Fig. 22*
New England Mutual Life Insurance Co. 190
Newman, Helena 8
New York City Housing Authority 90
New York State Housing 14-15, 19, 101
Nolen, John 11

Olmsted, Frederick Law *Fig. 25,* pp. 11, 15-16, 49
Operation-maintenance costs 229-234

Parkchester 16
Parker, Barry 16
Peets, Elbert 8, 185, 187
Pencil Points 209
Perry, Clarence 15, 17, 150
PHIPPS GARDEN APARTMENTS (I) 24, 86-91
balconies *Fig. 72*
building technology 90-91
conclusions 91
costs 89-90
four-room apartments *Fig. 71*

general plan   87-88
great central court   *Fig. 70,* pp. 87-88
origin   87
plot plan   *Fig. 73*
public and private gardens   *Fig. 70*
site   87-88
two T-units combined   *Fig. 69*
unit plans   *Figs. 69, 71,* pp. 88-89
walk-up or elevator apartments   88-91
PHIPPS GARDEN APARTMENTS (II)   8, 108-113
block plan   *Fig. 95*
Dutch Garden   *Fig. 96*
four-room apartments   *Fig. 97*
inner court   *Fig. 93*
origins   109
general plan   111-112
typical apartment plans   *Figs. 97, 98,* p. 109
typical entrance   *Fig. 94*
Pomeroy, Hugh   8
Production costs, relative   220
Public Housing Administration   119, 133, 150, 160, 168,
   172-173
Public Works Administration   12, 95, 137

RADBURN, N. J.   8, 15-17, 19, 22, 37-73, 119, 189
adult cultural life   60, 65
air view, 1929   *Fig. 23*
air view, 1955   *Fig. 49*
apartment buildings   *Fig. 46,* p. 66
building of Radburn   57, 59
Burnham Place   *Figs. 33, 34, 36,* pp. 66-67
children, care of   *Figs 31, 32, 38, 39, 40, 43, 44, 51,*
   pp. 52, 59, 63-66
church   65
Citizens' Association   60, 62, 65
community life   59-65
conclusions   72-73
culs-de-sac   44, 48, 56-57, 67
economic background   37, 39, 41, 59-61, 67-69, 72-73
economy of Radburn plan   48, 57, 66
education   63
elements of Radburn plan   41, 44, 47-48, 66, 72
experimental plan of four houses   *Fig. 30*
family at work   *Fig. 41*
formal playground   *Fig. 44*
friction with Fairlawn   61
garages, importance of   *Fig. 48,* pp. 47, 54 ,57, 66
general plan showing neighborhoods   *Fig. 27*
Government Community Organization   57, 61, 73
houses and landscape   *Fig. 17*
house turned around, the   44, 47-48, 51
how the Radburn Plan worked   51
inner park   *Figs. 18, 19, 31, 42, 47,* pp. 44, 48, 51,
   60-61, 65-68, 72
lane, typical, plan   *Fig. 19*
   transverse section   *Fig. 20*
overpass   47, 52

park paths   *Figs. 40, 45*
path from houses to park   *Fig. 35*
plan of development, 1930   *Fig. 26*
plan of Radburn neighborhoods   *Fig. 27,* pp. 41, 48,
   51, 66
plan of residential districts   *Fig. 21*
plan for complete town   *Fig. 28,* pp. 39, 41, 48, 51, 67
play places   44, 47-48, 51-52, 63
private garden   *Fig. 37*
public services   61-62, 69
Radburn Association   61-63, 65
Radburn Idea, the   41, 47-48, 60, 67, 72, 119
Radburn revisited   65
recreation   *Fig. 38,* pp. 60, 63-66
residents   59-60, 62, 65
row houses   *Fig. 50,* pp. 54-55, 66-67
safety for children   *Figs. 24, 32,* pp. 41, 44, 51-52, 54,
   65
sand box   *Fig. 43*
schools   49, 51-52, 61-63, 65-66, 73
separation of means of communication   *Fig. 25,* pp. 44,
   47, 65
service lanes   *Fig. 36,* pp. 41, 48, 52, 54, 67
single family house   54, 57, 65-66
site   44, 48, 57, 59, 69.
sketch map by Emmerich   *Fig. 16*
specialized highways   41, 47-48, 51-52
stores   51, 57, 65, 69
success or failure   67
superblock   *Fig. 18,* pp. 39, 41, 48, 51, 65-67, 72
swimming pools   *Fig. 39,* pp. 52, 60, 63, 66
typical plan of early house   *Fig. 29*
underpass   *Figs. 24, 45,* pp. 52, 66
unit plans   52, 55, 57
wading pool   *Fig. 51,* pp. 63, 66
Reed, Mrs.   157
Regional Plan Association of N. Y.   13-14
Regional Planning Association of America   14-15, 19
Resettlement Administration   118-177, 182
   reports   162, 228-248
Roosevelt, Franklin D.   12, 14-16, 93, 119

Sage, Russell, Foundation   14, 17
Schofield, Ernest   8, 88, 110
Smith, Chloethiel Woodard   12
Smith, Geddes   44
Smith, Governor Alfred   13, 19
Stanislas   198
Starrett Brothers and Eken   93, 100
Stein, Clarence S.
   by Lewis Mumford   11-19
   Architect, Hillside Homes   93
   Architect, Phipps Garden Apartments   87, 109
   Architect, Valley Stream Project   114
   Architect and Town Planner, Chatham Village   74
   Chief Architect and Town Planner, Radburn   37
   Chief Architect and Town Planner, Sunnyside   21

Consulting Architect, Baldwin Hills   188
Stephenson, Gordon   7-8, 11, 229
Stockholm, Radburn Plan in   9, 72
Stokes, I. N. Phelps   45
Straus, Nathan   8, 93
Strong, William A.   178
Stuyvesant Town   16
SUNNYSIDE GARDENS   8, 11, 13, 16-17, 19, 21-36, 57, 59, 61, 68-69, 78, 85, 87
    basements   31
    brick, use of   31
    children's playground, 1924   *Fig. 8,* p. 34
    community association   31-32, 34
    conclusions   35
    court opening off street   *Fig. 14*
    courts and gardens   27, 35
    first unit   *Fig. 5*
    garage compounds   24, 27
    general plan   *Figs. 2, 3,* pp. 23, 34
    group plans   24, 34, 27-28, 34-35
    house types   *Fig. 10,* pp. 27-28, 35
    inner courts   *Figs. 9, 11, 12, 13,* p. 24
    interior of block   *Fig. 6*
    land cost   22
    life in Sunnyside   31-32
    origins   21
    plan of superblock with inner court   *Fig. 18*
    plan of two blocks with inner courts   *Fig. 9*
    planning economies   27-28, 35, 37
    purpose   22
    site   21
    typical Long Island City street   *Fig. 7*
    unit plans   28
Superblocks   *Figs. 4, 17, 18,* pp. 9, 11, 16, 39, 41, 48, 51, 65-67, 72, 76, 95, 128, 136, 189, 202, 219

Tassel, Gretchen van   8
Tennessee Valley Authority   15, 119
Thomas, Andrew J.   *Fig. 6,* p. 37

Thomas, Walter G.   185
Thomson, James Renwick   *Fig. 71,* p. 37
Tucker, Lawrence   8
Tugwell, Rexford Guy   120, 130
Tyrone, New Mexico   13

Unwin, (Sir) Raymond   7, 12, 16, 19, 22, 47, 76

VALLEY STREAM PROJECT   114-117
    choice of location   114
    community facilities   117
    cost studies   117
    general plan   *Fig. 99,* p. 115
    house types   117
    objects   114
    proposed layout   *Fig. 100*
    service and garden courts   *Fig. 100*
    site   114-115
Vaux, Calvert   11, 44
Veblen, Thorstein   14
Veiller, Lawrence   13
Vinton, Warren   121
Virginia, University of   11
Vitolo, Frank   13, 100, 114, 246

Wadsworth, R. J.   119
Walker, Hale   119
Walker, Major John O.   61, 117, 170, 174, 221
Wank, Roland A.   8, 178
Welwyn Garden City   19, 44, 149
Whitaker, Charles Harris   11, 14, 19
White Tenements, Brooklyn   11
Wilson, Lewis   8
Wilson, Merrill and Alexander   188
Wood, Edith Elmer   14
Wright, Henry   *Figs. 18, 40,* pp. 7, 11-28, 37, 47-48, 74, 76, 182, 221

Yorkship Village near Camden   12

THE M.I.T. PAPERBACK SERIES

1 **Computers and the World of the Future** edited by Martin Greenberger

2 **Experiencing Architecture** by Steen Eiler Rasmussen

3 **The Universe** by Otto Struve

4 **Word and Object** by Willard Van Orman Quine

5 **Language, Thought, and Reality** by Benjamin Lee Whorf

6 **The Learner's Russian-English Dictionary** by B. A. Lapidus and S. V. Shevtsova

7 **The Learner's English-Russian Dictionary** by S. Folomkina and H. Weiser

8 **Megalopolis** by Jean Gottmann

9 **Time Series** by Norbert Wiener

10 **Lectures on Ordinary Differential Equations** by Witold Hurewicz

11 **The Image of the City** by Kevin Lynch

12 **The Sino-Soviet Rift** by William E. Griffith

13 **Beyond the Melting Pot** by Nathan Glazer and Daniel Patrick Moynihan

14 **A History of Western Technology** by Friedrich Klemm

15 **The Dawn of Astronomy** by Norman Lockyer

16 **Information Theory** by Gordon Raisbeck

17 **The Tao of Science** by R. G. H. Siu

18 **A History of Civil Engineering** by Hans Straub

19 **Ex-Prodigy** by Norbert Wiener

20 **I am a Mathematician** by Norbert Wiener

21 **The New Architecture and the Bauhaus** by Walter Gropius

22 **A History of Mechanical Engineering** by Aubrey F. Burstall

23 **Garden Cities of Tomorrow** by Ebenezer Howard

24 **Brett's History of Psychology** edited by R. S. Peters

25 **Cybernetics** by Norbert Wiener

26 **Biological Order** by André Lwoff

27 **Nine Soviet Portraits** by Raymond A. Bauer

28 **Reflexes of the Brain** by I. Sechenov

29 **Thought and Language** by L. S. Vygotsky

30 **Chinese Communist Society: The Family and the Village** by C. K. Yang

31 **The City: Its Growth, Its Decay, Its Future** by Eliel Saarinen

32 **Scientists as Writers** edited by James Harrison

33 **Candidates, Issues, and Strategies: A Computer Simulation of the 1960 and 1964 Presidential Elections** by I. de S. Pool, R. P. Abelson, and S. L. Popkin

34 **Nationalism and Social Communication** by Karl W. Deutsch

35 **What Science Knows About Life: An Exploration of Life Sources** by Heinz Woltereck

36 **Enzymes** by J. B. S. Haldane

37 **Universals of Language** edited by Joseph H. Greenberg

38 **The Psycho-Biology of Language: An Introduction to Dynamic Philology** by George Kingsley Zipf

39 **The Nature of Metals** by Bruce A. Rogers

40 **Mechanics, Molecular Physics, Heat, and Sound** by R. A. Millikan, D. Roller, and E. C. Watson

41 **North American Trees** by Richard J. Preston, Jr.

42 **God & Golem, Inc.** by Norbert Wiener

43 **The Architecture of H. H. Richardson And His Times** by Henry-Russell Hitchcock

44 **Toward New Towns For America** by Clarence Stein

45 **Man's Struggle For Shelter In An Urbanizing World** by Charles Abrams

46 **Science And Economic Development** by Richard L. Meier

47 **Human Learning** by Edward Thorndike

48 **Pirotechnia** by Vannoccio Biringuccio

49 **A Theory of Natural Philosophy** by Roger Joseph Boscovich

50 **Bacterial Metabolism** by Marjory Stephenson